SIDE
by SIDE

TEACHER'S GUIDE
Second Edition

2

Steven J. Molinsky
Bill Bliss

Contributing Authors

Mary Ann Perry / John Kopec

 PRENTICE HALL REGENTS Englewood Cliffs, New Jersey 07632

Editorial/production supervision: Janet Johnston
Art supervision: Karen Salzbach
Manufacturing buyers: Laura Crossland, Peter Havens
Cover illustration: Richard E. Hill
Cover design: Kenny Beck

Printed in the United States of America

10 9 8 7 6 5 4 3 2

ISBN 0-13-811282-7

Prentice-Hall International (UK) Limited, *London*
Prentice-Hall of Australia Pty. Limited, *Sydney*
Prentice-Hall Canada Inc., *Toronto*
Prentice-Hall Hispanoamericana, S.A., *Mexico*
Prentice-Hall of India Private Limited, *New Delhi*
Prentice-Hall of Japan, Inc., *Tokyo*
Simon & Schuster Asia Pte. Ltd., *Singapore*
Editora Prentice-Hall do Brasil, Ltda., *Rio de Janeiro*

CONTENTS

INTRODUCTION

Side by Side is an English language program for young-adult and adult learners from beginning to high-intermediate levels. The program consists of Student Books 1, 2, 3, 4 and accompanying Activity Workbooks, Teacher's Guides, an Audio Program, a Picture Program, and a Testing Program.

Side by Side offers students a dynamic, communicative approach to the language. Through the methodology of Guided Conversations, *Side by Side* engages students in meaningful conversational exchanges within carefully structured grammatical frameworks, and then encourages students to break away from the textbook and *use* these frameworks to create conversations *on their own*. All the language practice that is generated through the texts results in active communication taking place between students...practicing speaking together, "side by side."

The texts provide all-skills language practice through reading, writing, and listening activities that are totally integrated with the conversational exercises. Short reading selections offer enjoyable reading practice that simultaneously reinforces the grammatical focus of each chapter. *Check-Up* activities provide focused practice in reading comprehension and vocabulary development. *Listening* exercises enable students to develop their aural comprehension skills through a variety of listening activities. And *In Your Own Words* activities provide topics and themes for student compositions and classroom discussions in which students write about their friends, families, homes, schools, and themselves.

The goal of *Side by Side* is to engage students in active, meaningful communicative practice with the language. The aim of the *Side by Side Teacher's Guides* is to offer guidelines and strategies to help achieve that goal.

STUDENT TEXT OVERVIEW

Chapter Opening Pages

The opening page of each chapter provides an overview of the new grammatical structures treated in the chapter.

Conversation Lessons

1. GRAMMATICAL PARADIGMS

A new grammatical structure appears first in the form of a grammatical paradigm, or "grammar box"—a simple schema of the structure. (Grammar boxes are in a light blue tint.) These paradigms are meant to be a reference point for students as they proceed through a lesson's conversational activities. While these paradigms highlight the structures being taught, they are not intended to be goals in themselves. Students are not expected to memorize or parrot back these rules. Rather, we want students to take part in conversations that show they can *use* these rules correctly.

2. MODEL GUIDED CONVERSATIONS

Model Guided Conversations serve as the vehicles for introducing new grammatical structures, as well as many communicative uses of English. Since the model becomes the basis for all of the exercises that follow, it is essential that students be given sufficient practice with it before proceeding with the lesson.

3. SIDE BY SIDE EXERCISES

In the numbered exercises that follow the model, students pair up and work "side by side," placing new content into the given conversational framework. These exercises form the core learning activity of each conversation lesson.

Reading Lessons

1. READING SELECTIONS

Short reading selections offer enjoyable reading practice that simultaneously reinforces the grammatical focus of each chapter. Accompanying illustrations serve as visual cues that guide learners through the reading and help to clarify both context and new vocabulary.

2. CHECK-UP

Check-Up exercises provide focused practice in reading comprehension and vocabulary development. Also, listening exercises enable students to develop their aural comprehension skills through a variety of listening activities.

3. IN YOUR OWN WORDS

These activities provide topics and themes for student compositions and classroom discussions. Students write about their friends, families, homes, schools, jobs, and themselves.

On Your Own and How About You? Activities

These student-centered activities give students valuable opportunities to apply lesson content to their own lives and experiences and to share opinions in class. Through these activities, students bring to the classroom new content, based on their interests, their backgrounds, and their imaginations. Activities include role plays, questions about the students' real world, and topics for discussion and debate.

Summary Pages

Summary pages at the end of each chapter highlight functional language and grammatical structures covered in that chapter. They are useful as a review and study guide after students have completed the chapter.

ANCILLARY MATERIALS

Activity Workbooks

The Activity Workbooks offer a variety of exercises for reinforcement, fully coordinated with the student texts. A special feature of the Activity Workbooks is the inclusion of rhythm, stress, pronunciation, and intonation exercises. Periodic check-up tests are also included.

Audio Program

The Student Text tapes are especially designed to serve as a student's speaking partner, making conversation practice possible even when the student is studying alone. In addition to the guided conversation exercises, the tapes contain the listening comprehension exercises along with recordings of all of the reading selections in the text.

The Activity Workbook tapes contain the listening, pronunciation, rhythm, stress, and intonation exercises in the workbooks.

Picture Program

Side by Side Picture Cards illustrate key concepts and vocabulary items. They can be used for introduction of new material, for review, for enrichment, and for role-playing activities. Suggestions for their use are included in the Teacher's Guide. Also, the Appendix to the Teacher's Guide contains a triple listing of the Picture Cards: numerically, alphabetically, and by category.

Testing Program

The *Side by Side* Testing Program offers a placement test as well as mid-term and final examinations for each level of the program.

FORMAT OF THE TEACHER'S GUIDE

Chapter Overview

The Chapter Overview provides the following:

- Functional and grammatical highlights of the chapter
- A listing of new vocabulary and expressions
- Language and culture notes that apply to the chapter as a whole

Step-by-Step Lesson Guide

Included for each conversation lesson are the following:

- FOCUS of the lesson
- GETTING READY: suggestions for introducing the new concepts in the lesson
- INTRODUCING THE MODEL: steps for introducing the model conversation
- SIDE BY SIDE EXERCISES: suggestions for practicing the exercises, as well as a listing of new vocabulary
- LANGUAGE AND CULTURE NOTES
- WORKBOOK: page references for exercises in the Activity Workbook that correspond to the particular lesson
- EXPANSION ACTIVITIES: optional activities for review and reinforcement of the content of the lesson

Included for each reading lesson are the following:

- FOCUS of the lesson
- NEW VOCABULARY contained in the reading
- PREVIEWING THE STORY: an optional preliminary stage before students begin to read the selection
- READING THE STORY: suggestions for presenting the story as well as questions to check students' comprehension
- CHECK-UP: answer keys and listening scripts for check-up exercises
- IN YOUR OWN WORDS: suggestions for doing these writing and discussion exercises

Workbook Answer Key and Listening Scripts

Answers and listening scripts for all exercises contained in the Activity Workbooks are provided at the end of each chapter of the Teacher's Guide.

GENERAL TEACHING STRATEGIES

Introducing the Model

Since the model conversation forms the basis of each lesson, it is essential that students practice the model several times in a variety of ways before going on to the exercises. The following eight steps are recommended for introducing a model conversation. Of course, you should feel free to modify them to suit your own particular teaching style and the needs of your students.

1. Have students look at the model illustration. This helps establish the context of the conversation.

2. *Set the scene.* For every model, one or two lines are suggested in this Teacher's Guide for you to use to "set the scene" of the dialog for your students.

3. *Present the model.* With books closed, have students listen as you present the model or play the tape one or more times. To make the presentation of the model as realistic as possible, you might draw two stick figures on the board to represent the speakers in the dialog. You can also show that two people are speaking by changing your position or by shifting your weight from one foot to the other as you say each speaker's lines.

4. *Full-Class Choral Repetition.* Model each line and have the whole class repeat in unison.

5. Have students open their books and look at the dialog. Ask if there are any questions, and check understanding of new vocabulary. (All new vocabulary in the model is listed here. The illustration and the context of the dialog normally help to clarify the meaning of new words.)

6. *Group Choral Repetition.* Divide the class in half. Model line A and have Group 1 repeat; model line B and have Group 2 repeat. Continue this with all the lines of the model.

7. *Choral Conversation.* Groups 1 and 2 practice the dialog twice, without teacher model. First Group 1 is Speaker A and Group 2 is Speaker B; then reverse.

8. Call on one or two pairs of students to present the dialog.

In steps 6, 7, and 8 you should encourage students to look up from their books and *say* the lines rather than read them. (Students can of course refer to their books when necessary.) *The goal here is not memorization or complete mastery of the model.* Rather, students should become familiar with the model and feel comfortable saying it.

At this point, if you feel that additional practice is necessary before going on to the exercises, you can do Choral Conversation in small groups or by rows.

Side by Side Exercises

The numbered exercises that follow the model form the core learning activity in each conversation lesson. Here students use the pictures and word cues to create conversations based on the structure of the model. Since all language practice in these lessons is conversational, you will always call on a pair of students to do each exercise. *Your* primary role is to serve as a resource to the class: to help with the structures, new vocabulary, intonation, and pronunciation.

The following three steps are recommended in each lesson for practicing the *Side by Side* exercises. (Students should be given thorough practice with the first two exercises before going on.)

1. Exercise 1: Introduce any new vocabulary in the exercise. Call on two students to present the dialog. Then do Choral Repetition and Choral Conversation Practice.

2. Exercise 2: Same as for Exercise 1.

3. For the remaining exercises, there are two options: either Full-Class Practice or Pair Practice.

   Full-Class Practice: Call on a pair of students to do each exercise. Introduce new vocabulary one exercise at a time. (For more practice, call on other pairs of students, or do Choral Repetition or Choral Conversation.)

Pair Practice: Introduce new vocabulary for all the exercises. Next have students practice all the exercises in pairs. Then have pairs present the exercises to the class. (For more practice, do Choral Repetition or Choral Conversation.)

The choice of Full-Class Practice or Pair Practice should be determined by the content of the particular lesson, the size and composition of the class, and your own teaching style. You might also wish to vary your approach from lesson to lesson.

Suggestions for Pairing Up Students: Whether you use Full-Class Practice or Pair Practice, you can select students for the pairs in various ways. You might want to pair students by ability, since students of similar ability might work more efficiently together than students of dissimilar ability. On the other hand, you might wish to pair a weaker student with a stronger one. The slower student benefits from this pairing, while the more advanced student strengthens his or her abilities by helping the partner.

You should also encourage students to *look at* each other when speaking. This makes the conversational nature of the language practice more realistic. One way of ensuring this is *not* to call on two students who are sitting next to each other. Rather, call on students in different parts of the room and encourage them to look at each other when saying their lines.

Presenting New Vocabulary

Many new vocabulary words are introduced in each conversation lesson. The illustration normally helps to convey the meaning, and the new words are written for students to see and use in these conversations. In addition, you might:

1. write the new word on the board or on a word card,
2. say the new word several times and ask students to repeat chorally and individually, and
3. help clarify the meaning with *Side by Side* Picture Cards or your own visuals (pictures from magazines, newspapers, or your own drawings).

Students might also find it useful to keep a notebook in which they write each new word, its meaning, and a sentence using that word.

Open-Ended Exercises (the ''Blank Box'')

In many lessons, the final exercise is an open-ended one. This is indicated in the text by a blank box. Here the students are expected to create conversations based on the structure of the model, but with vocabulary that they select themselves. This provides students with an opportunity for creativity, while still focusing on the particular structure being practiced. These open-ended exercises can be done orally in class and/or assigned as homework for presentation in class the next day. Encourage students to use dictionaries to find new words they want to use.

On Your Own

On Your Own activities offer students the opportunity to contribute content of their own within the grammatical framework of the lesson. You should introduce these activities in class and assign them as homework for presentation in class the next day. In this way, students will automatically review the previous day's grammar while contributing new and inventive content of their own.

These activities are meant for simultaneous grammar reinforcement and vocabulary building. Students should be encouraged to use a dictionary when completing the *On Your Own* activities. In this way, they will not only use the words they know, but the words they would *like* to know in order to really bring their interests, backgrounds, and imaginations into the classroom.

As a result, students will teach each other new vocabulary and also share a bit of their lives with others in the class.

How About You?

How About You? activities are intended to provide students with additional opportunities to tell about themselves. Have students do these activities in pairs or as a class.

Expansion Activities

For each conversation lesson, the Teacher's Guide contains ideas for optional review and reinforcement activities. Feel free to pick and choose or vary the activities to fit the particular needs and learning styles of students in your class. The ideas are meant to serve as a springboard for developing your own learning activities.

General Guiding Principles for Working with Guided Conversations

1. When doing the exercises, students should practice *speaking* to each other, rather than *reading* to each other. Therefore, while students will need to refer to the text to be able to practice the conversations, they should not read the lines word by word. Rather, they should practice scanning a full line and then look up from the book and *speak* the line to another person.

2. Throughout, teachers should use the book to teach proper intonation and gesture. (Capitalized words are used to indicate spoken emphasis.) Students should be encouraged to truly *act out* the dialogs in a strong and confident voice.

3. Use of the texts should be as *student-centered* as possible. Modeling by the teacher should be efficient and economical, but students should have every opportunity to model for each other when they are capable of doing so.

4. Vocabulary can and should be effectively taught in the context of the conversation being practiced. Very often it will be possible to grasp the meaning from the conversation or its accompanying illustration. Teachers should spend time drilling vocabulary in isolation *only* if they feel it is absolutely essential.

5. Students need not formally study or be able to produce grammatical rules. The purpose of the texts is to engage students in active communicative practice that gets them to *use* the language according to these rules.

6. Students should be given every opportunity to apply their own lives and creative contributions to the exercises. This is directly provided for in the blank boxes at the end of many lessons as well as in the *On Your Own* and *How About You?* activities, but teachers can look to *all* exercises with an eye toward expanding them to the real world of the classroom or to the students' real lives.

Introducing Reading Selections

You may wish to preview each story either by briefly setting the scene or by having students talk about the illustrations or predict the content of the story from the title. You may also find it useful to introduce new vocabulary items before they are encountered in the story. On the other hand, you may prefer to skip the previewing step and instead have students experience the subject matter and any unfamiliar words in the context of the initial reading of the story.

There are many ways in which students can read and talk about the stories. Students may read silently to themselves or follow along as the story is read by you, by one or more students, or on the tape. You should then ask students if they have any questions and check understanding of new vocabulary. For each reading selection, the Teacher's Guide provides a list of questions based on the story. You may wish to check students' comprehension by asking these questions before going on to the Check-Up exercises.

Q & A Exercises

Q & A exercises are included as part of the Check-Up after many of the reading selections. These exercises are designed to give students conversation practice based on information contained in the stories. Italic type in the Q & A model highlights the words to be replaced by different information contained in the reading.

Call on a pair of students to present the Q & A model. Have students work in pairs to create new dialogs based on the model, and then call on pairs to present their new dialogs to the class.

In Your Own Words

These activities are designed to guide students in their creation of original stories. Students are asked to write about topics such as their homes, schools, friends, families, and themselves.

You should go over the instructions for the activities and make sure students understand what is expected. Students should do the activity as written homework, using a dictionary for any new words they wish to use. Then have students present and discuss what they have written, in pairs or as a class.

Activity Workbooks

The exercises in the Activity Workbooks are fully coordinated with the student texts. For each conversation lesson in the student text, the Teacher's Guide indicates which particular workbook exercises provide supplementary practice. This cross-referencing information can also be found at the back of the workbooks.

The workbooks provide intensive practice in grammar reinforcement, reading, writing, listening, and pronunciation. A special feature is the inclusion of exercises in rhythm, stress, and intonation of English. In these exercises, black dots are used as a kind of musical notation system to indicate the number of "beats" on each line. The dots also serve to indicate the primary word stresses and graphically show the reduced emphasis on the surrounding, unstressed words. Have students first listen to these exercises on tape, and then practice saying them. For each exercise, establish the rhythm for the students by clapping, tapping, or finger-snapping on each "beat," as indicated by the black dots. Students also enjoy doing this as they perform these exercises.

In conclusion, we have attempted to make the study of English a lively and relevant experience for our students. While we hope that we have conveyed to you the substance of our textbooks, we also hope that we have conveyed the spirit: that learning the language can be interactive . . . student-centered . . . and fun.

Steven J. Molinsky
Bill Bliss

CHAPTER 1 OVERVIEW: *Text Pages 1–8*

1

GRAMMAR

Like to

I We You They	like to	watch TV.
He She It	likes to	

I We You They	don't like to	watch TV.
He She It	doesn't like to	

Future: Going to

Am	I	
Is	he she it	going to eat?
Are	we you they	

Yes,	I	am.
	he she it	is.
	we you they	are.

No,	I'm	not.
	he she it	isn't.
	we you they	aren't.

Simple Past Tense

I He She It We You They	cooked spaghetti last night.

Indirect Object Pronouns

He's going to give	me him her it us you them	a present.

Time Expressions

I studied English	last week. last weekend. last month. last year.	last Sunday. last Monday. : last Saturday.	last spring. last summer. last fall (autumn). last winter.	last January. last February. : last December.

FUNCTIONS

Inquiring about Intention

Are you going to *cook spaghetti this week*?

What are you going to *give your wife for her birthday*?

Expressing Dislikes

I don't like to *cook spaghetti* very often.

Expressing Inability

I can't *give her a necklace*.

Suggesting

How about *flowers*?

Expressing Uncertainty

I don't know.

Attracting Attention

Harry!

Describing Feelings·Emotions

I'm really upset!

NEW VOCABULARY

advice
ago
Alabama
anniversary
anything
bought (buy)
Canada
doll
down south
East Coast
even though
far apart
give

give advice
"Happy Birthday"
into
last month
last week
last weekend
last year
lent (lend)
like to
lost (lose) *his* job
Minnesota
necktie
painting (n)
perfume

Philadelphia
plant (n)
present (n)
receive
San Diego
send
silk (adj)
silver (adj)
sold (sell)
south
up north
West Coast
wish (v)

Text Pages 2–3: *Are You Going to Cook Spaghetti This Week?*

FOCUS

- Introduction of *like to*
- Review of the simple past tense and future: *going to*
- Time expressions

GETTING READY

1. Review tenses.

   a. Write on the board:

      He _____ every day.
      He _____ yesterday.
      He _____ tomorrow.

   b. Have students complete these sentences, using each of the following verbs: *study, work, go skiing.* For example:

      "He studies every day."
      "He studied yesterday."
      "He's going to study tomorrow."

2. Introduce *like to.*

   a. Tell about yourself and a friend. For example:

      "I like to cook."
      "I don't like to wash the dishes."
      "I like to go to the beach, but I don't like to swim."
      "My friend George likes to speak English, but he doesn't like to study."

   b. Make sentences with forms of *like to*; have students repeat. For example:

"I like to (*swim*)."	"I don't like to (*talk*)."
"We like to (*ski*)."	"You don't like to (*watch TV*)."
"You like to (*drive*)."	"We don't like to (*cook*)."
"They like to (*play soccer*)."	"They don't like to (*clean*)."
"He likes to (*sing*)."	"He doesn't like to (*go skiing*)."
"She likes to (*dance*)."	"She doesn't like to (*read*)."

INTRODUCING THE MODEL

1. Have students look at the model illustration.
2. Set the scene: "Two friends are talking."
3. With books closed, have students listen as you present the model or play the tape one or more times.
4. **Full-Class Choral Repetition:** Model each line and have students repeat.
5. Have students open their books and look at the dialog. Ask students if they have any questions; check understanding of vocabulary.

6. **Group Choral Repetition:** Divide the class in half. Model line A and have Group 1 repeat; model line B and have Group 2 repeat.

7. **Choral Conversation:** Groups 1 and 2 practice the dialog twice, without teacher model. First Group 1 is Speaker A and Group 2 is Speaker B; then reverse.

8. Call on one or two pairs of students to present the dialog.

   (For additional practice, do Choral Conversation in small groups or by rows.)

9. Review the expressions *yesterday morning, afternoon, evening; last night.* Introduce the new expressions:

   > *last weekend, month, year*
   > *last Sunday, Monday, . . . , Saturday*
   > *last spring, summer, fall (autumn), winter*
   > *last January, February, . . . , December*

   Have pairs of students practice the model again, using some of these expressions in place of *last week.*

SIDE BY SIDE EXERCISES

Examples

---

1. A. Are you going to study English this weekend?
   B. No, I'm not. I studied English LAST weekend, and I don't like to study English very often.

2. A. Are you going to watch TV tonight?
   B. No, I'm not. I watched TV LAST night, and I don't like to watch TV very often.

---

1. **Exercise 1:** Call on two students to present the dialog. Then do Choral Repetition and Choral Conversation Practice.

2. **Exercise 2:** Same as above.

3. **Exercises 3–12:**

New vocabulary: 10. *Canada*

Language Note

> Exercises 9, 11, 12: The expression *going to* is commonly used to mean *going to go to.* For example, *Are you going skiing this February? Are Mr. and Mrs. Smith going to London this summer?*

Either

Full-Class Practice: Call on a pair of students to do each exercise. Introduce the new vocabulary before doing Exercises 5 and 10. (For more practice, call on other pairs of students, or do Choral Repetition or Choral Conversation.)

or

Pair Practice: Introduce the new vocabulary. Next, have students practice all of the exercises in pairs. Then, have pairs present the exercises to the class. (For more practice, do Choral Repetition or Choral Conversation.)

WORKBOOK

Pages 1–6

Exercise Notes

> Workbook p. 2: In Exercise B, students contrast *like to* and *likes to*. In Exercise C, students practice negatives with *like to* and *going to* in the 1st person singular. In Exercise D, they practice the 3rd person singular.

> Workbook p. 6: Students practice the contrast between *going to* and the past tense.

EXPANSION ACTIVITIES

1. *Students Talk about Themselves*

Have students use the structures on text pages 2 and 3 to talk about themselves.

a. Put on the board:

> A. What did you do last weekend?
> B. I _____.
> A. Are you going to _____ this weekend?
> B. { Yes, I am. I like to _____.
> { No, I'm not. I don't like to _____ very often.

b. Call on pairs of students to create conversations, using the model on the board. You can use Full-Class Practice or Pair Practice. For example:

> A. What did you do last weekend?
> B. I went swimming.
> A. Are you going to go swimming this weekend?
> B. { Yes, I am. I like to go swimming.
> { No, I'm not. I don't like to go swimming very often.

2. *Chain Game: On the Weekend*

Use a chain game to have students tell what they like to do on the weekend. You start. For example:

> You: I like to go to the beach on the weekend.
> What do *you* like to do?
>
> Student A: I like to play soccer.
> What do *you* like to do?
>
> Student B: I like to . . .

3. *Guess Who: Class Survey—Review of Tenses and Vocabulary*

a. Before you do this exercise, have each student write a true statement about himself or herself. For example:

> I live on the 3rd floor of my apartment building.
> I have four sisters.
> I visited Tokyo last fall.
> I'm going to study music next year.
> I like to go jogging.

b. Collect these statements. Then write them all on the board or on a large poster, or make copies of the statements for all the students.

c. Students must then find out who these statements are about by going around the room and asking their classmates questions. For example:

> "Do you live on the 3rd floor of your apartment building?"
> "Do you have four sisters?"
> "Did you visit Tokyo last fall?"
> "Are you going to study music next year?"

This exercise can be done as a game where the *winner* is the person who identifies all the people first.

Text Page 4: *What Are You Going to Give Your Wife for Her Birthday?*

FOCUS

> - Introduction of indirect objects: *I gave her a necklace.*
> - Irregular verb: *give–gave*

GETTING READY

1. Make sentences with indirect objects; use names of students in your class. For example:

    "I'm going to give (Mary) a pencil."
    "I'm going to give her a pencil."

    "I'm going to give (John) a pencil."
    "I'm going to give him a pencil."

2. Say a sentence with an indirect object noun and have students say the sentence with a pronoun. For example:

    You: "I'm going to give *Bill* a book."
    Student: "I'm going to give *him* a book."

    Other possible sentences:

    "I'm going to give *Mary* a pencil."
    "I'm going to give *Bill and Mary* two books."
    "He's going to give *Martha* a present."
    "They're going to give *Joe* a necktie."
    "We're going to give *our parents* a new TV."

3. Read the sentences in the box at the top of the page and have students repeat.

INTRODUCING THE MODEL

1. Have students look at the model illustration.
2. Set the scene: "Two friends are talking. One doesn't know what to give his wife for her birthday."
3. With books closed, have students listen as you present the model or play the tape one or more times.
4. **Full-Class Choral Repetition:** Model each line and have students repeat.
5. Have students open their books and look at the dialog. Ask students if they have any questions; check understanding of new vocabulary: *give, ago.*

    ### Culture Note

    In the United States people usually give gifts to family members and close friends on their birthdays. Birthdays are also often celebrated with a party.

6. **Group Choral Repetition:** Divide the class in half. Model line A and have Group 1 repeat; model line B and have Group 2 repeat, and so on.
7. **Choral Conversation:** Groups 1 and 2 practice the dialog twice, without teacher model. First, Group 1 is Speaker A, and Group 2 is Speaker B; then reverse.
8. Call on one or two pairs of students to present the dialog.

    (For additional practice, do Choral Conversation in small groups or by rows.)

SIDE BY SIDE EXERCISES

Examples

---

1. A. What are you going to give your husband for his birthday?
   B. I don't know. I can't give him a new shirt. I gave him a new shirt LAST YEAR.
   A. How about a necktie?
   B. No. I can't give him a necktie. I gave him a necktie TWO YEARS ago.
   A. Well, what are you going to give him?
   B. I don't know. I really have to think about it.

2. A. What are you going to give your girlfriend for her birthday?
   B. I don't know. I can't give her perfume. I gave her perfume LAST YEAR.
   A. How about a bracelet?
   B. No. I can't give her a bracelet. I gave her a bracelet TWO YEARS ago.
   A. Well, what are you going to give her?
   B. I don't know. I really have to think about it.

---

1. **Exercise 1:** Introduce the new word *necktie*. Call on two students to present the dialog. Then do Choral Repetition and Choral Conversation Practice.

2. **Exercise 2:** Introduce the new word *perfume*. Same as above.

3. **Exercises 3–5:**

New vocabulary: 5. *doll*

Either

Full-Class Practice: Call on a pair of students to do each exercise. Introduce the new vocabulary before doing Exercise 5. (For more practice, call on other pairs of students or do Choral Repetition or Choral Conversation.)

or

Pair Practice: Introduce the new vocabulary. Next, have students practice all of the exercises in pairs. Then, have pairs present the exercises to the class.

(For more practice, do Choral Repetition or Choral Conversation.)

4. **Exercise 6:** Have students use the model as a guide to create their own conversations, using vocabulary of their choice. Encourage students to use dictionaries to find new words they want to use. This exercise can be done orally in class or for written homework. If you assign it for homework, you should do one example in class to make sure students understand what's expected. Have students present their conversations in class the next day.

WORKBOOK

Pages 7–8

Exercise Note

Workbook p. 8: Students practice indirect object pronouns.

EXPANSION ACTIVITY

What Can I Give Them?

1. Put on the board:

---
1. friend / 45 years old / likes to eat
2. aunt / 65 / likes to read
3. roommate / 25 / likes to go jogging
4. little sister / 10 / likes to paint
5. cousin / 18 / likes to listen to music
6. friend / 17 / lazy / doesn't like to work
7. _____
---

2. Tell your students:

> "This month, many people I know are going to have birthdays. I'm very worried because I have to give them presents. My friend Albert is 45 years old. He likes to eat. What can I give him?"

Have students answer by suggesting any gift they wish. For example:

> "You can give him candy."

3. Tell about the other people on the board and have students suggest gifts.

4. For Number 7 on the board, have students make up information about someone who is having a birthday. Other students in the class then suggest gifts.

Text Page 5: *Harry! I'm Really Upset!*

FOCUS

- Indirect objects with the verbs *send, give, buy, wish*
- Talking about birthdays
- Expressing dates: *January 23rd*

INTRODUCING THE MODEL

1. Have students look at the model illustration.
2. Set the scene: "Harry's wife is talking. She's very upset."
3. With books closed, have students listen as you present the model or play the tape one or more times.
4. **Full-Class Choral Repetition:** Model each line and have students repeat.
5. Have students open their books and look at the model. Ask students if they have any questions; check understanding of new vocabulary: *send, wish, Happy Birthday.*
6. Call on one or two pairs of students to present the dialog.
7. Practice with key words on the board.

   Write on the board:

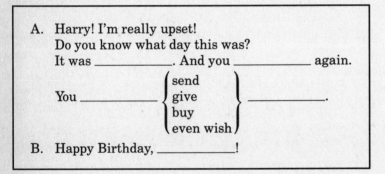

8. With their books closed, have students role play, using these key words as cues. (Have students use their own names.) This can be done as Full-Class Practice or as Pair Practice.

WHY IS SHE UPSET WITH HARRY?

Answer Key

1. He didn't send her flowers.
2. He didn't give her candy.
3. He didn't buy her a present.
4. He didn't even wish her *Happy Birthday*.

1. *Writing Practice*

   Have students write these sentences for homework.
   and/or

2. *Oral Practice*

   Have students say these sentences aloud.

ON YOUR OWN: *Birthdays*

1. Practice saying dates.

   a. Write ordinal numbers *1st* through *31st* on the board or on word cards.

   b. Have students repeat chorally and individually.

   c. Point to dates on a calendar and have students say them chorally and individually. For example:

      "June 1st," "June 10th," "June 23rd."

2. Go over the questions in the **On Your Own** exercise.

   a. Ask several students: "When is your birthday?" Then have students ask each other.

   b. Introduce the new vocabulary *receive, get, anything special*.

3. For homework, have students write answers to the questions.

4. In the next class, have students ask and answer the questions without referring to their written answers.

   This can be Full Class Practice or Pair Practice. If Pair Practice, have students report back to the class. For example:

      "Mary's family cooked a special dinner for her.
      They gave her wonderful presents.
      Her boyfriend took her to the movies."

WORKBOOK

Pages 9–10

   ### *Exercise Note*

      Workbook p. 9: For additional oral practice with Exercise M, ask students about people in the building. For example: "Where does Peter Jones live?" "Where's the flower shop?" "Who works on the 7th floor?"

EXPANSION ACTIVITY

Listening Practice: Indirect Object Pronouns

1. Put on the board:

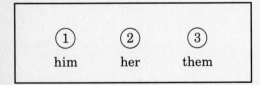

2. Read the sentences below. Have students say or write the number of the indirect object pronoun they can substitute for the noun in each sentence.

   a. I gave *my wife* a sweater.
   b. She's going to buy *her brother* a TV.
   c. They bought *Mr. Jones* a radio.
   d. I didn't send *my parents* a present.
   e. Did you wish *your sister* "Happy Birthday"?
   f. We didn't give *my friends* any dessert.
   g. I can't send *my aunt* flowers.
   h. She always gives *her husband* clothes.
   i. She always gives *her children* candy.

3. Read the sentences below. Have students say or write the number of the indirect object pronoun they hear.

   a. I gave her a sweater.
   b. She's going to buy him a TV.
   c. They bought him a radio.
   d. I didn't send them a present.
   e. Did you wish her Happy Birthday?
   f. We didn't give them any dessert.
   g. I can't send her flowers.
   h. She always gives him clothes.
   i. She always gives them candy.

READING: *Very Good Friends:* **East and West**
Very Good Friends: **North and South**

FOCUS

- Review of tenses: simple present, simple past
- Indirect object pronouns

NEW VOCABULARY

Story 1		Story 2	
advice	lost (lose *his* job)	Alabama	Minnesota
East Coast	Philadelphia	anniversary	painting
even though	San Diego	bought (buy)	plant (n)
far apart	silk	down south	sold (sell)
give advice	silver	into	up north
lent (lend)	West Coast		

PREVIEWING THE STORIES (optional)

Have students talk about the story titles and/or illustrations. Introduce new vocabulary.

READING THE STORIES

1. Have students read silently, or follow along silently as the stories are read aloud by you, by one or more students, or on the tape.
2. Ask students if they have any questions; check understanding of vocabulary.
3. Check students' comprehension, using some or all of the following questions:

Story 1:

a. What does he write her letters about?
b. What does she write him letters about?
c. What did he send her last year on her birthday?
d. What did she send him last year on his birthday?
e. How did he help her last year?
f. How did she help him last year?

Story 2:

a. What do we write them letters about?
b. What do they write us letters about?
c. What did we send them last year on their anniversary?
d. What did they send us last year on our anniversary?
e. How did we help them last year?
f. How did they help us last year?

CHECK-UP

True or False?

1.	False	6.	False
2.	True	7.	False
3.	True	8.	True
4.	False	9.	True
5.	True	10.	True

Choose

1. b
2. d
3. c
4. c
5. b

Listening

Have students complete the exercises as you play the tape or read the following:

Listen and choose the best answer.

1. What are you going to cook tomorrow? (b)
2. What did you give your husband for his birthday? (a)
3. When did you plant these flowers? (a)
4. What do you do in the winter? (b)
5. Where did your parents go on their vacation? (a)
6. How often do they write to each other? (b)
7. What did he send her? (a)
8. When are you going to move? (b)

IN YOUR OWN WORDS

1. Make sure students understand the instructions.
2. Have students do the activity as written homework, using a dictionary for any new words they wish to use.
3. Have students present and discuss what they have written, in pairs or as a class.

WORKBOOK ANSWER KEY AND LISTENING SCRIPTS

Page 1 A. LIKES AND DISLIKES

1. likes to play
2. doesn't like to teach
3. like to eat
4. don't like to dance
5. likes to visit
6. doesn't like to study
7. like to watch
8. don't like to bake
9. likes to write to
10. doesn't like to wait for

Page 3 F. DAY AFTER DAY

1. talks
   talked to his girlfriend
   he's going to talk to his girlfriend
2. clean
   cleaned their bedroom
   they're going to clean their bedroom
3. washes
   washed his car
   he's going to wash his car
4. write
   wrote to my son
   I'm going to write to my son
5. sing
   sang together
   we're going to sing together
6. cries
   cried
   she's going to cry
7. eat
   ate dessert
   they're going to eat dessert
8. get up
   got up at 8:00
   I'm going to get up at 8:00
9. reads
   read the newspaper
   she's going to read the newspaper
10. go
    went to the movies
    they're going to go to the movies
11. buys
    bought bananas
    he's going to buy bananas
12. brush
    brushed their teeth
    they're going to brush their teeth
13. takes
    took the bus
    she's going to take the bus
14. do
    did
    we're going to do our exercises

Page 7 H. WHAT'S JUDY GOING TO GIVE HER FAMILY?

1. She's going to give him a football.
2. She's going to give her a book.
3. She's going to give them candy.
4. She's going to give her a record.
5. She's going to give him a watch.
6. She's going to give her a blouse.
7. She's going to give them a suitcase.
8. She's going to give him a dog.

Page 7 I. PRESENTS

1. gave, I'm going to give him
2. gave, she's going to give her
3. gave, he's going to give him
4. gave, he's going to give them
5. gave, they're going to give him
6. gave, he's going to give her
7. gave, we're going to give them

Page 9 K. LISTEN

Listen and write the correct activity under the appropriate date.

John is busy this month.

On July 2nd he's going bowling.
On July 4th he's going to a concert.
On July 8th he's going to the dentist.
On July 11th he's going sailing.
On July 16th he's going to a football game.
On July 20th he's going to a party.
On July 27th he's going swimming.
On July 29th he's going to the doctor.
On July 31st he's going to a wedding.

			JULY			
SUNDAY	MONDAY	TUESDAY	WEDNESDAY	THURSDAY	FRIDAY	SATURDAY
				1	2 bowling	3
4 concert	5	6	7	8 dentist	9	10
11 sailing	12	13	14	15	16 football game	17
18	19	20 party	21	22	23	24
25	26	27 swimming	28	29 doctor	30	31 wedding

Page 9 L. LISTEN

Listen and write the ordinal number you hear.

Many people live and work in this building in New York City.

1. Peter Jones lives in an apartment on the 4th floor.
2. The Smith family lives in an apartment on the 14th floor.
3. The PRESTO Company has an office on the 19th floor.
4. Mary Nelson works in an office on the 7th floor.
5. There's a drug store on the 1st floor.
6. There's a dentist's office on the 35th floor.
7. Barbara Harris and her son live on the 30th floor.
8. Mr. and Mrs. Brown live in an apartment on the 13th floor.
9. Dr. Johnson has an office on the 28th floor.
10. Mr. Jackson works in an office on the 10th floor.
11. Hilda Green lives in a small apartment on the 46th floor.
12. There's a flower shop on the 2nd floor.
13. Dr. Rinaldi has an office on the 15th floor.
14. The Larson family lives on the 41st floor.
15. Mrs. Nathan has an office on the 12th floor.
16. There's a French restaurant on the 50th floor.

Answers

1.	4th	2.	14th
3.	19th	10.	10th
4.	7th	11.	46th
5.	1st	12.	2nd
6.	35th	13.	15th
7.	30th	14.	41st
8.	13th	15.	12th
9.	28th	16.	50th

Page 10 M. JOHNNY'S BIRTHDAYS

1.	took	15.	baked
2.	went	16.	wished
3.	ate	17.	loved
4.	loved	18.	dance
5.	buy	19.	sat
6.	had	20.	talked
7.	played	21.	watched
8.	went	22.	have
9.	loved	23.	went
10.	like	24.	had
11.	gave	25.	give
12.	wanted	26.	bake
13.	had	27.	danced
14.	cooked		

1. He was upset because his mother didn't buy him any candy at the zoo.
2. He was upset because he didn't like his presents.
3. He was upset because the girls didn't dance at his party. (They sat and talked and watched TV.)
4. He wasn't upset because his girlfriend danced with him all night.

GRAMMAR

Count/Non-Count Nouns

There isn't any	bread. lettuce. flour.

There aren't any	apples. eggs. lemons.

How much	milk coffee ice cream	do you want?
How many	cookies french fries meatballs	

Not too	much. many.

Just	a little. a few.

FUNCTIONS

Suggesting

Let's *make sandwiches for lunch*!

Asking for and Reporting Information

There isn't any *bread*.
There aren't any *apples*.

My doctor says that *too many potatoes are bad for my health*.

Inquiring about Want-Desire

How much *milk* do you want?
How many *cookies* do you want?

Inquiring about Satisfaction

How do you like *the potatoes*?

Expressing Satisfaction

I think it's *delicious*.
I think they're *delicious*.

Offering

Would you care for some more?

Expressing Inability

We can't.

Expressing Gratitude

Thanks.

NEW VOCABULARY

a few
a little
apple
bag
beans
beer
bread
butter
cake
care
celery
cheese
chicken
chocolate
chocolate cake
chocolate chip cookie
cookie
cracker
delicious
dollar
egg
fish
flour
french fries
fresh

garlic
good for
grapes
groceries
hamburger
how much
jam
jelly
just
lemon
let's
lettuce
make
mayonnaise
meat
meatballs
melon
milk
omelette
onion
orange
orange juice
pepper
pizza

potato
rice
salad
salt
sandwich
soda
some more
spend
sugar
taste
Thanks.
think so
tomato
too many
too much
vegetable
want
yogurt

bad for my health
Here you are.
Just a few.
Just a little.
Would you care for some more?

LANGUAGE NOTE

Distinguishing Count and Non-Count Nouns

1. A count noun refers to something we can count. For example:

    I have an apple.
    I have two apples.

2. A non-count noun refers to something that cannot be counted. For example:

            I have rice, or *I have some rice.*
    NOT: *I have a rice,* or *I have two rices.*

    The quantity of a non-count noun is described with *partitive* expressions, such as measurements or containers. For example:

    I have a box of rice.
    I have two boxes of rice.

    Partitive expressions are introduced in Chapter 3.

Text Page 10: *What's in Henry's Kitchen?*

FOCUS

> Introduction of count and non-count nouns

WHAT'S IN HENRY'S KITCHEN?

Use *Side by Side* Picture Cards 172–202 or your own visuals; or bring products from home to introduce the food items on text page 10:

Count Nouns	Non-Count Nouns	
apples	beer	lettuce
beans	bread	mayonnaise
cookies	butter	milk
crackers	celery	orange juice
eggs	cheese	pepper
melons	flour	rice
onions	garlic	salt
pears	jam	soda
tomatoes	jelly	sugar
		yogurt

1. Write on the board:

> 1. There are some _____.   2. There's some _____.

2. Have students look at the illustration on text page 10 as you ask the question "What's in Henry's kitchen?" Point to the food items as you introduce the 4 count nouns in the left column.

   Use sentence 1 on the board and have students repeat:

   > "There are some *tomatoes*."
   > "There are some *eggs*."
   > "There are some *bananas*."
   > "There are some *apples*."

3. Point to the food items as you introduce the 4 non-count nouns in the right column. Use sentence 2 on the board and have students repeat:

   > "There's some *cheese*."
   > "There's some *milk*."
   > "There's some *ice cream*."
   > "There's some *bread*."

4. Introduce all the other food items in Henry's refrigerator the same way. Have students repeat each sentence and write the new food item in their books or notebooks under the categories *count* and *non-count*.

There are some crackers.	There's some milk.
There are some beans.	There are some apples.
There's some garlic.	There's some wine.
There's some rice.	There are some eggs.
There's some flour.	There's some lettuce.
There are some cookies.	There are some melons.
There's some ice cream.	There are some apples.
There's some yogurt.	There are some pears.
There's some soda.	There's some celery.
There's some orange juice.	There's some sugar.
There's some cheese.	There's some bread.
There's some jam.	There's some coffee.
There's some jelly.	There's some salt.
There's some butter.	There's some tea.
There's some beer.	There are some onions.
There are some tomatoes.	There's some pepper.
There's some mayonnaise.	There are some bananas.

5. Use *Side by Side* Picture Cards 172–202, your own visuals, or products from home to review the food items.

   Point to each food item. Have students say the word and make a sentence. For example:

   > "rice: There's some rice."
   > "flour: There's some flour."
   > "cookies: There are some cookies."

6. Write the following on the board:

in the refrigerator
in the cupboard on the left
in the cupboard on the right

   Ask about the location of the food items in Henry's kitchen and have students answer, using the expressions on the board. For example:

   A. Where's the ice cream?
   B. It's in the refrigerator.

   A. Where are the crackers?
   B. They're in the cupboard on the left.

   A. Where's the bread?
   B. It's in the cupboard on the right.

WORKBOOK

Pages 11–12

EXPANSION ACTIVITY

Students Talk about Foods They Like and Dislike

Practice count and non-count nouns with visuals or word cards for the foods on text page 10.

1. Write on the board:

```
A.  I  ⎧ like       ⎫
       ⎨ don't like ⎬  _____. Do you like _____?
       ⎪ love       ⎪
       ⎩ hate       ⎭

B.  I  ⎧ like       ⎫
       ⎨ don't like ⎬  (it/them).
       ⎪ love       ⎪
       ⎩ hate       ⎭
              or
       ⎧ It's   ⎫  okay.
       ⎨ They're ⎬
```

2. Hold up a visual or word card for a food item and call on a pair of students to create a conversation, using the model on the board. For example:

   cue: *garlic*
   A. I love garlic. Do you like garlic?
   B. I hate it. (or) I love it. (or) It's okay. (or) I like it. (or) I don't like it.

   cue: *beans*
   A. I hate beans. Do you like beans?
   B. I love them. (or) I hate them. (or) They're okay. (etc.)

   cue: *eggs*
   A. I like eggs. Do you like eggs?
   B. I don't like them. (etc.)

   cue: *melon*
   A. I don't like melon. Do you like melon?
   B. I like it. (etc.)

Text Page 11: *Let's Make Sandwiches for Lunch!*

FOCUS

> • Non-count nouns: *There isn't any bread.*
> • Count nouns: *There aren't any apples.*

INTRODUCING THE MODEL

There are two model conversations. Introduce and practice each separately. For each model:

1. Have students look at the model illustration.
2. Set the scene: "People are talking about food they want to make."
3. With books closed, have students listen as you present the model or play the tape one or more times.
4. **Full-Class Choral Repetition:** Model each line and have students repeat.
5. Have students open their books and look at the dialog. Ask students if they have any questions; check understanding of new vocabulary:

   1st model: *let's, make, sandwich, for lunch*
   2nd model: *for dessert*

6. **Group Choral Repetition:** Divide the class in half. Model line A and have Group 1 repeat; model line B and have Group 2 repeat, and so on.
7. **Choral Conversation:** Groups 1 and 2 practice the dialog twice, without teacher model. First, Group 1 is Speaker A, and Group 2 is Speaker B; then reverse.
8. Call on one or two pairs of students to present the dialog.

   (For additional practice, do Choral Conversation in small groups or by rows.)

SIDE BY SIDE EXERCISES

Examples

> 1. A. Let's make a salad for dinner!
>   B. Sorry, we can't. There isn't any lettuce.
>
> 2. A. Let's make an omelette for breakfast!
>   B. Sorry, we can't. There aren't any eggs.

1. **Exercise 1:** Introduce the new vocabulary *salad, for dinner, lettuce*. Call on two students to present the dialog. Then do Choral Repetition and Choral Conversation Practice.
2. **Exercise 2:** Introduce the new vocabulary *omelette, for breakfast*. Same as above.
3. **Exercises 3–8:**

   > **New vocabulary:**   3. *fresh, lemon*   4. *cake*   5. *pizza*   6. *orange*
   >   7. *chicken*   8. *french fries, hamburger, potato*

Culture Note

French fries, hamburgers (Exercise 8): These foods are extremely common in the United States, especially in what are called *fast food* restaurants, where food is prepared beforehand and served quickly.

Either Full-Class Practice or Pair Practice.

4. **Exercise 9:** Call on pairs of students to create new conversations based on the model.

WORKBOOK

Pages 13–15 (Exercises C, D, E)

Exercise Note

Workbook p. 13: For additional oral practice with Exercise C, have students role play the conversations between customers and the waitress at *Ed's Restaurant.*

EXPANSION ACTIVITY

Role Play: In a Restaurant

Use the following conversational model and word cards as cues to role play ordering food in a restaurant.

1. Write on the board:

> A. Can I have some _____ with my _____, please?
> B. I'm sorry. There _____ any _____.

2. Set the scene: "A customer is ordering food in a restaurant."

3. Hold up a word card showing two food items often eaten together. For example:

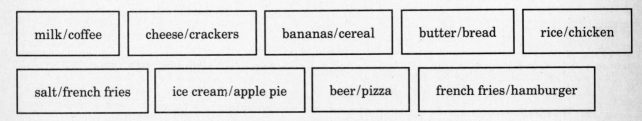

| milk/coffee | cheese/crackers | bananas/cereal | butter/bread | rice/chicken |

| salt/french fries | ice cream/apple pie | beer/pizza | french fries/hamburger |

Call on two students to create a conversation. For example:

cue: *milk/coffee*
   A. Can I have some *milk* with my *coffee*, please?
   B. I'm sorry. There isn't any *milk*.

cue: *crackers/cheese*
   A. Can I have some *crackers* with my *cheese*, please?
   B. I'm sorry. There aren't any *crackers*.

Text Page 12: *How Much Milk Do You Want?*

FOCUS

> - Expressions with *much* and *a little* with non-count nouns
> - Expressions with *many* and *a few* with count nouns

GETTING READY

1. Introduce non-count nouns.

   a. Write the following conversation on the board and have students repeat after you:

      > A. Do you want some milk?
      > B. Okay, but just a little.

   b. Put the following non-count nouns on the board or on word cards for students to use as cues for creating similar conversations: *ice cream, bread, coffee, orange juice.*

2. Introduce count nouns.

   a. Write the following conversation on the board and have students repeat after you:

      > A. Do you want some cookies?
      > B. Okay, but just a few.

   b. Put the following count nouns on the board or on word cards for students to use as cues for creating similar conversations: *crackers, eggs, potatoes, beans.*

INTRODUCING THE MODEL

There are two model conversations. Introduce and practice each separately. For each model:

1. Have students look at the model illustration.
2. Set the scene:

   1st model: "A mother and daughter are talking."
   2nd model: "Two friends are talking."

3. Present the model.
4. Full-class Choral Repetition.
5. Ask students if they have any questions; check understanding of new vocabulary:

   1st model: *how much, too much, just, a little, Here you are, Thanks*
   2nd model: *how many, too many, a few*

6. Group Choral Repetition.
7. Choral Conversation.
8. Call on one or two pairs of students to present the dialog.

   (For additional practice, do Choral Conversation in small groups or by rows.)

SIDE BY SIDE EXERCISES

Examples

> 1. A. How much coffee do you want?
>   B. Not too much. Just a little.
>   A. Okay. Here you are.
>   B. Thanks.
>
> 2. A. How many french fries do you want?
>   B. Not too many. Just a few.
>   A. Okay. Here you are.
>   B. Thanks.

1. **Exercise 1:** Call on two students to present the dialog. Then do Choral Repetition and Choral Conversation Practice.

2. **Exercise 2:** Same as above.

3. **Exercises 3–5:**

> **New vocabulary:** 5. *meatballs*

Either Full-Class Practice or Pair Practice.

4. **Exercise 6:** Have students use the model as a guide to create their own conversations, using vocabulary of their choice. (They can use any foods they wish.) Encourage students to use dictionaries to find new words they want to use. This exercise can be done orally in class or for written homework. If you assign it for homework, you should do one example in class to make sure students understand what's expected. Have students present their conversations in class the next day.

WORKBOOK

Pages 15–17 (Exercises F, G)

Exercise Note

Workbook p. 17: Students practice count/non-count nouns with *a few/a little* and *many/much*.

EXPANSION ACTIVITIES

1. Review Count and Non-Count Nouns

Say the nouns below. After each word have students respond either "How much?" (for non-count) or "How many?" (for count).

1.	french fries	(How many?)	8.	butter	(How much?)
2.	rice	(How much?)	9.	orange juice	(How much?)
3.	sugar	(How much?)	10.	crackers	(How many?)
4.	hamburgers	(How many?)	11.	apples	(How many?)
5.	sandwiches	(How many?)	12.	eggs	(How many?)
6.	flour	(How much?)	13.	bread	(How much?)
7.	mayonnaise	(How much?)	14.	onions	(How many?)

2. *Practice* A Little *and* A Few

a. Write the following conversational model on the board:

> A. Do you want a lot of _____?
> B. No, thanks. Just (a few/a little).
> A. Are you sure?
> B. Yes.
> A. Okay. { Here's a little _____.
>   Here are a few _____. }

b. Hold up word cards for pairs of students to use as cues for creating conversations based on the model:

> *rice, crackers, lettuce, potatoes, cheese, chicken, meatballs, cookies*

3. *Practice* Too Much *and* Too Many

Use the conversational model below and word cues to have students create conversations.

a. Write on the board:

> A. You look terrible! What's the matter?
> B. I have a very bad _____.
> A. Why?
> B. Because I _____ too (much/many) _____ last night.

b. Set the scene: "Two friends are talking; one of them feels terrible."

c. Hold up a word card showing key words such as those below. Call on two students to create a conversation.

Key words:

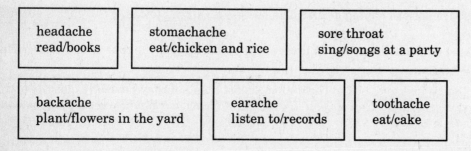

headache read/books	stomachache eat/chicken and rice	sore throat sing/songs at a party
backache plant/flowers in the yard	earache listen to/records	toothache eat/cake

For example:

> A. You look terrible! What's the matter?
> B. I have a very bad headache.
> A. Why?
> B. Because I read too many books last night.

d. Call on pairs of students to create similar conversations, using any vocabulary they wish.

Text Page 13

ON YOUR OWN: *Would You Care for Some More?*

FOCUS

> Review of count and non-count nouns

INTRODUCING THE MODEL

Introduce the conversational model with Exercises 1 and 2. Introduce and practice each separately.

Answer Key

> 1. A. How do you like the potatoes?
>   B. I think they're delicious.
>   A. I'm glad you like them. Would you care for some more?
>   B. Yes, please. But not too many. Just a few.
>   My doctor says that too many potatoes are bad for my health.
>
> 2. A. How do you like the chocolate cake?
>   B. I think it's delicious.
>   A. I'm glad you like it. Would you care for some more?
>   B. Yes, please. But not too much. Just a little.
>   My doctor says that too much chocolate cake is bad for my health.

For each conversation:

1. Have students look at the illustration.
2. Set the scene: "Some friends are having dinner. The hostess is talking to one of the guests about the food."
3. With books closed, have students listen as you present the model or play the tape one or more times.
4. Full-Class Choral Repetition.
5. Have students open their books and look at the dialog. Ask students if they have any questions; check understanding of new vocabulary: *How do you like* _____*?, delicious, Would you care for some more? bad for my health, chocolate.*
6. Group Choral Repetition.
7. Choral Conversation.
8. Call on one or two pairs of students to present the dialog.

   (For additional practice, do Choral Conversation in small groups or by rows.)

SIDE BY SIDE EXERCISES

1. **Exercises 3 and 4:** Either Full-Class Practice or Pair Practice.
2. **Exercise 5:** For homework, have students use the model as a guide to write two *dinner table* conversations: one using a non-count noun, and the other using a count noun. Have students present their conversations in class the next day without referring to their written homework. (For added realism you can set up a dinner table in front of the class with *props* such as plates, silverware and cups.)

WORKBOOK

Pages 18–21

Exercise Notes

Workbook p. 18: For additional oral practice, have pairs of students act out the conversations.

Workbook p. 20: Students practice count/non-count nouns with *a few* and *a little*.

Workbook p. 21: Students practice count/non-count nouns with *there isn't* and *there aren't*.

EXPANSION ACTIVITY

Table Talk

Use *Side by Side* Picture Cards 172–202, your own visuals, or word cards of count and non-count food items.

1. Write on the board:

   > A. Would you care for some more _____?
   > B. Just (a little/a few), thank you. (It's/They're) delicious.

2. Set the scene: "A friend is having dinner at your house."

3. Hold up a visual or word card. Call on two students to create a conversation. For example:

   > cue: *cake*
   > A. Would you care for some more cake?
   > B. Just a little, thank you. It's delicious.

4. Practice this way with as many food items as possible.

Text Page 14:

READING: *Two Bags of Groceries*

FOCUS

Count/Non-count nouns

NEW VOCABULARY

bag	fish	groceries
dollar	grapes	meat

PREVIEWING THE STORY (optional)

Have students talk about the story title and/or illustration. Introduce new vocabulary.

READING THE STORY

1. Have students read silently, or follow along silently as the story is read aloud by you, by one or more students, or on the tape.
2. Ask students if they have any questions; check understanding of vocabulary.
3. Check students' comprehension:

   a. Why is Henry upset?
   b. What did he buy?

CHECK-UP

Q & A

1. Call on a pair of students to present the model.
2. Have students work in pairs to create new dialogs.
3. Call on pairs to present their new dialogs to the class.

Listening

Have students complete the exercises as you play the tape or read the following:

Listen and choose what the people are talking about.

1. A. How much do you want?
   B. Just a little, please. (a)

2. A. Do you want some more?
   B. Okay. But just a few. (b)

3. A. These are delicious!
   B. I'm glad you like them. (a)

4. A. I ate too many.
   B. How many did you eat? (b)

5. A. They're bad for my health.
   B. Really? (a)

6. A. It's very good.
   B. Thank you. (a)

7. A. Would you care for some more?
   B. Yes, but not too much. (b)

8. A. There isn't any.
   B. There isn't?! (a)

HOW ABOUT YOU?

Have students do the activity in pairs or as a class.

Text Page 15

READING: *Delicious!*
Tastes Terrible!

FOCUS

Count/Non-count nouns

NEW VOCABULARY

Story 1	Story 2
chocolate chip cookie	care
think so	good for
	taste
	vegetable

PREVIEWING THE STORIES (optional)

Have students talk about the story titles and/or illustrations. Introduce new vocabulary.

READING THE STORIES

1. Have students read silently, or follow along silently as the stories are read aloud by you, by one or more students, or on the tape.
2. Ask students if they have any questions; check understanding of vocabulary.
3. Check students' comprehension, using some or all of the following questions:

Story 1
   a. What does Peter like?
   b. How do you know?
   c. What do his friends often tell him?
   d. Does Peter think so?

   e. What does Gloria like?
   f. How do you know?
   g. What does her doctor often tell her?
   h. Does Gloria think so?

Story 2
   a. Does Sally like vegetables?
   b. How do you know?
   c. What do her parents often tell her?
   d. Does Sally care?

   e. Does Michael like yogurt?
   f. How do you know?
   g. What does his daughter often tell him?
   h. Does Michael care?

IN YOUR OWN WORDS

1. Make sure students understand the instructions.
2. Have students do the activity as written homework, using a dictionary for any new words they wish to use.
3. Have students present and discuss what they have written, in pairs or as a class.

WORKBOOK ANSWER KEY AND LISTENING SCRIPTS

Page 11   A.   MISSING LABELS

1. MILK	2. APPLES	3. COOKIES
4. BREAD	5. ONIONS	6. SODA
7. CHEESE	8. BANANAS	9. BUTTER
10. EGGS	11. ICE CREAM	12. SUGAR

Page 12   B.   LOOKING FOR FOOD

1. There are, there's
   there are
2. There's, there's
   there's, there are
   there's, there are
3. There's, there's
   there's
4. There's, there's
5. There's, there's
6. There's, there are
   there's, there are
   there are, there are
   there's
7. There's, there's
   there's, there's
   there's

Page 13   C.   I'M SORRY, BUT . . .

1. there aren't
   any beans
2. there isn't
   any beer
3. there isn't
   any yogurt
4. there isn't
   any lemonade
5. there aren't
   any french fries
6. there isn't
   any cake
7. there aren't
   any cookies
8. there isn't
   any wine
9. there isn't
   any jam
10. there aren't
   any crackers

Page 14   D.   LISTEN: *I'm Sorry, but There _____ Any.*

Listen and put a circle around the correct word.

1. May I have some milk?
2. I'm looking for some tomatoes.
3. I'm looking for some bread.
4. I want some eggs.
5. I want some lettuce.
6. Let's have some chicken!
7. May I have some beans?
8. I'm looking for some mayonnaise.
9. May I have some flour?
10. I'm looking for some crackers.
11. I want some cheese.
12. Let's have some rice!
13. I want some pears.
14. May I have some beer?
15. I'm looking for some onions.
16. May I have some orange juice?

Answers

1.	isn't	9.	isn't
2.	aren't	10.	aren't
3.	isn't	11.	isn't
4.	aren't	12.	isn't
5.	isn't	13.	aren't
6.	isn't	14.	isn't
7.	aren't	15.	aren't
8.	isn't	16.	isn't

Page 14   E.   WHAT DO YOU WANT TO EAT?

1. aren't any eggs
   cereal
2. isn't any chicken
   hamburgers
3. isn't any wine
   coffee
4. aren't any bananas
   oranges
5. aren't any cookies
   cake
6. aren't any potatoes
   bread
7. isn't any ice cream
   yogurt
8. isn't any milk
   soda

Page 15   F.   HOME FROM VACATION

1.	much	8.	many
2.	much	9.	many
3.	much	10.	many
4.	many	11.	much
5.	much	12.	much
6.	much	13.	many
7.	much	14.	many

1. He ate so much dessert that he's in bed today with a stomachache.
2. She ate so much bread that she can't wear the new clothes she bought on vacation.
3. He wrote so many letters that he's never going to write a letter again.
4. He drank so much coffee that he has a headache today.
5. She bought so many presents that she's going to have to work hard every day after school this month.

Page 18   H.   AT THE DINNER TABLE

1. little
   much
3. This, is
   it
   little
5. little
   it's
7. it's
   it

2. few
   many
4. These, are
   them
   few
6. them
   they're
   few
8. many
   they're
   few
   few

9. this, it's
   it, little
   it's
   it isn't, It's, it's

Page 19   I.   LISTEN

Listen and put a check next to the correct picture.

1. A. Would you care for some more?
   B. Yes, please. But not too many.
2. I like it, but it's bad for my health.
3. My doctor says they're good for my health.
4. A. These are really delicious.
   B. I'm glad you like them.
5. A. How many did you eat?
   B. I ate so many that I have a stomachache.
6. I bought it this morning, and it's very fresh. Would you care for a little?

Answers

1.	✔	____	2.	____	✔
3.	____	✔	4.	____	✔
5.	____	✔	6.	✔	____

TEACHER'S NOTES

GRAMMAR

Count/Non-Count Nouns

Lettuce Butter Milk	is	very expensive this week.
Apples Carrots Onions	are	

Add	a little	salt. sugar. honey.
	a few	potatoes. nuts. raisins.

I recommend our	chocolate ice cream. scrambled eggs.

Everybody says	it's they're	delicious.

Partitives

a bag of flour	**a loaf of** bread
a bottle of soda	**a pound (lb.) of** butter
a box of cereal	
a bunch of bananas	**a bowl of** chicken soup
a can of beans	**a cup of** coffee
a half pound (half a pound) of cheese	**a dish of** ice cream
	a glass of milk
a head of lettuce	**an order of** scrambled eggs
a jar of jam	**a piece of** apple pie

Imperatives

Please **give me** a dish of ice cream.
Put a little butter into a saucepan.
Cook for 3 hours.

FUNCTIONS

Inquiring about Want-Desire

Do we need anything from *the supermarket*?

What would you like *for dessert*?

Expressing Want-Desire

We need *a loaf of bread.*

I'm looking for *a head of lettuce.*

Please give me *a dish of chocolate ice cream.*
I'd like *a glass of tomato juice.*

Asking for and Reporting Information

How much does *a head of lettuce* cost?
  Ninety-five cents.

Lettuce is very *expensive this week.*
Apples are very *expensive this week.*

There isn't any more *lettuce.*
There aren't any more *bananas.*

Everybody says *it's delicious.*

Expressing Surprise-Disbelief

NINETY-FIVE CENTS?!   That's a lot of money!

Asking for a Suggestion

What do you recommend?

Offering a Suggestion

I recommend *our chocolate ice cream.*

Inquiring about Satisfaction

How is *the vegetable soup*?

Expressing Satisfaction

It's *delicious.*

Instructing

Put a little butter into a saucepan.
Chop up a few onions.

Checking Understanding

A loaf of bread?
There isn't?
There aren't?

NEW VOCABULARY

add
appetite
baked (adj)
baking soda
bottle
bowl
box
broiled (adj)
bunch
can (n)
carrot
cents
chicken soup
chop up
cost (v)
cut up
decide
disappointed
dozen
everybody
excellent
fantastic
fruitcake
get there
glass
go to bed

had to
half a pound
half pound
head
honey
hot chocolate
hour
jar
loaf/loaves
magnificent
main course
mix (in)
mixing bowl
mushroom
need
nuts
open (v)
order (n)
order (v)
overtime
pancakes
piece
pound (lb.)
pour (in)
put
quart

raisin
recipe
recommend
romantic
saucepan
scrambled eggs
shopping list
sit down
slice
strawberry
Swiss cheese
table
tasty
tomato juice
vanilla ice cream
vegetable soup
vegetable stew
wedding anniversary
white bread
whole wheat bread

Anything else?
lost *her* appetite
out of this world
What would you like *for dessert?*

Text Page 18: *Do We Need Anything from the Supermarket?*

FOCUS

Introduction of partitives:

a bag of	a jar of
a bottle of	a loaf of (two loaves of)
a bunch of	a pound (lb.) of
a box of	a half pound of/half a pound of
a can of	a quart of
a head of	a dozen

GETTING READY

1. Use *Side by Side* Picture Cards for foods, or your own visuals; or bring real food items to class to introduce the vocabulary in **My Shopping List.**

New vocabulary:

bag	carrot	pound: (abbreviation) lb. *
bottle	dozen	half pound: ½ lb. *
box	head	white bread
bunch	jar	whole wheat bread
can	loaf (loaves)	

lb.: This abbreviation for pound is commonly used on price labels.
For example, 45¢/lb. = *forty-five cents a pound.*

a. With students' books closed, point to a visual of each item, introduce the new expression, and have students repeat chorally and individually.

b. Have students look at the shopping list in the book; model each item again and have students repeat.

c. Point to each visual and have students tell what it is.

d. Practice plural forms.

1. Model singular and plural partitives. Say: "a can of beans"—"two cans of beans." Have students repeat.
2. Give the singular form of the other items on the shopping list, and have students give the plural.

INTRODUCING THE MODEL

1. Have students look at the model illustration.
2. Set the scene: "A husband and wife are talking."
3. Present the model.
4. Full-Class Choral Repetition.
5. Ask students if they have any questions; check understanding of new vocabulary: *need, anything else.*

Supermarket: Most people in the United States shop for food in supermarkets, where they can buy all their groceries in one store. Supermarkets typically have separate departments for foods such as baked goods, meat, fruit, and vegetables.

6. Group Choral Repetition.
7. Choral Conversation.
8. Call on one or two pairs of students to present the dialog.

   (For additional practice, do Choral Conversation in small groups or by rows.)

SIDE BY SIDE EXERCISES

Examples

---

1. A. Do we need anything from the supermarket?
   B. Yes. We need a box of cereal.
   A. A box of cereal?
   B. Yes.
   A. Anything else?
   B. No. Just a box of cereal.

2. A. Do we need anything from the supermarket?
   B. Yes. We need a jar of jam.
   A. A jar of jam?
   B. Yes.
   A. Anything else?
   B. No. Just a jar of jam.

---

1. **Exercise 1:** Call on two students to present the dialog. Then do Choral Repetition and Choral Conversation Practice.
2. **Exercise 2:** Introduce the new word *jam.* Same as above.
3. **Exercises 3–7:**

   New vocabulary: 5. *vegetable soup*

   Either Full-Class Practice or Pair Practice.

4. **Exercise 8:** Have students use the model as a guide to create their own conversations, using vocabulary of their choice. (They can use any food products they wish.) Encourage students to use dictionaries to find new words they want to use. This exercise can be done orally in class or for written homework. If you assign it for homework, you should do one example in class to make sure students understand what's expected. Have students present their conversations in class the next day.

HOW ABOUT YOU?

Have students do the activity in pairs or as a class.

WORKBOOK

Pages 22–23

Exercise Note

Workbook p. 22:   The answer key is based on containers practiced in the text. It's possible that these foods come in different containers in your country. Have students talk about this with their classmates.

EXPANSION ACTIVITIES

1. **Dictation**

   a. Set the scene: "Tomorrow my cousin is going to have lunch at my house. Tonight I'm going shopping, and here's what I'm going to buy:

1.	a pound of cheese	7.	a dozen eggs
2.	a loaf of white bread	8.	a bag of sugar
3.	a half pound of butter	9.	a bag of flour
4.	a quart of milk	10.	a jar of mayonnaise
5.	2 heads of lettuce	11.	a box of tea
6.	a bunch of carrots	12.	2 cans of chicken soup."

   b. After the dictation, review the shopping list. Call out each number and have students tell you the food item.

   c. Finally, have students look at the shopping list and guess what you are going to make for lunch. (For example, based on this list you can make soup, salad, and cheese sandwiches. For dessert you can make a cake.)

2. **Chain Game: Our Shopping List**

   Make a chain game where students add new items to a shopping list in increasing quantities. For example:

   You ask Student A:
You:	Do we need anything from the supermarket?
Student A:	Yes, we need a box of cereal.

   A asks B:
Student A:	Do we need anything from the supermarket?
Student B:	Yes, we need a box of cereal and 2 quarts of milk.

   B asks C:
Student B:	Do we need anything from the supermarket?
Student C:	Yes, we need a box of cereal, 2 quarts of milk, and 3 cans of beans.

3. **Menus**

   a. Have students prepare menus for breakfast, lunch, dinner, and a snack. For example:

Lunch	*A snack*
a cup of chicken soup	a bowl of popcorn (with butter and salt)
a tuna fish salad sandwich	a soft drink
a green salad	potato chips
fresh fruit	

b. Have others in the class tell them what food they will have to buy at the supermarket. For example:

Lunch	*A snack*
a can of chicken soup	a bag of popcorn
a can of tuna fish	three cans of a soft drink
a jar of mayonnaise	a bag of potato chips
a loaf of bread	a stick of butter
a head of lettuce	a box of salt
a bottle of salad dressing	
half a pound of apples	
a bunch of grapes	
four oranges	

Encourage students to practice using the different partitives in this exercise.

Text Page 19: *How Much Does a Head of Lettuce Cost?*

FOCUS

> - Practice with partitives
> - Asking about prices

GETTING READY

Practice saying prices.

> **New vocabulary:** *cents   dollar*

1. Put prices on the board or on word cards. For example:

25¢	$1.00
50¢	$1.50
95¢	$2.25
	$4.50

2. Say each price and have students repeat chorally and individually.
3. Point to a price and have students say it.

INTRODUCING THE MODEL

There are two model conversations. Introduce and practice each separately. For each model:

1. Have students look at the model illustration.
2. Set the scene: "A customer is talking to a clerk in a supermarket."
3. Present the model.
4. Full-Class Choral Repetition.
5. Ask students if they have any questions; check understanding of new vocabulary:

> Model 1: *cost, cents*
> Model 2: *dollar*

Language Note

> *Expressing prices:* Prices are often expressed informally. For example:
>
> > $1.25—a dollar twenty-five
> > $2.25—two twenty five.
>
> A more formal way of expressing prices is:
>
> > $1.25—one dollar and twenty-five cents
> > $2.25—two dollars and twenty-five cents.

6. Group Choral Repetition.

7. Choral Conversation.

8. Call on one or two pairs of students to present the dialog.

9. Have pairs of students practice the models using other prices, such as those listed below the second model.

   (For additional practice, do Choral Conversation in small groups or by rows.)

SIDE BY SIDE EXERCISES

In these exercises, students use any prices they wish.

Examples

> 1. A. How much does a pound of butter cost?
>   B. A dollar seventy-five ($1.75).
>   A. A DOLLAR SEVENTY-FIVE?! That's a lot of money!
>   B. You're right. Butter is very expensive this week.
>
> 2. A. How much does a bunch of carrots cost?
>   B. Eighty cents (80¢).
>   A: EIGHTY CENTS?! That's a lot of money!
>   B. You're right. Carrots are very expensive this week.

1. **Exercise 1:** Call on two students to present the dialog. Then do Choral Repetition and Choral Conversation Practice.

2. **Exercise 2:** Same as above.

3. **Exercises 3–8:**

> **New vocabulary:**   5. *Swiss cheese*

   Either Full-Class Practice or Pair Practice.

4. **Exercise 9:** Have students use the model as a guide to create their own conversations, using vocabulary of their choice. (They can use any foods they wish.) Encourage students to use dictionaries to find new words they want to use. This exercise can be done orally in class or for written homework. If you assign it for homework, you should do one example in class to make sure students understand what's expected. Have students present their conversations in class the next day.

WORKBOOK

Pages 23–25 (Exercises B, C, D)

Exercise Notes

   Workbook p. 23: For additional oral practice with Exercise B, have students ask and answer questions about the prices of the pictured foods.

   Workbook p. 24: Students practice foods and their containers (loaves/cans/pounds/jars/quarts).

   Workbook p. 25: For additional oral practice with Exercise D, have students act out the conversations.

EXPANSION ACTIVITIES

1. ***Role Play:*** ***At the Supermarket***

Bring a variety of food items to class. You can also use *Side by Side* Picture Cards for *foods* (172–202) or your own visuals. Have students create role plays, using the conversational model below and the food items or visuals as *props*. Students can use any prices they wish.

a. Write on the board:

A. How much does _____ cost?

B. _____.

A. _____?! { That's a lot of money! }
            { That's a bargain! }

B. You're right.

_____ is/are very { expensive } this week.
                { cheap }

---

b. Introduce the new word *bargain*. Then call on pairs of students to role play the conversation using visuals or one of the props (such as a bottle of soda or a head of lettuce).

2. ***Food Advertisements***

Bring to class an English-language newspaper or a local newspaper that has grocery advertisements. Show the advertisements to the class. Have students ask questions about prices; be sure students practice partitives when appropriate. Other students can give answers. For example:

Advertisement	Students
bananas . . . 39¢ lb.	A. How much does a pound of bananas cost? B. Thirty-nine cents.
eggs . . . $1.10 doz.	A. How much does a dozen eggs cost? B. A dollar ten.
carrots . . . 40¢ bunch	A. How much does a bunch of carrots cost? B. Forty cents.

Text Page 20

READING: *Nothing to Eat for Dinner*

FOCUS

> - Partitives
> - Count/Non-count nouns

NEW VOCABULARY

appetite	go to bed	lost (lose) her appetite	overtime
disappointed	had to	open	sat (sit) down
get there			shopping list

PREVIEWING THE STORY (optional)

Have students talk about the story title and/or illustrations. Introduce new vocabulary.

READING THE STORY

1. Have students read silently, or follow along silently as the story is read aloud by you, by one or more students, or on the tape.
2. Ask students if they have any questions; check understanding of vocabulary.

   Culture Note

   Most Americans work eight hours a day. Sometimes there is a lot of work to finish, so the boss asks his or her employees to work *overtime*, additional hours.

3. Check students' comprehension, using some or all of the following questions:

   a. Why did Joan get home late?
   b. Why was she upset when she got home?
   c. What did she need from the supermarket?
   d. Why was she disappointed when she got to the supermarket?
   e. How did Joan feel?
   f. What did she do?

CHECK-UP

Q & A

1. Call on a pair of students to present each model.
2. Have students work in pairs to create new dialogs.
3. Call on pairs to present their new dialogs to the class.

Listening

Have students complete the exercises as you play the tape or read the following:

Listen and choose what the people are talking about.

1. A. How much does a pound cost?
   B. A dollar forty. (b)

2. A. How many loaves do we need?'
   B. Three. (a)

3. A. They're very expensive this week.
   B. You're right. (a)

4. A. Sorry. There isn't any more.
   B. There isn't? (b)

5. A. I need two quarts.
   B. Okay. (a)

6. A. I bought too many.
   B. Really? (a)

7. A. There weren't any in the refrigerator.
   B. Who ate them? (b)

8. A. How much does the large box cost?
   B. Two nineteen. (a)

Text Page 21: *What Would You Like?*

FOCUS

> Introduction of partitives:
> | | |
> |---|---|
> | *a bowl of* | *a glass of* |
> | *a cup of* | *an order of* |
> | *a dish of* | *a piece of* |

INTRODUCING THE MODEL

There are two model conversations. Introduce and practice each separately. For each model:

1. Have students look at the model illustration.
2. Set the scene:

1st model:	"A waiter is talking to a customer in a restaurant."
2nd model:	"A waitress is talking to a customer in a restaurant."

3. Present the model.
4. Full-Class Choral Repetition.
5. Ask students if they have any questions; check understanding of new vocabulary:

1st model:	*What would you like?, decide, recommend, everybody, a dish of*
2nd model:	*scrambled eggs, out of this world, an order of*

   ### Language Note

   An order of: This expression refers to servings of food in a restaurant. For example, *an order of pancakes, an order of french fries.*

6. Group Choral Repetition.
7. Choral Conversation.
8. Call on one or two pairs of students to present the dialog.
9. Introduce the new expressions *fantastic, wonderful, magnificent, excellent, out of this world.* Have pairs of students practice the model again, using these expressions in place of *delicious* (1st model) and *out of this world* (2nd model).

   (For additional practice, do Choral Conversation in small groups or by rows.)

SIDE BY SIDE EXERCISES

In these exercises, students can choose any adjectives for describing the food.

Examples

> 1. A. What would you like for dessert?
>   B. I can't decide. What do you recommend?
>   A. I recommend our apple pie. Everybody says it's (delicious).
>   B. Okay. Please give me a piece of apple pie.

2. A. What would you like for lunch?
    B. I can't decide. What do you recommend?
    A. I recommend our chicken soup. Everybody says it's (fantastic).
    B. Okay. Please give me a bowl of chicken soup.

1. **Exercise 1:** Introduce the new expression *a piece of.* Call on two students to present the dialog. Then do Choral Repetition and Choral Conversation Practice.

2. **Exercise 2:** Introduce the new expressions *a bowl of, chicken soup.* Same as above.

3. **Exercises 3–8:**

> **New vocabulary:**   4. *an order of pancakes*   5. *glass of*
>   6. *vanilla ice cream*   7. *hot chocolate*   8. *strawberry*

Either Full-Class Practice or Pair Practice.

4. **Exercise 9:** Have students use the model as a guide to create their own conversations, using vocabulary of their choice. (They can use any foods they wish.) Encourage students to use dictionaries to find new words they want to use. This exercise can be done orally in class or for written homework. If you assign it for homework, you should do one example in class to make sure students understand what's expected. Have students present their conversations in class the next day.

WORKBOOK

Pages 26–28

Exercise Notes

Workbook p. 26:   For additional oral practice with Exercise E, have students act out the conversation.

Workbook p. 28:   In Exercises G and H, students practice partitives.

EXPANSION ACTIVITIES

1. Role Play: At the Restaurant

a. Write on the board:

> A. What would you like $\begin{Bmatrix} \text{to} \\ \text{for} \end{Bmatrix}$ _____?
> B. I don't know. What do you recommend?
> A. How about a/an _____ of _____?
> B. No, thank you. I don't really like _____.
> A. Well, how about a/an _____ of _____?
> B. Okay. That's fine.

b. Call on two students to create a conversation using word cues: Student A is the waiter or waitress; Student B is the customer.

Give the waiter/waitress a word card with appropriate cues. Sample word cards:

breakfast pancakes cereal	drink coffee milk	dessert vanilla ice cream apple pie
breakfast cereal pancakes	drink wine tea	dessert chocolate cake strawberry ice cream

Example:

    A. What would you like for breakfast?
    B. I don't know. What do you recommend?
    A. How about an order of pancakes?
    B. No, thank you. I don't really like pancakes.
    A. Well, how about a bowl of cereal?
    B. Okay. That's fine.

2. *Students Talk about Local Restaurants*

Have students use a conversational model to talk about favorite places to eat, such as restaurants, coffee shops, pubs.

a. Write on the board:

    A. I like to eat at _____.
    B. Oh, really? What do you recommend?
    A. I recommend the _____. (It's/They're) _____.
       Where do you like to eat?
    B. I like to eat at _____. The _____ there (is/are) delicious.

---

b. Have pairs of students create conversations. Encourage students to expand the dialog in any way they wish. This can be done as Full-Class Practice or Pair Practice.

Example:

    A. I like to eat at Stanley's Restaurant.
    B. Oh, really? What do you recommend?
    A. I recommend the french fries. They're excellent.
       Where do you like to eat?
    B. I like to eat at Mr. Burger. The hamburgers there are delicious.

Text Page 22: *Stanley's Favorite Recipes*

FOCUS

- Introduction of imperatives to give instructions
- Practice with *a little* and *a few*

GETTING READY

1. Introduce the new word *mushrooms*.
2. Practice saying *a little* or *a few* with the foods below:

mushrooms	potatoes	salt
butter	wine	tomatoes
onions	carrots	pepper

Say each word and have students form expressions with *a little* or *a few*. For example:

"mushrooms": "a few mushrooms"
"butter": "a little butter"

STANLEY'S FAVORITE RECIPES

1st RECIPE

1. Have students follow along in the book as you read the introduction to the recipe at the top of the page.
2. Ask students if they have any questions; check understanding of new vocabulary: *recipe, vegetable stew.*
3. **Step 1 of the recipe:** Introduce the new words *put ____ into, saucepan.* Read the sentence and have students repeat.
4. **Step 2:** Introduce the new expression *chop up.* Same as above.
5. **Steps 3–10:**

> **New vocabulary:** 3. *cut up* 4. *pour in* 5. *slice* 6. *add* 10. *hour*

For each:

a. Introduce any new words.
b. Call on a student to say the sentence, filling in either *a little* or *a few*.
c. Do Full-Class Choral Repetition of each sentence.

Answer Key for 3–9

> 3. Cut up a few potatoes.   7. Chop up a few mushrooms.
> 4. Pour in a little wine.   8. Slice a few tomatoes.
> 5. Slice a few carrots.   9. Add a little pepper.
> 6. Add a little salt.

2nd RECIPE

1. Have students follow along in the book as you read the introduction to the recipe.
2. Check understanding of the new word *fruitcake*.
3. **Steps 1 and 2:** Introduce the new expression *mixing bowl*. Then read each sentence and have students repeat.
4. **Steps 3–10:**

New vocabulary: 5. *honey*   6. *baking soda*   7. *nuts*   9. *mix in, raisin*

For each:

a. Introduce any new words.
b. Call on a student to say the sentence, filling in either *a little* or *a few*.
c. Do Full-Class Choral Repetition of each sentence.

Answer Key for 3–9

---

3. Slice a few apples.
4. Cut up a few oranges.
5. Pour in a little honey.
6. Add a little baking soda.

7. Chop up a few nuts.
8. Add a little salt.
9. Mix in a few raisins.

HOW ABOUT YOU?

1. For homework, have students write their favorite recipes, using the models on text page 22 as a guide. Encourage students to use dictionaries to expand their vocabulary.
2. Have students present their recipes in class the next day. Students should write any new words on the board and introduce them to the class.

WORKBOOK

Page 29

EXPANSION ACTIVITY

What Is It?

Have students use word cues to present recipes to the class. Other students must then guess what the recipe is for.

1. Write the ingredients for recipes on word cards. Put the name of the recipe in parentheses at the bottom of each card. For example:

---

a quart/cold water
lemon juice
sugar

(lemonade)

---

5 eggs
milk
salt
pepper
cheese
butter   (omelette)

```
┌─────────────────────────┐   ┌─────────────────────────┐
│  lettuce                │   │  hot milk               │
│  tomatoes               │   │  chocolate              │
│  carrots                │   │  sugar                  │
│                         │   │                         │
│     (salad)             │   │     (hot chocolate)     │
└─────────────────────────┘   └─────────────────────────┘

┌─────────────────────────┐   ┌─────────────────────────┐
│  bread                  │   │  butter                 │
│  cheese                 │   │  onion                  │
│  butter or mayonnaise   │   │  2 cups/wine            │
│                         │   │  1 quart/water          │
│     (cheese sandwich)   │   │     (onion soup)        │
└─────────────────────────┘   └─────────────────────────┘

┌─────────────────────────┐   ┌─────────────────────────┐
│  butter                 │   │  butter                 │
│  flour                  │   │  onions                 │
│  eggs                   │   │  wine                   │
│  milk                   │   │  carrots                │
│  baking powder          │   │  salt                   │
│  salt                   │   │  mushrooms              │
│  chocolate              │   │  tomatoes               │
│                         │   │  pepper                 │
│     (chocolate cake)    │   │     (vegetable stew)    │
└─────────────────────────┘   └─────────────────────────┘
```

2. Give the cards to students and have them present the recipes, using the vocabulary on text page 22. For example:

   a. Pour in a quart of cold water. Add a little lemon juice. Mix in a little sugar. What is it?

   b. Put 5 eggs in a bowl. Mix in a little milk. Add a little salt and pepper. Put a little cheese on it. Cook it with a little butter for five minutes. What is it?

Text Page 23

READING: *At the Continental Restaurant*

FOCUS

- Partitives
- Count/Non-count nouns

NEW VOCABULARY

baked chicken	order (v)	tasty
broiled fish	romantic	tomato juice
main course	table	wedding anniversary

PREVIEWING THE STORY (optional)

Have students talk about the story title and/or illustration. Introduce new vocabulary.

READING THE STORY

1. Have students read silently, or follow along silently as the story is read aloud by you, by one or more students, or on the tape.
2. Ask students if they have any questions; check understanding of vocabulary.
3. Check students' comprehension, using some or all of the following questions:

   a. Where did Sherman and Dorothy Johnson go for dinner?
   b. Why?
   c. Where did they sit?
   d. What did they order?
   e. How was the food?

CHECK-UP

Q & A

1. Call on a pair of students to present each model.
2. Have students work in pairs to create new dialogs.
3. Call on pairs to present their new dialogs to the class.

HOW ABOUT YOU?

Have students answer the questions, in pairs or as a class.

WORKBOOK

Check-Up Test: Pages 30–31

WORKBOOK ANSWER KEY AND LISTENING SCRIPTS

Page 22   A.   SHOPPING LISTS

1. bottle of
    box of
    loaf of
    lb. (pound) of
    jar of

2. quart of
    dozen
    lb. (pound) of
    can of
    head of
    bunch of

3. bottles of
    cans/bottles of
    quart of
    boxes of
    lb. (pound) of
    lb. (pound)/ can/
      jar of
    bunches of

4. bag of
    dozen
    bag of
    lb. (pound) of
    lb. (pound) of
    loaves of
    jar of
    heads of
    bunches of
    bottles of

Page 23   B.   LISTEN

Listen and write the prices you hear.

1.   A bunch of carrots costs 55¢.
2.   A bag of potatoes costs $1.80.
3.   A box of cereal costs $2.15.
4.   A bunch of bananas costs 95¢.
5.   A loaf of bread costs 99¢.
6.   A pound of cheese costs $2.98.
7.   A quart of milk costs 89¢.
8.   A pound of butter costs $1.73.
9.   A bag of onions costs $1.19.
10.   A can of vegetable soup costs 67¢.
11.   A box of cookies costs $1.30.
12.   A bag of flour costs $1.20.

Answers

1.	55¢	2.	$1.80	3.	$2.15
4.	95¢	5.	99¢	6.	$2.98
7.	89¢	8.	$1.73	9.	$1.19
10.	67¢	11.	$1.30	12.	$1.20

Page 25   D.   SHOPPING FOR FOOD

1. much, bunch, cost
    bunch, bananas costs
    of
    are

2. much, quart, cost
    quart, costs
    Milk is

3. much does, loaf, cost
    loaf, bread costs
    loaves
    loaves, of
    bread is

4. much does, pound of
    cost
    pound, apples costs
    much
    Apples are, are
    pound

Page 26   E.   WHERE WOULD YOU LIKE TO GO FOR LUNCH?

1.	are	14.	It
2.	they	15.	much
3.	order	16.	many
4.	of	17.	piece
5.	are	18.	of
6.	bowl	19.	dish
7.	of	20.	of
8.	is	21.	bowl
9.	it	22.	of
10.	bowl	23	is
11.	of	24.	cups
12.	is	25.	of
13.	is	26.	coffee

Page 27   F.   LISTEN: *What Did They Have?*

Listen and write the missing words.

1.   David usually has two bowls of cereal for breakfast. This morning he got up late and had a glass of milk.
2.   Jane usually has a glass of orange juice with her lunch. Yesterday, she had two glasses of milk.
3.   Mr. Nelson usually has two cups of coffee with his dinner. Yesterday he visited his Japanese neighbors and had a cup of tea.

4. Peter usually has a bowl of soup for lunch. Yesterday he was very hungry, and he had three pieces of chicken.
5. Lois usually has a dish of yogurt for lunch. This afternoon she went to a restaurant and had two orders of french fries.
6. Marie usually has a piece of cheese for dessert. Yesterday she went to a party and had three dishes of ice cream.
7. Alice usually has a cup of hot chocolate for breakfast. Yesterday morning she went to a restaurant and had an order of pancakes.
8. Nancy usually has a piece of cake for dessert. Yesterday she visited her grandmother and had two pieces of pie and a bowl of strawberries.

Answers
1. bowls of
   glass, milk
2. glass of
   glasses, milk
3. cups, coffee
   cup of tea
4. bowl, soup
   pieces of
5. dish of
   orders of
6. piece, cheese
   dishes of
7. cup of
   order, pancakes
8. piece, cake
   pieces, pie, bowl of

Page 29 I. BETTY'S DELICIOUS STEW

1. little
2. few
3. little
4. little
5. little
6. few
7. few
8. little

1. Put a little
2. Chop up a few
   a little
3. Cut up
4. Add a little, a little
5. Cut up a few
6. Slice a few
7. Pour in a cup of
   a little
8. Cook the stew

CHECK-UP TEST: *CHAPTERS 1–3*

Page 30 A.

1. many
2. much
3. few
   them, they're
4. This, is
   little
5. much

Page 30 B.

1. bunch
   bananas
2. can
   soup
3. bag
   onions
4. bottles
   soda
5. boxes
   cereal
6. loaves
   bread

Page 30 C.

1. watched
   he's going to watch
2. talked
   I'm going to talk
3. drank
   he's going to drink
4. wrote
   we're going to write
5. had
   they're going to have
6. went
   we're going to go

Page 31 D.

1. we're going to give them
2. she's going to give him
3. he's going to give her

Page 31 E.

Listen and put a circle around the correct word.

Ex. I'm looking for some milk.

1. I'm looking for some crackers.
2. May I have some flour?
3. Let's have some cheese!
4. I want some eggs.
5. May I have some orange juice?

Answers
1. aren't
2. isn't
3. isn't
4. aren't
5. isn't

GRAMMAR

Future Tense: Will

(I will)	I'll	
(He will)	He'll	
(She will)	She'll	
(It will)	It'll	work.
(We will)	We'll	
(You will)	You'll	
(They will)	They'll	

I	
He	
She	
It	won't work.
We	
You	
They	

	I	
	he	
	she	
Will	it	arrive soon?
	we	
	you	
	they	

	I	
	he	
	she	
Yes,	it	will.
	we	
	you	
	they	

	I	
	he	
	she	
No,	it	won't.
	we	
	you	
	they	

Time Expressions

The train will arrive	in	a few — days. minutes. hours. months. seconds. weeks.
		a week. an hour. half an hour. a little while.
		at seven o'clock.

Might

I	
He	
She	
It	might clean it today.
We	
You	
They	

FUNCTIONS

Asking for and Reporting Information

Will *the train arrive* soon?
  Yes, *it* will.   *It'll arrive in five minutes.*

Inquiring about Probability

Do you think *it'll rain tomorrow*?

Expressing Probability

Maybe *it* will, and maybe *it* won't.

Expressing Possibility

I might *clean it today.*
You might *hurt your head.*

Inquiring about Intention

When are you going to *clean your apartment*?

Warning

Careful!
You might *hurt your head.*

Asking for Repetition

I'm sorry.   What did you say?

Expressing Gratitude

Thanks for *the warning*.

Extending an Invitation

Would you like to *go swimming* with me?

Accepting an Invitation

Okay.   I'll *go swimming* with you.

Declining an Invitation

No, I don't think so.

NEW VOCABULARY

absolutely
all over
any more
arm
be back
bloom (v)
break (v)
drown
either
fall (v)
fall asleep
fancy
feet
fight (v)
get carsick
get hit
get hurt
get out of
get seasick
get sick
go for a walk
grass
half an hour
have a baby
helmet
indoors
instead
jail

Japan
leg
machine
marry
maybe
measles
Mexico
might
might not
name (v)
nauseous
outdoors
pneumonia
pregnant
puppy
ready
return
ripe
safety glasses
season
second
smoke
snow (n)
some day
spot
step (v)
sunburn

take a ride
take a walk
tired of
touch
understand
war
warning (n)
wet
will
winter coat
won't
you two

Careful!
catch a cold
Don't worry!
I can't wait
I don't think so.
I'm positive!
in a little while
Just think . . .
sick and tired of
take chances
Thanks for *the warning*.
That's too bad.
We'll just have to wait and see.
What did you say?

Text Page 26: *Will the Train Arrive Soon?*

FOCUS

> - Introduction of the future tense with *will*
> - Time expressions:
>
>   *in a few days/minutes/months/seconds/weeks*
>   *in a week/an hour/half an hour/a little while*
>   *at seven o'clock*

GETTING READY

1. Introduce *will*. Make a few sentences with *will*, describing a regular, predictable event. For example:

   "Every day school ends at 3:00."
   "Tomorrow school will end at 3:00."

   "Every day our class begins at 10:00."
   "Tomorrow our class will begin at 10:00."

2. Practice the forms of *will* in the box at the top of the page.

   a. Form sentences with both the full forms and the contracted forms. Have students repeat. For example:

      "I will work."/"I'll work."
      "He will work."/"He'll work."

   b. Read the sentences below with the full forms of *will*; have students give the contracted forms.

      "I will arrive."   "We will have dinner."
      "He will work."   "You will get up."
      "She will be home."   "They will arrive."
      "It will rain."

   c. Practice short answers with *will*.

      1. Read the question and answer in the right-hand box at the top of the page; have students repeat chorally.

         "Will he work?"
         "Yes, he will."

      2. Substitute the other pronouns in the question form and have students respond with the appropriate short answer. For example:

         "Will she work?"   "Will it work?"
         "Yes, she will."   "Yes, it will."

INTRODUCING THE MODEL

1. Have students look at the model illustration.
2. Set the scene: "At the train station, a woman is asking for information about the train."
3. Present the model.
4. Full-Class Choral Repetition.
5. Ask students if they have any questions; check understanding of new vocabulary: *in five minutes*.

6. Group Choral Repetition.
7. Choral Conversation.
8. Call on one or two pairs of students to present the dialog.

(For additional practice, do Choral Conversation in small groups or by rows.)

SIDE BY SIDE EXERCISES

Examples

> 1. A. Will the soup be ready soon?
>   B. Yes, it will. It'll be ready in a few minutes.
>
> 2. A. Will Miss Blake return soon?
>   B. Yes, she will. She'll return in an hour.

1. **Exercise 1:** Introduce the new vocabulary *ready, in a few minutes*. Call on two students to present the dialog. Then do Choral Repetition and Choral Conversation Practice.

2. **Exercise 2:** Introduce the new expressions *return, in an hour*. Same as above.

3. **Exercises 3–10:**

> **New vocabulary:**   3. *in half an hour*   4. *in a few seconds*   5. *ripe, in a few weeks*
>   7. *in a little while*   8. *be back*   9. *get out of, in a few days*   10. *jail*

Either Full-Class Practice or Pair Practice.

WORKBOOK

Page 32

Exercise Note

Workbook p. 32:   Have students read the exercises aloud to give them practice pronouncing the contracted forms *I'll, he'll, she'll,* etc.

EXPANSION ACTIVITIES

1. Role Play: A Business Call

a. Put this conversational framework on the board:

> A. Hello. Can I speak to _____, please?
> B. I'm sorry. _____ isn't here right now.
> A. I see. When will _____ be back?
> B. _____'ll be back in _____.
> A. Okay. I'll call back then. Thank you.
> B. You're welcome. Good-bye.

b. Set the scene: "This is a business telephone call; 'A' is the caller and 'B' is the secretary."

c. Call on pairs of students to role play the telephone call, using any name and time expression. You can use Full-Class Practice or Pair Practice. For added realism, bring a telephone to class; have the *secretary* sit in front of the class and *answer the phone*. For example:

> A. Hello. Can I speak to Ms. Jones, please?
> B. I'm sorry. She isn't here right now.
> A. I see. When will she be back?
> B. She'll be back in two hours.
> A. Okay. I'll call back then. Thank you.
> B. You're welcome. Good-bye.

2. **Role Play: *Telling the Future***

Have students pretend to be fortune tellers predicting the future.

a. Divide the class into pairs. One person is the fortune teller, and the other is the client.

b. Write the following cues on the board:

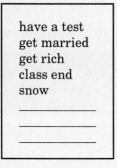

> have a test
> get married
> get rich
> class end
> snow
> _____
> _____
> _____

c. Have the client ask the fortune teller a question, using one of the cues on the board or any other he or she wishes. The fortune teller should answer, using one of the time expressions from the lesson. For example:

> A. Will we have a test soon?
> B. Yes, you will. You'll have a test in a few days.

> A. Will I get married soon?
> B. Yes, you will. You'll get married in a few weeks.

For fun, you may wish to bring in props such as a crystal ball, cards, or some tea leaves for the *fortune tellers* to use while they're making their predictions.

Text Page 27: *What Do You Think?*

FOCUS

> - Practice with *will*
> - Introduction of *won't*
> - Expressing possibility with *maybe*

GETTING READY

1. Review contractions with *will*. Say the full form with each pronoun; have students tell you the contracted form. For example:

   "I will work."   ("I'll work.")
   "He will work."   ("He'll work.")

2. Introduce *won't*.

   a. Form sentences with the words in the box at the top of the page. Use each pronoun to make a sentence with *will* and then with *won't*. Have students repeat chorally. For example:

      "I will work."/"I won't work."
      "He will work."/"He won't work."

   b. Make statements with *will* and have students negate them. For example:

      "I'll go soon."   ("I won't go soon.")
      "He'll work tomorrow."
      "She'll arrive in five minutes."
      "It'll be hot next week."
      "We'll be ready next week."
      "You'll be there."
      "They'll be on time."

INTRODUCING THE MODEL

1. Have students look at the model illustration.
2. Set the scene: "Two friends are talking."
3. Present the model.
4. Full-Class Choral Repetition.
5. Ask students if they have any questions; check understanding of new vocabulary: *maybe, We'll just have to wait and see.*
6. Group Choral Repetition.
7. Choral Conversation.
8. Call on one or two pairs of students to present the dialog.

   (For additional practice, do Choral Conversation in small groups or by rows.)

SIDE BY SIDE EXERCISES

Examples

> 1. A. Do you think Cynthia will marry Norman?
>   B. Maybe she will, and maybe she won't.
>   We'll just have to wait and see.
>
> 2. A. Do you think it'll be very cold this winter?
>   B. Maybe it will, and maybe it won't.
>   We'll just have to wait and see.

1. **Exercise 1:** Introduce the new word *marry*. Call on two students to present the dialog. Then do Choral Repetition and Choral Conversation Practice.

2. **Exercise 2:** Same as above.

3. **Exercises 3–8:**

> **New vocabulary:** 6. *have a baby*   8. *fight, war, some day*

Either Full-Class Practice or Pair Practice.

4. **Exercise 9:** Have pairs of students create dialogs about any future events.

WORKBOOK

Pages 33–35

Exercise Notes

Workbook p. 33:   Have students read the exercises aloud to give them practice pronouncing the contracted forms of *will*.

Workbook p. 34:   This exercise contrasts the full and contracted forms of *will*. Call on students to read the exercises aloud.

Workbook p. 35:   Students practice the future tense with *will*.

EXPANSION ACTIVITY

Students Make Predictions

1. Have each of your students write a sentence about the future, using *will*. Students can make *predictions* about anything they wish. For example:

   "My sister will get married next year."
   "It'll rain tonight."
   "Joe will find a job soon."
   "Class will start at 7:00 tomorrow morning."
   "Mary will buy a TV next month."
   "I'll marry a movie star."

2. Write this conversational framework on the board:

A. Do you really think _____ ?
B. $\left\{ \begin{array}{l} \text{Yes} \\ \text{No} \end{array} \right\}$, _____ probably $\left\{ \begin{array}{l} \text{will} \\ \text{won't} \end{array} \right\}$.

3. Have each student read his or her prediction. For each prediction call on two other students to create a conversation, using the framework on the board. You can do this activity as Full-Class Practice or divide students into groups of 3 and have them take turns reading and talking about their predictions. For example:

A. Do you really think it'll rain tonight?
B. Yes, it probably will.
   or
   No, it probably won't.

Text Page 28:

READING: *I Can't Wait for Spring to Come*

FOCUS

> Future tense: Will

NEW VOCABULARY

any more	grass	Just think . . .	snow (n)
bloom	I can't wait	outdoors	tired of
go for a walk	indoors	sick and tired of	winter coat

PREVIEWING THE STORY (optional)

Have students talk about the story title and/or illustration. Introduce new vocabulary.

READING THE STORY

1. Have students read silently, or follow along silently as the story is read aloud by you, by one or more students, or on the tape.
2. Ask students if they have any questions; check understanding of vocabulary.
3. Check students' comprehension, using some or all of the following questions:

   a. What's he tired of?
   b. Will it be winter in a few weeks?
   c. Will it be cold?
   d. Will it snow?
   e. Will he have to stay indoors?
   f. What will he do?
   g. What will he and his friends do?
   h. What will the neighborhood look like in a few weeks?
   i. What will his father do outdoors?
   j. What will his mother do outdoors?
   k. What won't they do on weekends?
   l. What will they do instead?

CHECK-UP

True, False, or Maybe?

> 1. False
> 2. False
> 3. Maybe
> 4. True
> 5. Maybe
> 6. False
> 7. True
> 8. Maybe

HOW ABOUT YOU?

Have students answer the questions, in pairs or as a class.

Text Page 29: *They Really Can't Decide*

FOCUS

> Introduction of *might* to express possibility

GETTING READY

1. Introduce *might*. Describe a possibility using *maybe;* then describe the same possibilty using *might*. For example:

   > "Maybe it'll rain tomorrow."
   > "It might rain tomorrow."

   > "Maybe I'll get married soon."
   > "I might get married soon."

2. Form sentences with the words in the box at the top of the page. Have students repeat. For example:

   > "I might clean it today."
   > "He might clean it today."

INTRODUCING THE MODEL

There are two model conversations. Introduce and practice each separately. For each model:

1. Have students look at the model illustration.
2. Set the scene: "People can't decide what they're going to do."
3. Present the model.
4. Full-Class Choral Repetition.
5. Ask students if they have any questions; check understanding of new vocabulary:

   2nd model: *Japan, Mexico*

6. Group Choral Repetition.
7. Choral Conversation.
8. Call on one or two pairs of students to present the dialog.
   (For additional practice, do Choral Conversation in small groups or by rows.)

SIDE BY SIDE EXERCISES

In these exercises, students use their own ideas to answer the questions, using the model as a guide.

Examples

1. A. What is he going to cook tonight?
   B. He doesn't know. He might cook (Italian) food, or he might cook (Greek) food.
      He really can't decide.

2. A. What color is she going to paint her kitchen?
   B. She doesn't know. She might paint it (blue), or she might paint it (green).
      She really can't decide.

3. A. What are they going to name their new daughter?
   B. They don't know. They might name her (Jane), or they might name her (Susan). They really can't decide.

Answer Key

4. We don't know. We might get married (this summer), or we might get married (this winter). We really can't decide.

5. I don't know. I might buy him (a necktie), or I might buy him (a belt). I really can't decide.

6. They don't know. They might (go to a concert), or they might (go to a movie). They really can't decide.

7. I don't know. I might (take the bus), or I might (ride my bicycle). I really can't decide.

8. He doesn't know. He might name it (Rover), or he might name it (Duke). He really can't decide.

9. I don't know. I might be (a teacher), or I might be (a singer). I really can't decide.

1. **Exercise 1:** Call on two students to present the dialog. Then do Choral Repetition and Choral Conversation Practice.

2. **Exercise 2:** Same as above.

3. **Exercises 3–9:**

> **New vocabulary:** 3. *name* (v)   4. *you two*   7. *come*   8. *puppy*

Language Note

    You two (Exercise 4):   This expression is an informal way of saying *the two of you*.

Either Full-Class Practice or Pair Practice.

WORKBOOK

Page 36

EXPANSION ACTIVITY

Role Play: Harry Can Never Decide

1. Set the scene: "My friend Harry can NEVER decide what to do. What's he going to do tonight? He doesn't know. He might go to the movies, or he might watch TV at home. He can't decide."

2. Have students pretend to be *Harry* and answer questions using any vocabulary they wish. For example:

> Teacher: Harry, what are you going to do this weekend?
> Harry: I don't know. I might (go swimming), or I might (go sailing). I can't decide.

Possible questions for Harry:

What are you going to do this weekend?
Where are you going to go for your vacation?
What are you going to name your new cat?

What are you going to study next year?
When are you going to get married?
How many children are you going to have?

3. Have students think of other questions to ask Harry.

Text Page 30: *Careful!*

FOCUS

- Practice with *might* to express possibility
- Expressing fear/concern: *I'm afraid I might . . .*

INTRODUCING THE MODEL

1. Have students look at the model illustration.
2. Set the scene: "Two co-workers are talking."
3. Present the model.
4. Full-Class Choral Repetition.
5. Ask students if they have any questions; check understanding of new vocabulary: *Careful!, helmet, What did you say?, Thanks for the warning.*
6. Group Choral Repetition.
7. Choral Conversation.
8. Call on one or two pairs of students to present the dialog.

   (For additional practice, do Choral Conversation in small groups or by rows.)

SIDE BY SIDE EXERCISES

Examples

1. A. Careful! The floor is wet!
   B. I'm sorry. What did you say?
   A. The floor is wet! You might fall.
   B. Oh. Thanks for the warning.

2. A. Careful! Don't stand there!
   B. I'm sorry. What did you say?
   A. Dont stand there! You might get hit.
   B. Oh. Thanks for the warning.

1. **Exercise 1:** Introduce the new word *fall*. Call on two students to present the dialog. Then do Choral Repetition and Choral Conversation Practice.
2. **Exercise 2:** Introduce the new expression *get hit*. Same as above.
3. **Exercises 3–5:**

   New vocabulary: 3. *smoke, start a fire*   4. *safety glasses*
        5. *touch, machine, get hurt*

4. **Exercise 6:** Have students use the model as a guide to create their own conversations, using vocabulary of their choice. Encourage students to use dictionaries to find new words they want to use. This exercise can be done orally in class or for written homework. If you assign it for homework, you

should do one example in class to make sure students understand what's expected. Have students present their conversations in class the next day.

WORKBOOK

Page 37

Exercise Note

Workbook p. 37:   Students practice pronouncing the [w] sound. Have several students read the sentences aloud. For additional practice, students can ask and answer questions about the pictures. Encourage students to ask questions with *what, where, when* and *why*, since these words also contain the [w] sound.

EXPANSION ACTIVITY

Warnings

1. Write the following list of suggestions or warnings on the board:

Take your umbrella!
Don't touch that dog!
Don't talk too loud!
Don't drink that!
Take a map!
Take ($5.00) more!
Take the key!
Don't talk!
Study every night!

2. In another column, write these words on the board:

be late
bite
disturb someone
get sick
have a quiz
hear you
get lost
need more money
rain

3. Have Student A say a sentence from the first list. Have Student B choose a logical answer from the second. For example:

Student A	Student B
Take a map!	You might get lost.
Don't talk!	You might disturb someone.
Don't drink that!	You might get sick.

4. Have students create their own warnings or suggestions and responses.

Text Page 31: *I'm Afraid I Might Drown*

FOCUS

- Practice with *might* and *will*
- Extending invitations: *"Would you like to _____?"*

INTRODUCING THE MODEL

1. Have students look at the model illustration.
2. Set the scene: "Two friends are talking."
3. Present the model.
4. Full-Class Choral Repetition.
5. Ask students if they have any questions; check understanding of new vocabulary: *Would you like to _____ with me?, I don't think so, drown, Don't worry!, I'm positive.*
6. Group Choral Repetition.
7. Choral Conversation.
8. Call on one or two pairs of students to present the dialog.

   (For additional practice, do Choral Conversation in small groups or by rows.)
9. Point out the alternative expression: *Do you want to go swimming with me?* Have students practice the model again, using this expression.

SIDE BY SIDE EXERCISES

Examples

1. A. Would you like to go skiing with me?*
   B. No, I don't think so.
   A. Why not?
   B. I'm afraid I might break my leg.
   A. Don't worry! You won't break your leg.
   B. Are you sure?
   A. I'm positive!
   B. Okay. I'll go skiing with you.

2. A. Would you like to go to a fancy restaurant with me?*
   B. No, I don't think so.
   A. Why not?
   B. I'm afraid I might get sick.
   A. Don't worry! You won't get sick.
   B. Are you sure?
   A. I'm positive!
   B. Okay. I'll go to a fancy restaurant with you.

*Or: Do you want to . . . ?

1. **Exercise 1:** Introduce the new words *break, leg.* Call on two students to present the dialog. Then do Choral Repetition and Choral Conversation Practice.

2. **Exercise 2:** Introduce the new words *fancy, get sick.* Same as above.

3. **Exercises 3–9:**

New vocabulary: 3. *sunburn*   4. *step, feet*   5. *take a walk, catch a cold*
   7. *get seasick*   8. *take a ride, get carsick*   9. *fall asleep*

Either Full-Class Practice or Pair Practice.

4. **Exercise 10:** Have students use the model as a guide to create their own conversations, using vocabulary of their choice. (Students may use any activities they wish.) Encourage students to use dictionaries to find new words they want to use. This exercise can be done orally in class or for written homework. If you assign it for homework, you should do one example in class to make sure students understand what's expected. Have students present their conversations in class the next day.

WORKBOOK

Pages 38–40

Exercise Note

Workbook p. 40: Students practice *might* and WH-questions.

EXPANSION ACTIVITIES

1. *Tell a Story: Jack's Parents Need a Vacation*

   a. Write these word cues on the board:

Might

1.   watch too much TV
2.   drink too much/many _____
3.   eat too much/many _____
4.   go _____ and get _____
5.   forget to _____

Might not

6.   do _____
7.   feed _____
8.   _____ on time

9.   _____

---

   b. Tell this story about Jack's parents, using the key words on the board and any vocabulary you wish to fill in the blanks. "Jack's parents really need a vacation, but they're afraid to go. They're worried about their son Jack. They don't want to leave him at home."

   1.   They're afraid he might watch too much TV.
   2.   They're afraid he might drink too (much soda).
   3.   They're afraid he might eat too (much candy).
   4.   They're also afraid he might go (to the beach) and get (a sunburn).
   5.   They're afraid he might forget to (brush his teeth).
   6.   They're afraid he might not do (his homework).
   7.   They're afraid he might not feed (the dog).
   8.   They're afraid he might not (get up) on time.

c. Point to the word cues on the board and call on students to retell each part of the story.

d. For number 9 on the board, have students think of other reasons why Jack's parents might be afraid to go on vacation.

e. Change *Jack's parents* to *Judy's parents* and have students create a new story using the key words on the board and any vocabulary they wish.

2. **Role Play:** **What's the Matter? What's Wrong?**

Practice *he/she* with *might*.

a. Have students work in groups of three. Give cue cards to two students and have them create role plays based on the situations.

Invite your friend to go swimming with you.	You don't like the water. You're afraid _____ might _____.
Invite your friend to go skiing with you.	You don't like to ski. You're afraid _____ might _____.
Invite your friend to go dancing with you.	You NEVER go dancing. You're afraid _____ might _____.
Invite your friend to go to the beach with you.	You don't like the beach. You're afraid _____ might _____.
Invite a friend to go to the movies with you.	You NEVER go to the movies. You're afraid _____ might _____.

b. Have the third student interrupt the conversation to find out what's wrong. For example:

A. Do you want to go swimming with me?
B. I don't think so. I'm afraid a fish might bite me.
A. Don't worry! A fish won't bite you!
C. Excuse me. What's the matter?
A. I want to go swimming, but he doesn't want to go with me.
   He's afraid a fish might bite him.

Students may continue the conversations any way they wish.

READING: *Just in Case*

FOCUS

Might

NEW VOCABULARY

absolutely	instead	pneumonia
all over	measles	pregnant
arm	might not	spot
either	nauseous	take chances

PREVIEWING THE STORY

Have students talk about the story title and/or illustrations. Introduce new vocabulary.

READING THE STORY

1. Have students read silently, or follow along silently as the story is read aloud by you, by one or more students, or on the tape.
2. Ask students if they have any questions; check understanding of vocabulary.
3. Check students' comprehension, using some or all of the following questions:

   a. Did Larry go to work today?
   b. Will he go to work tomorrow?
   c. What might he do instead?
   d. What's the matter with him?
   e. What does he think?
   f. Is he positive?

   g. Did Mrs. Randall go to the office today?
   h. Will she go to the office tomorrow?
   i. What might she do instead?
   j. What's the matter with her?
   k. What does she think?
   l. Is she positive?

   m. Did Tommy and Julie Harris go to school today?
   n. Will they go to school tomorrow?
   o. What might they do instead?
   p. What's the matter with them?
   q. What do Mr. and Mrs. Harris think?
   r. Are they positive?

CHECK-UP

Choose

1. can't
2. might
3. Are you
4. will
5. Will
6. might not

Listening

Have students complete the exercises as you play the tape or read the following:

I. Mrs. Harris is calling Tommy and Julie's school. Listen and choose the correct lines for Mrs. Harris.

1. Hello. Park Elementary School. (a)
2. Yes, Mrs. Harris. What can I do for you? (b)
3. Oh? What's the matter? (a)
4. That's too bad. Are you going to take them to the doctor? (b)
5. Well, I hope Tommy and Julie feel better soon. (a)

II. Choose the word you hear.

1. We'll be ready in half an hour. (b)
2. I want to come to work today. (b)
3. Don't smoke in here! (a)
4. They'll work in their yard every Saturday. (b)
5. Don't stand there! You might get hurt! (a)
6. I call the doctor when I'm sick. (b)
7. Careful! There are wet spots on the floor. (a)
8. I'm sick and tired of sailing. (a)

IN YOUR OWN WORDS

1. Make sure students understand the instructions.
2. Have students do the activity as written homework, using a dictionary for any new words they wish to use.
3. Have students present and discuss what they have written, in pairs or as a class.

WORKBOOK ANSWER KEY AND LISTENING SCRIPTS

Page 32   A.   SOON

1. it will, It'll
   begin
2. he will, He'll
   be here
3. they will, They'll
   return
4. Will, get up
   she will, She'll
5. Will, be ready
   it will, It'll
6. finish
   I will, I'll
7. Will, get
   married
   they will, They'll
8. Will, get out of the hospital
   I will, I'll

Page 33   B.   WHAT DO YOU THINK?

1. she'll study, she won't study
2. he'll call, he won't call
3. they'll have, they won't have
4. we'll go, we won't go
5. he'll live, he won't live
6. it'll be, it won't be
7. I'll finish, I won't finish
8. she'll go out, she won't go out
9. I'll get, I won't get
10. they'll plant, they won't plant
11. it'll arrive, it won't arrive
12. they'll move, they won't move
13. you'll finish, you won't finish

Page 34   C.   WRITE AND SAY IT

1. it'll arrive
2. he'll call
3. they'll move
4. she'll be
5. they'll be home
6. it'll be ready

Page 34   D.   LISTEN

Listen and put a circle around the words you hear.

1. I want to visit my cousin.
2. I won't visit my uncle.
3. We won't write to our sister.
4. We want to go to New York.
5. Peter and John won't go home.
6. They want to call their mother.
7. I want to walk to school.
8. Dan won't take the bus.
9. My mother and father want to live in Athens.
10. I won't drive your new car.
11. I want to eat a big dinner.
12. We want to get up at 7:00.
13. She won't wear her new blouse.
14. They won't get married soon.
15. They want to get married soon.

Answers

1. want to		9.	want to
2. won't		10.	won't
3. won't		11.	want to
4. want to		12.	want to
5. won't		13.	won't
6. want to		14.	won't
7. want to		15.	want to
8. won't			

Page 36   F.   WE DON'T KNOW

1. I might do my homework tonight, I might do my homework tomorrow
2. He might go sailing, he might go swimming
3. She might get up at 10:00, she might get up at 11:00
4. We might go to Paris, we might go to London
5. She might visit her grandmother, she might visit her aunt
6. I might give her a necklace, I might give her a bracelet
7. They might listen to music, they might play cards
8. We might eat Chinese food, we might eat Greek food
9. He might be a doctor, he might be a dentist
10. They might get back on Sunday, they might get back next week

1. Williams, wearing
   warm winter

2. Winston won't
   walk
   wet

3. William wasn't
   Wednesday
   well

4. William, wife
   wash, windows
   Wednesday

5. Walter
   war, wife
   will, wait

6. We wanted
   swimming
   weather wasn't
   warm

1. he's afraid he might get seasick
2. he's afraid he might get a backache
3. she's afraid she might catch a cold
4. we're afraid we might have noisy neighbors
5. she's afraid she might break her leg
6. he's afraid he might get a sunburn
7. he's afraid it might rain
8. she's afraid she might get carsick
9. she's afraid she might have too much homework
10. he's afraid he might get fat
11. they're afraid they might miss their train
12. he's afraid he might step on her feet
13. he's afraid he might fall asleep
14. he's afraid he might look terrible
15. he's afraid he might get home very late
16. I'm afraid I might go to jail

GRAMMAR

Comparatives

| My new apartment is | colder
larger
bigger
prettier | than my old apartment. |
| | more comfortable
more attractive | |

Should

| Should | I
he
she
it
we
you
they | study? |

| I
He
She
It
We
You
They | should study. |

Possessive Pronouns

| This dog is much friendlier than | mine.
his.
hers.
ours.
yours.
theirs. |

FUNCTIONS

Describing

It was *fast/large/comfortable/interesting*.
My new _____ is *faster/larger/more comfortable/ more interesting*.

My dog isn't as *friendly* as *your dog*.
They aren't as *clean* as they used to be.

Bicycles are *safer* than *motorcycles*.
Yours is much *friendlier* than mine.

Asking for Advice

Should I *buy a bicycle or a motorcycle*?

Offering Advice

I think you should *buy a bicycle*.

Inquiring about an Opinion

Do you think *the weather in Miami is better than the weather in Honolulu*?

Expressing an Opinion

In my opinion, *New York is more interesting than San Francisco*.
I think *San Francisco is much more interesting than New York*.

Inquiring about Agreement

Don't you agree?

Expressing Agreement

That's right.
I agree.
I agree with you/him/her/John/. . . .
I think so.

Expressing Disagreement

I disagree.
I disagree with you/him/her/John/. . . .
No.   I don't think so.

Asking for and Reporting Information

Why?
Why do you say that?
What makes you say that?
How come?

Initiating a Topic

You know, . . .

Inquiring about Certainty

Do you really think so?

Expressing Certainty

Definitely!

Expressing Dissatisfaction

I'm very upset about *the streets here in Brownsville*.

NEW VOCABULARY

across the street	hers	rainy	useful
air conditioner	high	real	vote (for)
although	hire	reliable	wealthy
around the corner	his	rocking chair	wide
attractive	honest	roommate	wig
because of	hospitable	rug	yours
better	intelligent	safe	
black-and-white TV	Latin	San Francisco	Definitely!
bus system	lazy	satisfied	Do you think . . . ?
capable	light (adj)	should	Don't be ridiculous!
change (v)	lively	smart	Don't you agree?
changes (n)	mayor	snowy	go out on a date with
color TV	mine	soft	How come?
definitely	modern	sports car	I agree.
down the street	more	sympathetic	I disagree.
exciting	motorcycle	talented	in my opinion
fan	neat	talkative	no matter how
fashionable	ours	tennis racket	on the air
fast	polite	theirs	they say
friendly	powerful	understanding (adj)	What makes you say that?
fur	president	up the street	Why do you say that?
grades	pronunciation	used to	You know . . .
hand			

LANGUAGE NOTES

Guidelines for Forming Comparative Adjectives

1. Add -er to one-syllable adjectives:

   cold–colder

2. Add -r to one-syllable adjectives that end in -e:

   nice–nicer

3. Double the final consonant and add -er to one-syllable adjectives that end in a single consonant preceded by a single vowel:

   big–bigger

4. Change y to i and add -er to two-syllable adjectives that end in y preceded by a consonant:

   easy–easier

5. Place *more* before adjectives that have three or more syllables:

   beautiful–more beautiful

6. The comparatives of two-syllable adjectives that don't end in y are less predictable. Some are formed with *more*, some are formed with -er, and some are formed with either *more* or -er:

   honest–more honest
   simple–simpler

   handsome– $\begin{cases} \textit{more handsome} \\ \textit{handsomer} \end{cases}$

7. Irregular comparative:

   good–better

8. *Much* is used to make a comparison stronger:

   Your dog is much friendlier than mine.

Text Page 36: *My New Apartment Is Larger*

FOCUS

Introduction of comparative adjectives formed by adding *-er* (see **Chapter Overview**)

GETTING READY

1. Introduce comparative adjectives with *-er* endings.

    a. Draw 2 buildings and 2 people on the board:

    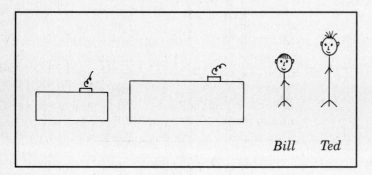

    b. Point and say: "This building is big."
    "That building is bigger."

    "Bill is tall."
    "Ted is taller."

    c. Say these sentences again and have students repeat chorally.

2. Read the adjectives in the boxes at the top of the page. Have students repeat chorally. Introduce the new word *safe*.

INTRODUCING THE MODEL

1. Have students look at the model illustration.
2. Set the scene: "Two friends are talking."
3. Present the model.
4. Full-Class Choral Repetition.
5. Ask students if they have any questions; check understanding of new vocabulary: *That's right.*
6. Group Choral Repetition.
7. Choral Conversation.
8. Call on one or two pairs of students to present the dialog.

    (For additional practice, do Choral Conversation in small groups or by rows.)

SIDE BY SIDE EXERCISES

Examples

> 1. A. I think you'll like my new bicycle.
>   B. But I liked your OLD bicycle. It was fast.
>   A. That's right. But my new bicycle is faster.
>
> 2. A. I think you'll like my new refrigerator.
>   B. But I liked your OLD refrigerator. It was big.
>   A. That's right. But my new refrigerator is bigger.

> **Answer key to comparative adjectives 3–9:**   3. *friendlier*   4. *safer*
> 5. *softer*   6. *fancier*   7. *lighter*   8. *easier*   9. *prettier*

1. **Exercise 1:** Introduce the new word *fast*. Call on two students to present the dialog. Then do Choral Repetition and Choral Conversation Practice.
2. **Exercise 2:** Introduce the new word *refrigerator.* Same as above.
3. **Exercises 3–9:**

> **New vocabulary:**   3. *friendly*   4. *safe*   5. *rug, soft*   6. *sports car*
> 7. *tennis racket, light*   9. *wig*

Either Full-Class Practice or Pair Practice.

WORKBOOK

Page 41

EXPANSION ACTIVITIES

1.   Role Play: I Remember

a. Put the following conversational model on the board:

> A. I remember your _____. _____ $\left\{ \begin{array}{l} \text{was} \\ \text{were} \end{array} \right\}$ very _____.
>
> B. You're right. But YOUR _____ $\left\{ \begin{array}{l} \text{was} \\ \text{were} \end{array} \right\}$ _____er.

b. Put these word cues on the board or on word cards:

> 1. dog/ugly   5. sports car/fast
> 2. house/pretty   6. neighborhood/safe
> 3. cat/friendly   7. _____
> 4. uncle/rich

c. Set the scene: "Two old people are sitting in the park and talking about the past."

d. Call on pairs of students to role play the people, using the conversational model and word cues. You can use Full-Class Practice or Pair Practice. Two examples:

    1. A. I remember your dog. It was very ugly.
        B. That's right. But YOUR dog was uglier.

    2. A. I remember your house. It was very pretty.
        B. That's right. But YOUR house was prettier.

e. For Exercise 7, have several pairs of students create similar conversations, using any vocabulary they wish.

2. *Spelling Practice:* *Scrambled Comparatives*

a. Divide the class into small groups.

b. Put some or all of these scrambled words on the board. With books closed, have students work together in their small groups to unscramble the words. The first group to successfully unscramble them all wins.

1. fesra	(safer)	6. fosret	(softer)
2. leidnfreri	(friendlier)	7. rasfte	(faster)
3. tirrepte	(prettier)	8. canifre	(fancier)
4. gibgre	(bigger)	9. tohret	(hotter)
5. egrarl	(larger)	10. thiglre	(lighter)

3. *Word Associations*

Say an adjective and have students tell you some different things that adjective can describe. For example:

Teacher	Students
fast	car/bicycle/train/ . . .
friendly	boy/dog/person/ . . .
safe	neighborhood/car/street/ . . .
soft	rug/hair/chair/ . . .
fancy	car/dress/shoes/ . . .
easy	assignment/recipe/ . . .

Text Page 37: *My New Rocking Chair Is More Comfortable*

FOCUS

> - Introduction of comparative adjectives formed by adding *more* (see **Chapter Overview**)
> - Practice with *-er* comparatives

GETTING READY

1. Introduce comparative adjectives with *more*.

   a. Draw 2 houses and 2 cups on the board:

   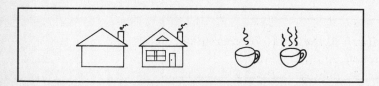

   b. Point and say: "This house is beautiful."
   "That house is more beautiful."

   "This coffee is delicious."
   "That coffee is more delicious."

   c. Say these sentences again and have students repeat chorally.

2. Read the adjectives in the boxes at the top of the page. Have students repeat chorally. Introduce the new word *intelligent*.

INTRODUCING THE MODEL

1. Have students look at the model illustration.
2. Set the scene: "Two friends are talking."
3. Present the model.
4. Full-Class Choral Repetition.
5. Ask students if they have any questions; check understanding of new vocabulary: *rocking chair.*
6. Group Choral Repetition.
7. Choral Conversation.
8. Call on one or two pairs of students to present the dialog.

   (For additional practice, do Choral Conversation in small groups or by rows.)

SIDE BY SIDE EXERCISES

Examples

> 1. A. I think you'll like my new girlfriend.
>   B. But I liked your OLD girlfriend. She was intelligent.
>   A. That's right. But my new girlfriend is more intelligent.

2. A. I think you'll like my new boyfriend.
   B. But I liked your OLD boyfriend. He was handsome.
   A. That's right. But my new boyfriend is more handsome.

Answer key to comparative adjectives 3–11:   3. *more beautiful*   4. *larger*
5. *more attractive*   6. *smarter*   7. *more interesting*   8. *nicer*
9. *more powerful*   10. *quieter*   11. *more delicious*

---

1. **Exercise 1:** Call on two students to present the dialog. Then do Choral Repetition and Choral Conversation Practice.

2. **Exercise 2:** Same as above.

3. **Exercises 3–11:**

New vocabulary: 5. *attractive*   6. *smart*   7. *roommate*
9. *powerful*   10. *air conditioner*

Either Full-Class Practice or Pair Practice.

4. **Exercise 12:** Have students use the model as a guide to create their own conversations, using vocabulary of their choice. (They can use any adjectives they wish.) Encourage students to use dictionaries to find new words they want to use. This exercise can be done orally in class or for written homework. If you assign it for homework, you should do one example in class to make sure students understand what's expected. Have students present their conversations in class the next day.

WORKBOOK

Page 42

EXPANSION ACTIVITIES

1. *Role Play:* *I'll Never Forget*

   a. Put the following conversational model on the board:

   A. I'll never forget your _____. _____ {was / were} really _____.

   B. Do you really think so? I think YOUR _____ {was / were} _____.

---

   b. Put these word cues on the board or on word cards:

---

   1. father/energetic   5. 16th birthday party/nice
   2. boss/interesting   6. wedding/beautiful
   3. cat/smart   7. _____
   4. pet bird/cute

---

c. Set the scene: "Two old friends are sitting in a restaurant and talking about the past."

d. Call on pairs of students to role play the two people, using the conversational model and word cues. You can use Full-Class Practice or Pair Practice. Two examples:

   1. A. I'll never forget your father. He was really energetic.
      B. Do you really think so? I think YOUR father was more energetic.

   2. A. I'll never forget your boss. He/She was really interesting.
      B. Do you really think so? I think YOUR boss was more interesting.

e. For Exercise 7, have students create similar conversations, using any vocabulary they wish.

2. Review of Comparatives

Make a list of adjectives or use the list below. Say an adjective and have students give the correct comparative form.

Teacher	Students
attractive	more attractive
beautiful	more beautiful
big	bigger
comfortable	more comfortable
delicious	more delicious
easy	easier
fancy	fancier
fast	faster
friendly	friendlier
intelligent	more intelligent
interesting	more interesting
large	larger
light	lighter
nice	nicer
powerful	more powerful
pretty	prettier
quiet	quieter
safe	safer
smart	smarter
soft	softer

If you wish, you can do this as a game. Divide the class into two teams. Each team gets a point for giving the correct form. The team with the most points wins the game.

3. Word Associations

Say an adjective and have students tell you some different things that adjective can describe. For example:

Teacher	Students
comfortable	chair/sofa/ . . .
attractive	woman/man/house/ . . .
interesting	person/book/movie/ . . .
powerful	computer/air conditioner/motorcycle/ . . .
delicious	food/recipe/cake/ . . .
quiet	person/car/air conditioner/ . . .

Text Page 38

READING: *Brownsville*

FOCUS

Comparatives

NEW VOCABULARY

although	definitely
because of	hospitable
bus system	polite
change (v)	real
changes (n)	reliable
	used to

PREVIEWING THE STORY (optional)

Have students talk about the story title and/or illustrations. Introduce new vocabulary.

READING THE STORY

1. Have students read silently, or follow along silently as the story is read aloud by you, by one or more students, or on the tape.
2. Ask students if they have any questions; check understanding of vocabulary.
3. Check students' comprehension, using some or all of the following questions:

    a. Why was Brownsville a very good place to live?
    b. Describe Brownsville today.
    c. Where did the Taylor family move?
    d. Why?
    e. Why were the Taylors happier in Brownsville?

CHECK-UP

Q & A

Culture Note

Radio talk-shows are very popular in the United States. Also known as *call-in programs,* these shows offer listeners the opportunity to call the radio station and talk with the program host or a featured guest during the broadcast. In many cities, local officials serve as program hosts or guests, in order to give residents an opportunity to speak directly with the politicians they have elected.

1. Call on a pair of students to present the model.
2. Have students work in pairs to create new dialogs.
3. Call on pairs to present their new dialogs to the class.

Text Pages 39–40: *Bicycles Are Safer Than Motorcycles*

FOCUS

> • Introduction of *should*
> • Comparative expressions with *than*

GETTING READY

1. Introduce *should*. Describe several problems and give advice using should. For example:

   "Jane is very hungry."
   "She should eat lunch."

   "Bill is sick today."
   "He should go to the doctor."

2. Form sentences using the words in the box at the top of the page and have students repeat.
   For example:

   "I should study."
   "He should study."

INTRODUCING THE MODEL

There are two model conversations. Introduce and practice each separately. For each model:

1. Have students look at the model illustration.
2. Set the scene: "This person can't decide what to do."
3. Present the model.
4. Full-Class Choral Repetition.
5. Ask students if they have any questions; check understanding of new vocabulary:

   1st model: *motorcycle*
   2nd model: *useful, Latin*

6. Group Choral Repetition.
7. Choral Conversation.
8. Call on one or two pairs of students to present the dialog.
9. Introduce the new expressions *Why do you say that? What makes you say that? How come?* Have pairs of
   students practice the models again, using these expressions in place of *Why?*

   (For additional practice, do Choral Conversation in small groups or by rows.)

SIDE BY SIDE EXERCISES

Examples

> 1. A. Should I buy a dog or a cat?
>   B. I think you should by a dog.
>   A. Why?/Why do you say that?/What makes you say that?/How come?
>   B. Dogs are friendlier than cats.

2. A. Should he buy a used car or a new car?
   B. I think he should buy a used car.
   A. Why?/Why do you say that?/What makes you say that?/How come?
   B. Used cars are cheaper than new cars.

Answer key to comparatives 3–16:

3. more honest	10. more talented
4. more interesting	11. fancier
5. more intelligent	12. cleaner
6. cheaper	13. warmer
7. quieter	14. more convenient
8. more attractive	15. more capable
9. prettier	16. lazier

---

1. **Exercise 1:** Call on two students to present the dialog. Then do Choral Repetition and Choral Conversation Practice.

2. **Exercise 2:** Introduce the new expression *used car*. Same as above.

3. **Exercises 3–16:**

New vocabulary: 3. *vote for, honest* 4. *go out on a date with*
6. *black-and-white TV, color TV* 7. *fan* 10. *talented* 11. *left hand, right hand*
12. *up the street, down the street* 13. *fur, leather*
14. *across the street, around the corner* 15. *hire, capable* 16. *fire*

Either Full-Class Practice or Pair Practice.

4. **Exercise 17:** Have students use the model as a guide to create their own conversations, using vocabulary of their choice. Encourage students to use dictionaries to find new words they want to use. This exercise can be done orally in class or for written homework. If you assign it for homework, you should do one example in class to make sure students understand what's expected. Have students present their conversations in class the next day.

WORKBOOK

Pages 43–48

Exercise Notes

Workbook p. 45: In Exercise E, students practice comparatives with *-er*. In Exercise F, they practice comparatives with *more*. In Exercise G, students practice *should*.

Workbook p. 46: There are two correct answers for every question. Have students talk about their choices.

Workbook p. 47: For additional oral practice with Exercise I, have students talk about the pictures, using comparatives.

Workbook p. 48: Students practice *should* and comparatives.

EXPANSION ACTIVITIES

1. **Role Play: *Going to a Party***

   a. Put the following conversational model and word cues on the board:

   > A. Should I _____ or _____?
   > B. I think you should _____ because _____.

   > 1. wear/old shoes/new shoes
   > 2. take/candy/flowers
   > 3. wear/sweater/jacket and a tie
   > 4. take/bus/subway
   > 5. take/wine/soda
   > 6. take/classical records/popular records
   > 7. _____

   b. Set the scene: "We're going to go to a party."

   c. Have pairs of students create conversations in which they ask for and give advice, using the word cues and conversational model on the board. Students can use any vocabulary they wish in giving reasons for their answers. For example:

   > A. Should I wear my old shoes or my new shoes?
   > B. I think you should wear your old shoes because they're more comfortable than your new shoes.
   >   or
   >   I think you should wear your new shoes because they're more attractive than your old shoes.

   d. For Exercise 7, have students make up their own questions.

2. **Giving Advice: *What Should They Do?***

   a. Write each of the *problems* below on an index card. (You can also make up other problems for your students to talk about.)

   > Michael doesn't have any friends. What should he do?

   > Steve and Betty are bored. What should they do?

   > Mr. and Mrs. Green can't find their dog. What should they do?

   > My TV is broken. What should I do?

   > Our neighbors are very noisy. What should we do?

> Carol wants to be rich some day. What should she do?

> Toshi wants to visit the United States. What should he do?

  b. Have students draw a card and read the problem.

  c. Call on several students to give advice. Encourage students to be imaginative and *playful*.

3. ***Practice Comparatives with Key Words on the Board***

   Have students make comparisons between different things they might buy or do. Write the key words below on the board and ask the following questions (students can answer using the adjectives on the board or any others they wish).

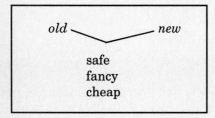

1. Should I buy an old car or a new car?

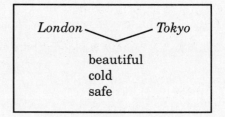

2. Should I buy a sports car or a truck?

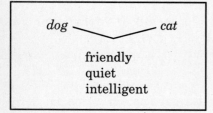

3. Should Joe get a dog or a cat?

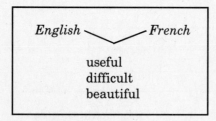

4. Should the Smiths go to London or Tokyo for their vacation?

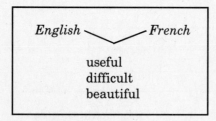

5. Should Martha study English or French?

Examples of answers:

   I think you should buy a new car because new cars are safer than old cars.

   or

   I think you should buy a new car because new cars are fancier than old cars.

   or

   I think you should buy a new car because old cars aren't as safe as new cars.

   or

   I think you should buy an old car because old cars are cheaper than new cars.

Text Page 41

READING: *It Isn't Easy Being a Teenager*
It Isn't Easy Being Parents

FOCUS

- Should
- Comparatives

NEW VOCABULARY

Story 1	Story 2
better	fashionable
hard	sympathetic
neat	understanding
no matter how	
satisfied	

PREVIEWING THE STORIES (optional)

Have students talk about the story titles and/or illustrations. Introduce new vocabulary.

READING THE STORIES

1. Have students read silently, or follow along silently as the stories are read aloud by you, by one or more students, or on the tape.
2. Ask students if they have any questions; check understanding of vocabulary.
3. Check students' comprehension:

   Story 1: What do his parents think?
   Story 2: What do their children think?

CHECK-UP

Choose

1. b
2. c
3. d
4. a
5. b

Listening

Have students complete the exercises as you play the tape or read the following:

Listen and choose what the people are talking about.

1. A. I think it should be shorter.
   B. But it's very short now! (a)

2. A. I like it. It's fast.
   B. It is. It's much faster than my old one. (b)

3. A. Why can't they be more polite?
   B. It isn't easy. (a)

4. A. Is it reliable?
   B. Yes, but it isn't as reliable as my old one. (a)

5. A. They aren't as good as they were last time.
   B. Don't worry. They'll be better next time. (a)

6. A. Which one should I buy?
   B. Buy this one. It's more powerful than that one. (b)

Text Page 42: *Don't Be Ridiculous!*

FOCUS

> * Introduction of possessive pronouns
> * New expressions:
>
>   isn't/aren't as _____ as
>   much $\left\{\dfrac{\underline{\quad\quad\quad}er}{more\underline{\quad\quad}}\right\}$ than

GETTING READY

1. Introduce possessive pronouns. Make sentences with the words in the box at the top of the page. Have students repeat each sentence with a possessive pronoun. For example:

    "This is my book. This is mine."
    "This is his book. This is his."
    "This is her book. This is hers."
    "This is our book. This is ours."
    "This is your book. This is yours."
    "This is their book. This is theirs."

2. Practice using possessive pronouns. Ask about objects in the classroom, and have students answer using possessive pronouns. For example, point to Student B's pencil and ask Student A:

    You: That pencil isn't mine. Is it yours?
    A: No, it isn't mine. It's hers/his.

INTRODUCING THE MODEL

There are two model conversations. Introduce and practice each separately. For each model:

1. Have students look at the model illustration.
2. Set the scene:

    1st model: "Two people are taking a walk in the park with their dogs."
    2nd model: "A husband and wife are talking. The husband is a writer, and he's talking about his books."

3. Present the model.
4. Full-Class Choral Repetition.
5. Ask students if they have any questions; check understanding of new vocabulary:

    1st model: *as _____ as, Don't be ridiculous!, much _____ than*
    2nd model: *Ernest Hemingway*

Culture Note

   Ernest Hemingway: A famous 20th-century U.S. author and journalist.

6. Group Choral Repetition.
7. Choral Conversation Practice.
8. Call on one or two pairs of students to present the dialog.

    (For additional practice, do Choral Conversation in small groups or by rows.)

SIDE BY SIDE EXERCISES

Examples

> 1. A. You know, my car isn't as fast as your car.
>   B. Don't be ridiculous! Yours is MUCH faster than mine.
>
> 2. A. You know, my furniture isn't as comfortable as your furniture.
>   B. Don't be ridiculous! Yours is MUCH more comfortable than mine.

1. **Exercise 1:** Call on two students to present the dialog. Then do Choral Repetition and Choral Conversation Practice.

2. **Exercise 2:** Same as above.

3. **Exercises 3–8:**

> **New vocabulary:**   7. *good–better, pronunciation*   8. *President*

   Either Full-Class Practice or Pair Practice.

4. **Exercise 9:** Have students use the model as a guide to create their own conversations, using vocabulary of their choice. Encourage students to use dictionaries to find new words they want to use. This exercise can be done orally in class or for written homework. If you assign it for homework, you should do one example in class to make sure students understand what's expected. Have students present their conversations in class the next day.

WORKBOOK

Pages 49–51

Exercise Note

Workbook p. 51:   In Exercises N and O, students practice possessive pronouns.

EXPANSION ACTIVITY

Practice Comparatives with Magazine Pictures

1. Find magazine pictures that represent two styles or kinds of the same things. For example, find pictures of two different houses, cars, watches, dogs, dresses, appliances, suits.

2. Give these sets of pictures to pairs of students; have them create conversations in which they compare their pictures, using possessive pronouns and any vocabulary they know. You can use Full-Class Practice or Pair Practice. For example:

   A. Your (house) is larger than mine.
   B. Yes, but yours is more beautiful than mine.
   A. I think yours is more interesting.
   B. But yours is more expensive.

Text Page 43

ON YOUR OWN: *Cities*

FOCUS

- Review of comparatives
- Students express their opinions about places they know

ON YOUR OWN ACTIVITY

1. There are three dialogs. Introduce and practice each separately. For each dialog:

   a. Set the scene: "People are talking about places they know."

   b. Read each line and have students repeat chorally and individually.

   c. Ask students if they have any questions; check understanding of new vocabulary:

      1st dialog: *in my opinion, disagree*
      2nd dialog: *I don't think so.*
      3rd dialog: *agree*

   d. Call on one or two pairs of students to present the dialog.

2. Introduce the suggested topics for conversation.

   New vocabulary: *wide, high, modern, rainy, snowy, hospitable, talkative, wealthy, lively, exciting*

---

3. Go over the expressions at the bottom of the page.

   a. Read the expressions and have students repeat chorally.

   b. Check understanding of the new expressions: *Don't you think . . . ?, Don't you agree? I agree/disagree with _____, I think so.*

4. Have pairs of students create conversations about two cities. Encourage students to express their opinions and agree or disagree with other students, using the expressions at the bottom of the page.

5. For homework, have students write a short dialog in which people compare two cities. Have students present their dialogs in the next class.

WORKBOOK

Pages 52–53

Exercise Note

Workbook p. 52: For additional oral practice with Exercise P, have students act out the conversation.

EXPANSION ACTIVITY

Students State Their Opinions, Using Comparatives

1. Have each student write a statement expressing an opinion, using a comparative.
2. Collect all the statements, mix them up, and have each student draw one.
3. Next, have students read the statements they've drawn, and call on one or two other students to respond by *agreeing* or *disagreeing* and telling why. For example:

> A. I think our class is smarter than Mrs. Smith's class.
> B. I agree. Our class is much smarter.
>   or
>   I disagree. I think her class is smarter than ours.

Page 41 A. OLD AND NEW

1. larger
2. faster
3. softer
4. cleaner
5. lighter
6. fancier
7. friendlier
8. bigger
9. safer
10. cheaper
11. prettier
12. easier
13. warmer
14. noisier
15. heavier
16. quieter
17. busier
18. whiter
19. hungrier
20. shorter
21. fatter

Page 42 B. THEY'RE DIFFERENT

1. more energetic
2. more delicious
3. more intelligent
4. more comfortable
5. more handsome
6. smarter
7. richer
8. hungrier
9. more attractive
10. lighter
11. dirtier
12. whiter
13. more beautiful
14. shorter
15. older
16. hotter
17. thinner
18. more expensive
19. healthier
20. larger

Page 43 C. WHAT SHOULD THEY DO?

1. He should call the plumber.
2. She should go to the dentist.
3. They should move to a new apartment.
4. He should go on vacation.
5. He should buy new clothes.
6. She should go to the doctor.
7. He should call a mechanic.
8. You should drink tea.
9. They should call the police.
10. She should get a job.
11. You should get a wig.

Page 44 D. PUZZLE

Crossword puzzle answers:

1. newer
2. larger
3. easier
4. healthier
5. friendlier
6. safer
7. safer
8. hotter
9. dirtier
10. taller
11. fancier
12. older
13. richer
14. poorer

(Crossword grid words: newer, larger, healthier, friendlier, hotter, dirtier, safer, fancier, older, richer, poorer)

Page 47 I. LISTEN

Listen and put a circle around the correct answer.

1. George is noisier than Jennifer.
2. Albert is richer than John.
3. Ted's dog is bigger than Fred and Sally's dog.
4. Robert is happier than Nancy.
5. Edward's English test was more difficult than his French test.
6. Margaret is older than Alice.
7. Eggs are cheaper than bread this week.
8. Bob is shorter and heavier than Bill.

Answers

1. yes
2. yes
3. no
4. no
5. no
6. yes
7. yes
8. no

Page 49 K. WHAT'S THE WORD?

1. his
2. theirs
3. hers
4. yours
5. his
6. hers
7. ours

Page 49 L. DIFFERENT, BUT OKAY

1. isn't as rich as, happier
2. isn't as clean as, more comfortable
3. aren't as intelligent as, healthier
4. isn't as large as, prettier
5. isn't as safe as, more interesting
6. isn't as smart as, friendlier
7. isn't as handsome as, nicer
8. isn't as powerful as, cheaper
9. isn't as new as, shinier
10. isn't as young as, more energetic
11. isn't as expensive as, softer
12. isn't as big as, better

Page 50 M. YOU'RE RIGHT

1. more talented than
2. more difficult than
3. busier than
4. as noisy as
5. as big as
6. more beautiful than
7. as light as
8. as nice as

Page 52 P. WHO SHOULD WE HIRE?

1. more interesting
2. smarter
3. smart
4. livelier
5. capable
6. more talented
7. more polite
8. friendlier
9. intelligent
10. talkative
11. better

Page 53 Q. DO YOU AGREE?

1. He thinks Chinese food is more delicious than Italian food.
2. No, he doesn't.

4. No, he doesn't.
5. He thinks cats are much smarter than dogs.

7. He thinks English is more useful than Latin.
8. No, she doesn't.
9. He agrees with Robert.

TEACHER'S NOTES

GRAMMAR

Superlatives

He's	the smartest the nicest the biggest the busiest	person I know.
	the most talented the most interesting	

FUNCTIONS

Describing

I think *your cousin* is very *kind/friendly/energetic/generous*.
He's *the kindest/the friendliest/the most energetic/the most generous* person I know.

This is the *smallest* one we have.

Expressing an Opinion

I think *your friend Margaret is very smart.*

Initiating a Topic

You know . . .

Expressing Agreement

I agree.
You're right.

Offering to Help

May I help you?

Expressing Want-Desire

I want to buy *a small radio.*

Asking for and Reporting Information

Don't you have *a smaller one*?

Who is *the most popular actress in your country*?
What is *the best city in your country*?

Expressing Gratitude

Thank you anyway.

Apologizing

Sorry *we can't help you.*

NEW VOCABULARY

anyway
appliance
ashamed
bargain
best
boring
bright
come
complain
compliment (v)
dependable
downstairs
elegant
evening gown
funny
generous
girl
helpful

history
kind (adj)
location
mean (adj)
miserable
most
museum
obnoxious
older
one
patient (adj)
price
produce
proud
reasonable
record player
salespeople
sell

sloppy
stingy
stubborn
tape recorder
tourist sight
twin
upstairs
vacation place
visitor
worse
worst
younger

besides that
I'm afraid not.
in addition
Thank you anyway.
you can see why

LANGUAGE NOTES

Guidelines for Forming Superlative Adjectives

1. Add -est to one-syllable adjectives:

    kind–the kindest

2. Add -st to one-syllable adjectives that end in -e:

    nice–the nicest

3. Double the final consonant and add -est to one-syllable adjectives that end in a single consonant preceded by a single vowel:

    hot–the hottest

4. Change y to i and add -est to two-syllable adjectives that end in y preceded by a consonant:

    happy–the happiest

5. Place *most* before adjectives that have three or more syllables:

    generous–the most generous

6. The superlatives of two-syllable adjectives that don't end in y are less predictable. Some two-syllable adjectives are formed with *most*, some are formed with -est, and some are formed with either *most* or -est:

    honest–the most honest
    simple–the simplest

    polite– $\begin{cases} \textit{the most polite} \\ \textit{the politest} \end{cases}$

7. Irregular superlatives:

    good–the best
    bad–the worst

Text Page 46:   *The Smartest Person I Know*

FOCUS

Introduction of superlative adjectives with *-est* (see **Chapter Overview**)

GETTING READY

1. Introduce superlative adjectives.

   a. Put on the board:

   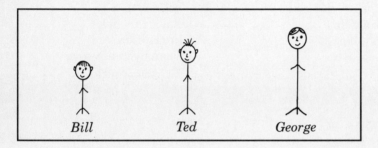

   b. Say: "Bill is tall."   "Ted is nice."
            "Ted is taller than Bill."   "George is nicer than Ted."
            "George is *the tallest.*"   "Bill is *the nicest.*"

   c. Say these sentences again and have students repeat chorally.

2. Read the adjectives in the boxes at the top of the page. Have students repeat chorally. Introduce the new word *kind.*

INTRODUCING THE MODEL

1. Have students look at the model illustration.
2. Set the scene: "Two people are talking."
3. Present the model.
4. Full-Class Choral Repetition.
5. Ask students if they have any questions; check understanding of the new vocabulary: *certainly.*
6. Group Choral Repetition.
7. Choral Conversation.
8. Call on one or two pairs of students to present the dialog.

   (For additional practice, do Choral Conversation in small groups or by rows.)

SIDE BY SIDE EXERCISES

Examples

1. A. I think your cousin is very friendly.
   B. He certainly is. He's the friendliest person I know.

2. A. I think your Uncle George is very funny.
   B. He certainly is. He's the funniest person I know.

Answer key to superlative adjectives 3–9:   3. *the kindest*   4. *the shyest*
5. *the prettiest*   6. *the laziest*   7. *the nicest*   8. *the coldest*   9. *the sloppiest*

---

1. **Exercise 1:** Call on two students to present the dialog. Then do Choral Repetition and Choral Conversation Practice.

2. **Exercise 2:** Introduce the new word *funny*. Same as above.

3. **Exercises 3–9:**

New vocabulary: 3. *kind*   4. *older, shy*   9. *younger, sloppy*

Language Note

Exercise 8: I think your Aunt Gertrude is very cold. The adjective *cold* is used here to mean *unfriendly*.

Either Full-Class Practice or Pair Practice.

WORKBOOK

Page 54

EXPANSION ACTIVITIES

1. *The People of Centerville*

   a. Put on the board:

Larry lazy	Sara smart	Karen kind
Sheila shy	Frank friendly	Ted tall
Phil funny	Slim sloppy	Herman heavy
Nancy nice	Rita rich	Clyde clean

   b. Set the scene: "Let's talk about the people who live in Centerville.
                         Larry is the laziest person in Centerville."

   c. Call on students to make similar statements about all the other people.

   d. Call on pairs of students to ask and answer questions about the people in Centerville. You can use Full-Class Practice or Pair Practice. For example:

   A. Who's the nicest person in Centerville?   A. Who's Rita?
   B. Nancy is the nicest person in Centerville.   B. She's the richest person in Centerville.

2. *Spelling Practice: Scrambled Superlatives*

a. Divide the class into small groups.

b. Put some or all of these scrambled words on the board. With books closed, have students work together in their small groups to unscramble the words. The first group to successfully unscramble them all wins.

1.	tepapsih	(happiest)	6.	delcots	(coldest)
2.	rotseths	(shortest)	7.	teyhss	(shyest)
3.	nusteinf	(funniest)	8.	silnerifdet	(friendliest)
4.	desktin	(kindest)	9.	slatelt	(tallest)
5.	postlepis	(sloppiest)	10.	shetnitn	(thinnest)

Text Page 47: *The Most Energetic Person I Know*

FOCUS

- Introduction of superlative adjectives with *most* (see **Chapter Overview**)
- Practice with *-est* superlatives

GETTING READY

1. Introduce superlative adjectives formed with *most*.

   a. Put on the board:

   b. Say: "Mary is talented."
       "Sue is more talented than Mary."
       "Jane is *the most talented*."

   c. Say these sentences again and have students repeat chorally.

2. Read the adjectives in the boxes at the top of the page. Have students repeat chorally.

INTRODUCING THE MODEL

1. Have students look at the model illustration.
2. Set the scene: "Two people are talking."
3. Present the model.
4. Full-Class Choral Repetition.
5. Ask students if they have any questions; check understanding of vocabulary.
6. Group Choral Repetition.
7. Choral Conversation.
8. Call on one or two pairs of students to present the dialog.
   (For additional practice, do Choral Conversation in small groups or by rows.)

SIDE BY SIDE EXERCISES

Examples

1. A. I think your son is very polite.
   B. He certainly is. He's the most polite person I know.

2. A. I think John is very stubborn.
   B. He certainly is. He's the most stubborn person I know.

1. **Exercise 1:** Introduce the new word *polite*. Call on two students to present the dialog. Then do Choral Repetition and Choral Conversation Practice.

2. **Exercise 2:** Introduce the new word *stubborn*. Same as above.

3. **Exercises 3–11:**

> **New vocabulary:**   3. *patient*   4. *bright*   6. *upstairs*   7. *downstairs, boring*
>   8. *twin*   9. *generous*   10. *stingy*

   Either Full-Class Practice or Pair Practice.

4. **Exercise 12:** Have students use the model as a guide to create 3 conversations, using vocabulary of their choice. (They may use any adjectives they wish.) Encourage students to use dictionaries to find new words they want to use. This exercise can be done orally in class or for written homework. If you assign it for homework, you should do one example in class to make sure students understand what's expected. Have students present their conversations in class the next day.

WORKBOOK

Pages 55–57

Exercise Note

Workbook p. 57: Students practice comparatives with *-est* and most.

EXPANSION ACTIVITIES

1. The People of Greenville

   a. Put on the board:

Peter polite	Tom talented	Stanley stingy
George generous	Betty boring	Inga important
Bill bright	Steven stubborn	Ted tall
Norman noisy	Frieda friendly	Dan dirty

   b. Set the scene: "Greenville is a city near Centerville. Let's talk about the people who live there. Peter is the most polite person in Greenville."

   c. Call on students to make similar statements about all the other people.

d. Call on pairs of students to ask and answer questions about the people in Greenville. You can use Full-Class Practice or Pair Practice. For example:

A. Who's the most polite person in Greenville?
B. Peter is the most polite person in Greenville.

A. Who's Betty?
B. She's the most boring person in Greenville.

2. **Review of Superlatives**

Make a list of adjectives or use the list below. Say an adjective and have students give the correct superlative form.

Teacher	Student
bright	the brightest
boring	the most boring
cold	the coldest
energetic	the most energetic
friendly	the friendliest
funny	the funniest
generous	the most generous
honest	the most honest
kind	the kindest
lazy	the laziest
nice	the nicest
noisy	the noisiest
patient	the most patient
polite	the most polite
pretty	the prettiest
shy	the shyest
sloppy	the sloppiest
stingy	the stingiest
stubborn	the most stubborn
talented	the most talented

If you wish, you can do this as a game. Divide the class into two teams. Each team gets a point for giving the correct form. The team with the most points wins the game.

3. **Our City**

a. Put a list of adjectives on the board. These adjectives should describe things in a city. For example:

tall	cheap	nice
long	expensive	modern
good	pretty	old
fast	ugly	busy

b. Set the scene:

"Let's talk about _____(name of your city)_____."
"_____(name of street)_____ is the busiest street in this city."

c. Call on students to make *superlative* statements about their city, using the list of adjectives on the board or any others they wish.

d. Write the following conversational model on the board:

A. What's the $\left\{\begin{array}{c}\text{most} \underline{\hspace{1cm}} \\ \underline{\hspace{1cm}}\text{est}\end{array}\right\}$ _____ in this city?

B. In my opinion, _____ is the $\left\{\begin{array}{c}\text{most} \underline{\hspace{1cm}} \\ \underline{\hspace{1cm}}\text{est}\end{array}\right\}$ _____.

Call on students to talk about their cities. For example:

A. What's the best hotel in this city?
B. In my opinion, the Plaza is the best hotel.

A. What's the cheapest restaurant in this city?
B. In my opinion, Joe's Diner is the cheapest restaurant.

e. If you wish, you may have students disagree with what others say. For example:

A. What's the best hotel in this city?
B. In my opinion, the Plaza is the best hotel.
C. I disagree. I think the Mayflower is the best hotel.

Text Page 48

READING: *The Nicest Person*
The Most Obnoxious Dog

FOCUS

> Superlatives

NEW VOCABULARY

Story 1	Story 2	
compliment (v)	ashamed	miserable
girl	complain	obnoxious
proud	mean	

PREVIEWING THE STORIES (optional)

Have students talk about the story titles and/or illustrations. Introduce new vocabulary.

READING THE STORIES

1. Have students read silently, or follow along silently as the stories are read aloud by you, by one or more students, or on the tape.
2. Ask students if they have any questions; check understanding of vocabulary.
3. Check students' comprehension, using some or all of the following questions:

Story 1	Story 2
a. Why are Mr. and Mrs. Jackson proud of their daughter?	a. Why are Mr. and Mrs. Hubbard ashamed of their dog?
b. What do the Jacksons' friends and neighbors say about Linda?	b. What do the Hubbards' friends and neighbors say about Rex?
c. According to them, what's she like?	c. According to them, what's he like?

CHECK-UP

Q & A

1. Call on a pair of students to present each model.
2. Have students work in pairs to create new dialogs.
3. Call on pairs to present their new dialogs to the class.

HOW ABOUT YOU?

Have students do the activity in pairs or as a class.

Text Pages 49–50: *I Want to Buy a Small Radio*

FOCUS

> - Expressions with *one:*
>
>   *this one*
>   *the _____ one*
>
> - Contrast of comparative and superlative adjectives:
>
>   *a small radio*
>   *the smallest one*

GETTING READY

Review comparative and superlative adjectives.

1. Read the expressions in the boxes at the top of the page.
2. Introduce the irregular superlative *good–(better)–best.*

INTRODUCING THE MODEL

1. Have students look at the model illustration.
2. Set the scene: "A salesman and a customer are talking in a department store."
3. Present the model.
4. Full-Class Choral Repetition.
5. Ask students if they have any questions; check understanding of new vocabulary: *this one, I'm afraid not, Thank you anyway, Please come again.*

   ### Language Note

   May I help you? Please come again. These expressions are commonly used by salespeople when talking with customers in stores.

6. Group Choral Repetition.
7. Choral Conversation.
8. Call on one or two pairs of students to present the dialog.

   (For additional practice, do Choral Conversation in small groups or by rows.)

SIDE BY SIDE EXERCISES

Examples

> 1. A. May I help you?
>   B. Yes, please. I want to buy a large refrigerator.
>   A. I think you'll like this one. It's VERY large.
>   B. Don't you have a larger one?
>   A. No, I'm afraid not. This is the largest one we have.
>   B. Thank you anyway.
>   A. Sorry we can't help you. Please come again.

2. A. May I help you?
   B. Yes, please. I want to buy a comfortable rocking chair.
   A. I think you'll like this one. It's VERY comfortable.
   B. Don't you have a more comfortable one?
   A. No, I'm afraid not. This is the most comfortable one we have.
   B. Thank you anyway.
   A. Sorry we can't help you. Please come again.

1. **Exercise 1:** Call on two students to present the dialog. Then do Choral Repetition and Choral Conversation Practice.

2. **Exercise 2:** Same as above.

3. **Exercises 3–11:**

   New vocabulary: 3. *record player* 7. *tape recorder* 9. *elegant, evening gown*

   Either Full-Class Practice or Pair Practice.

4. **Exercise 12:** Have students use the model as a guide to create their own conversations, using vocabulary of their choice. (They can use any *products* and adjectives they wish.) Encourage students to use dictionaries to find new words they want to use. This exercise can be done orally in class or for written homework. If you assign it for homework, you should do one example in class to make sure students understand what's expected. Have students present their conversations in class the next day.

WORKBOOK

Pages 58–61

Exercise Notes

Workbook p. 58: These exercises are TV commercials for PRESTO products. Have students act out these commercials, using *props* if possible.

Workbook p. 60: For additional oral practice with Exercise F, have students ask and answer questions about the pictures.

Workbook p. 61: Have students continue this playful exercise by having Student D point to Student E (*You're the best, better than the rest!*) and Student E point to Student F, etc.

EXPANSION ACTIVITIES

1. Vocabulary Practice

Ask about the items on text page 50.

   What's the largest item on the page?
   What's the smallest?
   What's the most expensive?
   What's the cheapest?
   What's larger than the _____?
   What's smaller than the _____?

2. *Shopping Advice about Your City*

a. Put this conversational model on the board:

A. I need a $\left\{ \dfrac{\underline{\hspace{2cm}}\text{er}}{\text{more} \underline{\hspace{2cm}}} \right\}$ _____.

B. Why don't you go to _____?

They have the $\left\{ \dfrac{\underline{\hspace{2cm}}\text{est}}{\text{most} \underline{\hspace{2cm}}} \right\}$ _____s in town.

b. Have students create conversations based on the model, using vocabulary of their choice. Encourage students to talk about local stores and the things they really need. If necessary, you can put word cues on the board to help students. For example:

comfortable/bed

A. I need a more comfortable bed.

B. Why don't you go to Joe's Furniture Store?
They have the most comfortable beds in town.

READING: *Bob's Bargain Department Store*
The Lord and Lady Department Store
The Super Saver Department Store

FOCUS

- Superlatives
- Comparatives

NEW VOCABULARY

Story 1		Story 2	Story 3
appliance	helpful	sell	in addition
bargain	location		price
besides that	product		reasonable
dependable	salespeople		you can see why
	worst		

PREVIEWING THE STORIES (optional)

Have students talk about the story titles and/or illustrations. Introduce new vocabulary.

READING THE STORIES

1. Have students read silently, or follow along silently as the stories are read aloud by you, by one or more students, or on the tape.
2. Ask students if they have any questions; check understanding of vocabulary.
3. Check students' comprehension, using some or all of the following questions:

   a. Why don't people shop at Bob's Bargain Department Store?
   b. Tell about the furniture, the clothes, the appliances, and the record players and tape recorders at Bob's Bargain Department Store.
   c. Tell about the location and the salespeople.

   d. What kind of products does the Lord and Lady Department Store sell?
   e. Tell about the furniture, the clothes, the appliances, and the record players and tape recorders at the Lord and Lady Department Store.
   f. Tell about the location and the salespeople.
   g. Why don't people shop there?

   h. Tell about the furniture at the Super Saver Department Store.
   i. Tell about the clothes.
   j. Tell about the appliances.
   k. Tell about the record players and tape recorders.
   l. Tell about the location and the salespeople.
   m. Why do people like to shop there?

CHECK-UP

True or False?

1. False
2. True
3. False
4. False
5. False

Listening

Have students complete the exercises as you play the tape or read the following:

Listen and choose the best answers to complete the commercial.

1. Good news for shoppers everywhere! Franklin's Department Store is having a big sale this week. Everything is on sale, and our products are very . . . (a)
2. Our products are also better than items at other stores. Our furniture is more . . . (a)
3. Our appliances are more . . . (b)
4. And everybody agrees our salespeople are more . . . (a)
5. Come on down to Franklin's Department Store! Don't shop at those other stores! We're the . . . (b)

HOW ABOUT YOU?

Have students answer the questions, in pairs or as a class.

Text Page 53

ON YOUR OWN: *In Your Opinion*

FOCUS

Students express opinions about people and places they know, using superlative adjectives

ON YOUR OWN ACTIVITY

1. Introduce the irregular adjective *bad–worse–worst*.
2. Introduce questions 1–15; check understanding of new vocabulary.

> **New vocabulary:**   5. *history*   8. *tourist sight, visitor, museum, monument*
>   9. *vacation place*

3. For homework, have students write answers to some or all of the questions. Have students present their opinions in the next class without referring to their written homework. You can use Full-Class Practice or Pair Practice.

   [Optional] Student Survey: Have students take a survey by asking friends, members of their families, or other students in the school the questions on text page 53. Compile the findings and *publish* the results.

WORKBOOK

Check-Up Test: Pages 62–63

WORKBOOK ANSWER KEY AND LISTENING SCRIPTS

Page 54   A.   WHAT DO YOU THINK?

1. the prettiest
2. the laziest
3. the largest
4. the kindest
5. the richest
6. the safest
7. the funniest
8. the sloppiest
9. the shyest
10. the biggest

Page 55   B.   WHAT'S THE WORD?

1. polite
   the most polite
2. talented
   the most talented
3. generous
   the most generous
4. energetic
   the most energetic
5. lazy
   the laziest
6. stingy
   the stingiest
7. patient
   the most patient
8. boring
   the most boring
9. bright
   the brightest
10. honest
    the most honest
11. interesting
    the most interesting
12. stubborn
    the most stubborn

Page 56   C.   AROUND THE WORLD

1. the most attractive
2. the softest
3. the most beautiful
4. the warmest
5. the most modern
6. the most elegant
7. the prettiest
8. the best
9. the safest
10. the most reliable

Page 58   E.   WONDERFUL PRESTO PRODUCTS

1. more delicious
   the most delicious
2. faster
   the fastest
3. more attractive
   the most attractive
4. lighter
   the lightest
5. more exciting
   the most exciting
6. quieter
   the quietest
7. softer, shinier
   the softest, the shiniest
8. cleaner
   fresher
   the cleanest, the freshest
9. better
   the best
10. more beautiful
    the most beautiful

Page 60   F.   LOUD AND CLEAR

1. Robert, ironing
   favorite shirt
2. Our, brother
   write German
3. right
   recipe, rice
   better
4. mother, are
   arrive, Rome
   morning
5. received
   attractive
   racket, her
   thirtieth birthday
6. Mr., Roberts
   were very
   Friday, their
   radiator
   broken

CHECK-UP TEST: *CHAPTERS 4–6*

Page 62   A.

1. it will, It'll
2. she won't
3. I will, I'll
4. he won't
5. they will, They'll

Page 62 B.

1. might
2. Should
3. might
   might
4. should

Page 62 C.

1. his
2. mine
3. theirs
4. yours

Page 62 D.

1. taller than
2. more capable than
3. friendlier than
4. faster than
5. more delicious than

Page 63 E.

1. isn't as interesting as
   safer
2. isn't as nice as
   more talented
3. isn't as young as
   healthier

4. isn't as elegant as
   bigger
5. isn't as new as
   better

Page 63 F.

1. the nicest
2. the most intelligent
3. the largest
4. the most interesting
5. the most honest

Page 63 G.

Listen and put a circle around the correct answer.

Ex. Alice is younger than Margaret.

1. Bob is taller than Bill.
2. Tea is more expensive than champagne.
3. David is heavier than Herman.
4. Stockholm is colder than Madrid.
5. Carl's homework is more difficult than Jack's homework.

Answers
1. Yes
2. No
3. No
4. Yes
5. Yes

GRAMMAR

Imperatives

> **Walk** up Main Street.
> **Turn** right.
> **Drive** along Second Avenue to River Street.

FUNCTIONS

Asking for Directions

Can you tell me
Could you please tell me
Would you please tell me
 how to get to the laundromat from here?

Can you tell me how to get there?

What's the best/easiest/fastest/most direct/
 quickest/shortest way to get to *Peter's Pet Shop*?

Giving Directions

Walk up
Walk down } *Main Street.*
Walk along

You'll see the *laundromat* { on the right / on the left },

{ across from *the drug store.*
 next to *the high school.*
 between *the museum* and *the park.*
 at the corner of *Brighton Boulevard*
  and *Twelfth Street.*

Walk up *Park Street* to *Second Avenue* and
 { turn right.
  turn left.

Drive along *Second Avenue* to *River Street* and
 { turn right.
  turn left.

Take *the Main Street bus* and get off at *First
Avenue.*

Attracting Attention

Excuse me.

Expressing Gratitude

Thank you.
Thanks.
Thank you very much.
Thanks very much.
 You're welcome.

Asking for a Suggestion

Can you recommend *a good hotel*?

Describing

The Bellview is a good *hotel.*

I think it's one of the best *hotels* in *town.*

NEW VOCABULARY

along
block (n)
boulevard
butcher shop
candy store
completely
concert hall
courthouse
direct (adj)
directions
follow

get lost
get off
hardware store
last
motel
news stand
pet shop
playground
road
stadium
stop (n)

stupid
such
turn (v)
TV station
university
way
wrong

in a hurry
You're welcome.

Text Page 56: *Can You Tell Me How to Get to the Laundromat from Here?*

FOCUS

Introduction of the expressions:

Can you tell me how to get to _____ *from here?*
walk up   on the right
walk down   on the left

GETTING READY

1. Review the following locations in the community. Use *Side by Side* Picture Cards or your own visuals. Say each word or expression and have students repeat chorally and individually.

bakery	*clinic*	*laundromat*	*post office*
bank	*drug store*	*library*	*shoe store*
barber shop	*high school*	*police station*	

    Introduce *butcher shop.*

2. Introduce the map of Main Street, using the illustration. Point to each location; say the word(s) and have students repeat.

3. Introduce the new expressions:

    walk up   on the left
    walk down   on the right

    a. Point to the map and gesture (↑) as you say, "Walk up Main Street." Have students repeat.

    b. Point to the map and gesture (↓) as you say, "Walk down Main Street." Have students repeat.

    c. Write on the board:

    > Walk _____ Main Street.
    > The _____ is on the right.
    > The _____ is on the left.

    Point to the map as you say these sentences and have students repeat:

"Walk up Main Street."	"Walk down Main Street."
"The shoe store is on the right."	"The bakery is on the right."
"The bakery is on the left."	"The shoe store is on the left."

    d. Call on students to make similar sentences.

4. Review the expressions *next to, across from,* and *between*. Have students make statements about the map, using these expressions. For example:

    > "The butcher shop is across from the barber shop."

INTRODUCING THE MODEL

There are two model conversations. Introduce and practice each separately. For each model:

1. Have students look at the model illustration.

2. Set the scene:

        1st model: "Two people are standing in front of the post office."
        2nd model: "Two people are standing in front of the drug store."

3. Present the model.
4. Full-Class Choral Repetition.
5. Ask students if they have any questions; check understanding of vocabulary.

Language Notes

Walk up, walk down, walk along: These three expressions are often used interchangeably when giving directions in a city.

Sure: The expression *Sure* is commonly used in informal conversation in place of *Yes* or *Yes, of course.*

6. Group Choral Repetition.
7. Choral Conversation.
8. Call on one or two pairs of students to present the dialog.
9. Call on another pair of students to present each dialog again. This time have them give alternate directions to the same places by substituting a different expression at the end. For example, an alternate way to present the 1st model is:

    "Walk up Main Street and you'll see the laundromat on the right, *next to the butcher shop.*"

(For additional practice, do Choral Conversation in small groups or by rows.)

SIDE BY SIDE EXERCISES

In these exercises, students can describe the location of buildings in several possible ways.

Examples

---

1. A. Excuse me. Can you tell me how to get to the shoe store from here?
   B. Sure. Walk up Main Street and you'll see the shoe store on the right, across from the bakery (OR next to the clinic/next to the butcher shop/between the clinic and the butcher shop).
   A. Thank you.

2. A. Excuse me. Can you tell me how to get to the police station from here?
   B. Sure. Walk down Main Street and you'll see the police station on the right, next to the library (OR next to the bank/between the library and the bank/across from the high school).
   A. Thank you.

---

1. **Exercise 1:** Call on two students to present the dialog. Then do Choral Repetition and Choral Conversation Practice. Ask students to tell you alternate directions to the same place.

2. **Exercise 2:** Same as above.

3. **Exercises 3–6:**

  Either Full-Class Practice or Pair Practice.

WORKBOOK

Page 64

EXPANSION ACTIVITIES

1. ***Role Play: Giving Directions***

    Have pairs of students role play the model conversation in front of the class. Put the map of Main Street on the board. Use *Side by Side* Picture Cards or word cards as cues for locations. For each pair:

    a. Set the scene by saying: "Student A is new in town; Student B lives here. They are talking in front of the _____ (any location on the map)."

    b. Give Student A a cue: either a *Side by Side* Picture Card or a word card for the location he or she is seeking.

2. ***Practice Following Directions: Where Are You?***

    Have students give the class directions to unknown locations; then have the class guess the locations. Use the map of Main Street in the book or make your own map on the board.

    a. Make word cards showing two locations: one the origin, the other the destination. Have students draw cards. For example:

    ┌────────────────────────────┐
    │   │
    │   bank → (butcher shop) │
    │   │
    └────────────────────────────┘

    b. You begin by telling the class *where they are*; then give directions to the *mystery* location. For example:

    > "You're at the bank. Walk up Main Street and you'll see it on the right between the laundromat and the shoe store."

    c. Ask "Where are you?" and have students tell you the location:

    > "The butcher shop."

    d. Call on students to do the same as above.

Text Page 57: *Could You Please Tell Me How to Get to the Hospital from Here?*

FOCUS

> Introduction of the expression *walk along*

GETTING READY

1. Review the following locations in the community. Use *Side by Side* Picture Cards or your own visuals. Say each word or expression and have students repeat chorally and individually.

gas station	*museum*
hospital	*park*
hotel	*zoo*

   Introduce *playground, university*.

2. Introduce the map of Central Avenue, using the illustration. Point to each location; say the word(s) and have students repeat.

3. Introduce the new expression *walk along*. Point to the map and gesture (⇄) as you say the expression. Have students repeat chorally and individually.

INTRODUCING THE MODEL

1. Have students look at the model illustration.
2. Set the scene: "Two people are talking in front of the parking lot."
3. Present the model.
4. Full-Class Choral Repetition.
5. Ask students if they have any questions.
6. Group Choral Repetition.
7. Choral Conversation.
8. Call on one or two pairs of students to present the dialog. Call on another pair of students to present the dialog again, using alternate locations. For example:

   "Walk along Central Avenue and you'll see the hospital on the left, across from the hotel."

   (For additional practice, do Choral Conversation in small groups or by rows.)

SIDE BY SIDE EXERCISES

As on text page 56, there is more than one correct answer for these exercises.

Examples

> 1. A. Excuse me. Could you please tell me how to get to the parking lot from here?
>   B. Sure. Walk along Central Avenue and you'll see the parking lot on the left, next to the gas station (OR across from the university).
>   A. Thanks.

2. A. Excuse me. Could you please tell me how to get to the university from here?
    B. Sure. Walk along Central Avenue and you'll see the university on the right, across from the parking lot (OR next to the museum).
    A. Thanks.

1. **Exercise 1:** Call on two students to present the dialog. Then do Choral Repetition and Choral Conversation Practice. Ask students to tell you alternate directions to the same place.

2. **Exercise 2:** Same as above.

3. **Exercises 3–6:**

    Either Full-Class Practice or Pair Practice.

WORKBOOK

Page 65

EXPANSION ACTIVITIES

1. *Role Play: Giving Directions*

    Have students role play the model conversation in front of the class. Put the map of Central Avenue on the board. For each pair:

    a. Set the scene by saying:

        "Student A is new in town; Student B lives here. They are talking in front of the _____ (any location on the map)."

    b. Give Student A a cue: either a *Side by Side* Picture Card or a word card for the location he or she is seeking.

    c. Have students role play the conversation. You might have students vary the question. For example:

        "How do I get to the _____ from here?"
        "Can you tell me how to get to the _____ from here?"

2. *Role Play: Directions in Our City*

    a. Make a map of the downtown area of your city—either on the board or on a large piece of paper.

    b. Set the scene: "Student A is a tourist in town; Student B lives here. They're talking in front of the _____ (any location on the map)."

    c. Give Student A a cue: a word card for the location he or she is seeking.

    d. Have students role play the conversations.

Text Pages 58–59: *Would You Please Tell Me How to Get to the Bus Station from Here?*

FOCUS

Introduction of the expressions:

turn right   *drive along/up/down*
turn left

GETTING READY

1. Introduce the new locations in the community. Use *Side by Side* Picture Cards or your own visuals. Say each word or expression and have students repeat chorally and individually.

New vocabulary:

candy store	*motel*
concert hall	*news stand*
courthouse	*pet shop*
hardware store	*TV station*

2. Introduce the map, using the illustration.

   a. Point to each location and street; say the word(s) and have students repeat.

   b. Familiarize students with the map by using the following model:

   Where's the _____?
   It's on _____ Street/Avenue.

   For example:

   > "Where's the hotel?"
   > "It's on Park Street."

   c. Call on pairs of students to ask and answer similar questions.

INTRODUCING THE MODEL

There are two model conversations. Introduce and practice each separately. For each model:

1. Have students look at the model illustration.
2. Set the scene:

   1st model: "Two people are standing in the park."
   2nd model: "Two people are talking in front of the department store. One of them is driving."

3. Present the model.
4. Full-Class Choral Repetition.

5. Ask students if they have any questions; check understanding of new vocabulary:

        1st model: *turn right*
        2nd model: *drive along/up, turn left*

Culture Note

Motels are roadside hotels with convenient parking facilities and overnight accommodations. (The word *motel* is a reduction of *mo*tor h*otel*.)

6. Group Choral Repetition.
7. Choral Conversation.
8. Call on one or two pairs of students to present the dialog.

   (For additional practice, do Choral Conversation in small groups or by rows.)

SIDE BY SIDE EXERCISES

In these exercises, there are many possible answers for each exercise.

Examples

---

1. A. Excuse me. Would you please tell me how to get to the shopping mall from here?
   B. Certainly. Drive up River Street to Third Avenue and turn left. Drive along Third Avenue and you'll see the shopping mall on the right, across from the motel.
   A. Thanks very much.

2. A. Excuse me. Would you please tell me how to get to the hardware store from here?
   B. Certainly. Walk along Third Avenue to Park Street and turn left. Walk down Park Street and you'll see the hardware store on the left, between the pet shop and the laundromat.
   A. Thanks very much.

---

1. **Exercise 1:** Call on two students to present the dialog. Then do Choral Repetition and Choral Conversation Practice.

2. **Exercise 2:** Same as above.

3. **Exercises 3–7:**

   Either Full-Class Practice or Pair Practice.

4. **Exercise 8:** Have students use the model as a guide to create their own conversations, using vocabulary of their choice. (They can use any locations they wish.) Encourage students to use dictionaries to find new words they want to use. This exercise can be done orally in class or for written homework. If you assign it for homework, you should do one example in class to make sure students understand what's expected. Have students present their conversations in class the next day.

WORKBOOK

Pages 66–68

EXPANSION ACTIVITY

Practice Following Directions: Where Are You?

Have students give the class directions to unknown locations; then have the class guess the locations. Use the illustration of the map in the book.

1. Make word cards showing two locations: one the origin, and the other the destination. Have students draw cards. For example:

    > concert hall → *(Chinese restaurant)*

2. Begin by telling the class *where they are*; then give directions to the *mystery* location. For example:

    > "You're at the concert hall. Walk up River Street to Third Avenue and turn left.
    > Walk along Third Avenue to Park Street and turn left. Walk down Park Street and you'll see *it* on the right, across from the hardware store."

3. Ask "Where are you?" and have students tell you the location:

    > "The Chinese restaurant."

4. Call on students to do the same as above.

Text Page 60: *Take the Main Street Bus and Get Off at First Avenue*

FOCUS

Directions for using public transportation:
take the bus/subway   get off at

INTRODUCING THE MODEL

There are two model conversations. Introduce and practice each separately. For each model:

1. Have students look at the model illustration.
2. Set the scene:

    1st model: "A woman wants to take her dog to Peter's Pet Shop."
    2nd model: "A man wants to take his son to Harry's Barber Shop."

3. Present the model.
4. Full-Class Choral Repetition.
5. Ask students if they have any questions; check understanding of new vocabulary:

    1st model: *the quickest way, get off, you're welcome*
    2nd model: *the easiest way*

6. Group Choral Repetition.
7. Choral Conversation.
8. Call on one or two pairs of students to present the dialog.

    (For additional practice, do Choral Conversation in small groups or by rows.)

SIDE BY SIDE EXERCISES

Answer Key

1. Take the 161st Street bus and get off at Jerome Avenue. Walk up Jerome Avenue and you'll see the baseball stadium on the left.

2. Take the subway and get off at Seventh Avenue. Walk down Seventh Avenue and you'll see Saint Andrew's Church on the right.

3. Take the subway and get off at Apple Road. Walk up Apple Road and you'll see the zoo on the left.

4. Take the 10th Avenue bus and get off at Station Street. Walk along Station Street and you'll see the train station on the right.

1. **Exercise 1:** Introduce the new word *stadium*. Call on two students to present the dialog. Then do Choral Repetition and Choral Conversation Practice.
2. **Exercise 2:** Same as above.
3. **Exercises 3–4:**

> **New vocabulary:**   3. *the most direct way*   4. *in a hurry, the shortest way*

Either Full-Class Practice or Pair Practice.

WORKBOOK

Pages 69–70

EXPANSION ACTIVITIES

1. *Students Talk about Transportation in Their City*

    For homework, have students write directions from their house to the school. Encourage students to use the dictionary to find new words. Have students present their directions in class the next day without referring to their written homework.

2. *Role Play: I'm Lost*

    Put a map of your city on the wall or have a student draw a simple map on the board. Put the following model on the board and call on pairs of students to role play:

> A. Excuse me, but I'm lost!
>   How do I get to _____?
> B. _____.
> A. Thank you for your help.

READING: *Harold Never Got There*

FOCUS

> Directions

NEW VOCABULARY

block	follow	stupid
completely	get lost	such
directions	stop	wrong

PREVIEWING THE STORY (optional)

Have students talk about the story title and/or illustrations. Introduce new vocabulary.

READING THE STORY

1. Have students read silently, or follow along silently as the story is read aloud by you, by one or more students, or on the tape.
2. Ask students if they have any questions; check understanding of vocabulary.
3. Check students' comprehension, using some or all of the following questions:

   a. Where did Harold want to go last night?
   b. Did he get there?
   c. Why not? What did he do?

CHECK-UP

True or False?

> 1. True
> 2. True
> 3. False
> 4. False
> 5. True
> 6. False

What's the Word?

1. to	4. of	7. on
2. to	5. off	8. to
3. at	6. at	9. from

Listening

Have students complete the exercises as you play the tape or read the following:

I. Listen and choose the word you hear.

1. The school is on the right, next to the post office. (a)
2. Walk up Town Road to Park Street. (b)
3. Drive along Fourth Avenue to Station Street. (b)
4. Take the subway to Bond Street. (a)
5. The bus stop is at the corner of Main and Fifth. (a)
6. Take this bus and get off at Rolling Road. (b)

II. Where is the conversation taking place? Listen and choose.

1. A. Please give me an order of chicken.
   B. An order of chicken? Certainly. (b)

2. A. Shh! Please be quiet! People are reading.
   B. Sorry. (b)

3. A. Do you want to buy these clothes?
   B. Yes, please. (a)

4. A. Can I visit my wife?
   B. Yes. She and the baby are in Room 407. (a)

5. A. How much does one head cost?
   B. Seventy-nine cents. (b)

IN YOUR OWN WORDS

1. Make sure students understand the instructions.
2. Have students do the activity as written homework, using a dictionary for any new words they wish to use.
3. Have students present and discuss what they have written, in pairs or as a class.

Text Page 63

ON YOUR OWN: *Can You Tell Me How to Get There?*

FOCUS

- Students practice asking for and giving directions to locations in their own community
- Introduction of the expressions:

$$\text{one of the} \left\{ \frac{\text{————— est}}{\text{most —————}} \right\}$$

at the corner of

ON YOUR OWN ACTIVITY

1. Have students look at the illustration.
2. Set the scene: "This family is visiting your town. They want to find a good hotel."
3. Present the dialog. Read each line and have students repeat chorally.
4. Ask students if they have any questions; check understanding of new vocabulary: *one of the best, boulevard, at the corner of.*
5. **Exercises 1–3:** Call on pairs of students to role play the conversations. Have students make recommendations about real places in their city.
6. **Exercise 4:** For homework, have students write a new conversation based on the model dialog. Encourage students to vary or expand the dialog in any way they wish. Have students present their dialogs in the next class.

WORKBOOK

Page 71

Exercise Note

Workbook p. 71: Pause after the first sentence of each exercise so that students can locate the starting place.

WORKBOOK ANSWER KEY AND LISTENING SCRIPTS

Page 64 A. HOW DO I GET THERE?

1. Walk up
   on the right
   clinic
2. Walk up
   on the right
   butcher shop
3. Walk up
   on the left
   clinic
4. Walk down
   on the left
   between
5. Walk up
   on the left
   across from

Page 65 B. WHICH WAY?

1. Walk along, on the right
   playground
2. Walk along
   on the left, university
3. Walk up
   on the left, across from
4. Walk down
   on the right, next to
5. Walk along
   on the right, library
6. Walk along
   on the left, between
   barber shop, museum

**Page 66 C. MRS. BROWN NEEDS
        YOUR HELP**

1. Walk up, turn right
   Walk along
   on the right, across from
2. Walk along, turn right
   Walk up
   on the right, between
3. Walk up, turn right
   Walk along
   on the left, across from

4. Walk along, turn left
   Walk down
   on the right, next to
5. Walk down, turn left
   Walk along, turn left
   Walk up, on the right
   between, courthouse, church

Page 69 E. IN A HURRY

1. Take, get off
   Walk up, on the right
2. Take, get off
   Walk up
   on the left
3. Take, get off
   Second Street, Walk down Second
   Street and you'll see Stanley's
   Restaurant on the right.

Page 71 H. LISTEN: *Where Did They Go?*

Listen and fill in the correct places.

1. John was at the restaurant on Maple Street.
   He walked up Maple Street to Grand Avenue
   and turned left. He walked along Grand
   Avenue to the building next to the post office.
   Where did he go?

2. Helen was at the shoe store on Brighton
   Boulevard. She walked along Brighton
   Boulevard to Elm Street and turned left. She
   walked up Elm Street to the building next to
   the Bellview Hotel. Where did she go?

3. Mr. and Mrs. Larson were at the motel on Elm
   Street. They walked down Elm Street to
   Brighton Boulevard and turned right. They
   walked along Brighton Boulevard to the
   building across from the museum. Where did
   they go?

4. Tommy was at the candy store on Maple
   Street. He walked up Maple Street to Grand
   Avenue and turned right. He walked along
   Grand Avenue to the building between the
   news stand and the butcher shop. Where did
   he go?

5. Julie was at the university on Brighton Boulevard. She walked along Brighton Boulevard to Maple Street and turned left. She walked up Maple Street to Grand Avenue and turned right. She walked along Grand Avenue to the building across from the pet shop. Where did she go?

6. Peggy and Paul were at the supermarket on Maple Street. They walked up Maple Street to Brighton Boulevard and turned right. They walked along Brighton Boulevard to Elm Street and turned left. They walked up Elm Street to the building next to the flower shop. Where did they go?

7. Mrs. Wilson and her son were at the laundromat on Brighton Boulevard. They walked along Brighton Boulevard to Maple Street and turned right. They walked up Maple Street to the building next to the restaurant at the corner of Maple Street and Grand Avenue. Where did they go?

Answers
1. department store
2. hardware store
3. courthouse
4. pet shop
5. hospital
6. TV station
7. post office

TEACHER'S NOTES

GRAMMAR

Adverbs

He works	slowly. terribly. sloppily. fast. hard. well.

Comparatives of Adverbs

He should try to work	more neatly. neater.
	more carefully. more politely.
	faster. harder. better.

Agent Nouns

dancer	skier
driver	teacher
painter	translator
player	worker
singer	

If-Clauses

If	I we you they	feel	better,	I'll we'll you'll they'll	go to work.
	he she it	feels		he'll she'll it'll	

If	I'm we're you're they're	tired,	I'll we'll you'll they'll	go to sleep early.
	he's she's it's		he'll she'll it'll	

FUNCTIONS

Describing

He's a *careless driver*.
He *drives* very *carelessly/slowly/fast/well/*....

Expressing an Opinion

I think *he's a careless driver*.

He should *try to speak slower*.

Expressing Agreement

I agree.
You're right.
You're probably right.

Asking for Feedback

Do I *type fast* enough?

Offering Feedback

You *type too slowly*.

Expressing Intention

I'll try to *type faster* in the future.
If *it rains*, I'll *take the bus*.

Inquiring about Intention

How are you going to *get to school tomorrow*?
What's *Fred* going to do *tomorrow*?
When are you going to *go to sleep tonight*?
What are you going to do *tonight* if *you have a lot of homework*?

Initiating a Topic

You know, . . .

Offering Advice

You shouldn't *drive so fast*.

Expressing Possibility

If you *drive too fast*, you might *have an accident*.

NEW VOCABULARY

accident	evict	luck	spoon
accurate	far away	mirror	stay up
Arizona	fast	New Jersey	superstition
awkward	fork	nightmare	tennis player
bad luck	four-leaf clover	open (v)	throw
bank account	furthermore	over	translator
beautiful	good luck	oversleep	ulcer
card player	graceful	painter	under
careful	headphones	player	until
careless	horseshoe	rent (n)	use
chess player	if	scary	worker
director	impolite	shoulder	worry
dishonest	in general	shouldn't	
dress (v)	itch (v)	skier	Hmm.
driver	knife	slow	Oh?
do well	ladder	somebody	Too bad!
ear	left	spill	You're probably right.
enough	lonely		

LANGUAGE NOTES

1. **Formation of Adverbs**

   a. An adverb of manner is formed by adding *-ly* to the corresponding adjective. For example:

   slow   – slowly
   careful – carefully

   For adjectives ending in *-y* preceded by a consonant, change the *-y* to *-i* and add *-ly:*

   lazy – lazily

   For adjectives ending in *-ble* or *-ple*, drop the *-le* and add *-ly:*

   terrible – terribly
   simple   – simply

   b. Irregular adverbs of manner:

   fast   – fast
   hard – hard
   good – well
   loud – loud/loudly

2. **Comparative Forms of Adverbs**

   a. Comparatives of adverbs of manner are commonly formed with *more:*

   carefully – more carefully

   b. Some comparative adverbs are formed either with *more* or by adding *-er* to the adjective form:

   slowly – $\begin{cases} more\ slowly \\ slower \end{cases}$

   c. Comparative forms of irregular adverbs of manner and adverbs of time are formed by adding *-er:*

   hard – harder   early – earlier

Text Page 66: *He Drives Very Carelessly*

FOCUS

```
• Introduction of adverbs
• Agent nouns
```

INTRODUCING THE MODEL

1. Have students look at the model illustration.
2. Set the scene: "Two people are talking about the man who is driving."
3. Present the model.
4. Full-Class Choral Repetition.
5. Ask students if they have any questions; check understanding of new vocabulary: *careless, driver, carelessly.*

   ### Culture Note

   The sign *Keep Off the Grass* is common on public lawns in the United States.

6. Group Choral Repetition.
7. Choral Conversation.
8. Call on one or two pairs of students to present the dialog.

   (For additional practice, do Choral Conversation in small groups or by rows.)
9. Practice the adverb forms in the boxes at the top of the page.

   a. Read each adjective–adverb pair and have students repeat chorally. Point out the irregular adverbs: *fast–fast, hard–hard, good–well.*

   b. Say each adjective and have students tell you the corresponding adverb.
10. Read the agent noun pairs in the box near the top of the page and have students repeat.

SIDE BY SIDE EXERCISES

Examples

```
1. A. I think he's a careless skier.
   B. I agree. He skis very carelessly.
2. A. I think he's a slow chess player.
   B. I agree. He plays chess very slowly.
```

1. **Exercise 1:** Introduce the new word *skier.* Call on two students to present the dialog. Then do Choral Repetition and Choral Conversation Practice.

2. **Exercise 2:** Introduce the new words *slow, player.* Same as above.

3. **Exercises 3–12:**

Language Note

Exercise 5: The *-or* ending in the word *translator* differs from the *er* ending of most agent nouns. Another example is *actor*.

Either Full-Class Practice or Pair Practice.

WORKBOOK

Pages 72–74

Exercise Note

Workbook p. 74: Students practice adverbs.

EXPANSION ACTIVITIES

1. ***Practice with Adverbs: I Had a Bad Day***

Use the conversational guide below to help students practice opposite adverbs.

a. Write these cues on word cards or on the board:

1. do my homework/carelessly/carefully
2. speak English/terribly/well
3. sing/badly/beautifully
4. play tennis/terribly/well
5. dance/badly/gracefully
6. work/slowly/fast
7. cook/badly/well
8. work/sloppily/carefully
9. type/sloppily/accurately
10. drive/ carelessly/_____
11. play tennis/badly/_____
12. _____

b. Write on the board:

> A. I'm upset! I _____ yesterday.
> B. That's strange. You usually _____ very _____.
> A. I know, but I had a bad day yesterday.

c. Call on pairs of students to create conversations using the cues. For example:

> A. I'm upset! I did my homework carelessly yesterday.
> B. That's strange. You usually do your homework very carefully.
> A. I know, but I had a bad day yesterday.

d. Call on pairs of students to create conversations for Number 12.

2. Making Choices

a. Put a list of adjectives on the board:

accurate	dishonest	graceful
beautiful	fast	hard
careful	good	sloppy
careless		slow

b. Based on the following list . . .

ski – skier	dance – dancer
paint – painter	sing – singer
work – worker	drive – driver
play – player	teach – teacher
translate – translator	

say a verb or noun and have students make a sentence, using either an appropriate adjective on the board or its adverb equivalent. For example:

Teacher	Student
skier	He's a slow skier.
ski	She skis very well.
dance	He dances very gracefully.

Encourage students to be creative. There are many possibilities for answers to this exercise.

Text Page 67: *He Should Try to Speak More Slowly*

FOCUS

> Introduction of the comparative forms of adverbs

INTRODUCING THE MODEL

1. Have students look at the model illustration.
2. Set the scene: "Two people are talking about Bob."
3. Present the model.
4. Full-Class Choral Repetition.
5. Ask students if they have any questions; check understanding of new vocabulary: *quickly, slower, more slowly.*
6. Group Choral Repetition.
7. Choral Conversation.
8. Call on one or two pairs of students to present the dialog using the adverb *slower;* then call on one or two pairs of students to present the dialog using *more slowly.*

   (For additional practice, do Choral Conversation in small groups or by rows.) Introduce the adverbs and comparative forms at the top of the page. Say each word and have students repeat chorally.

> **New adverbs:**
>
> *loud(ly)   politely*
> *neatly   softly*

SIDE BY SIDE EXERCISES

Examples

> 1. A. Linda speaks very softly.
>   B. You're right. She should try to speak louder/more loudly.
>
> 2. A. Ronald goes to bed very late.
>   B. You're right. He should try to go to bed earlier.

1. **Exercise 1:** Call on two students to present the dialog. Then do Choral Repetition and Choral Conversation Practice.
2. **Exercise 2:** Same as above.
3. **Exercises 3–9:**

> **New vocabulary:**   6. *dress* (v)   7. *impolite*

WORKBOOK

Pages 75–76

Exercise Notes

Workbook p. 75: Have students first fill in the grammar box at the top of the page and then use their answers to complete the dialog. For additional oral practice with the exercise, have students act out this conversation between Mr. Sharp and his boss.

Workbook p. 76: Students practice comparatives of adverbs.

EXPANSION ACTIVITIES

1. Review Adverbs

Write each of the following statements about people on word cards. Pass the cards out to students. Have each student read the statement on the card; then call on another student to make a similar statement, using *always* or *never* and the opposite adverb.

Example:

    (card):   Mary always speaks softly.
    (student):   "I know. She never speaks loud(ly)."

1. Ronald never goes to bed early.
2. Linda always plays her radio very loudly.
3. Your friends always come to class late.
4. Janet never speaks impolitely.
5. They always work very slowly.
6. Bill never dresses sloppily.
7. Karen always plays tennis well.
8. Mr. Jones always translates carefully.
9. They never play cards honestly.
10. Ralph never does his homework carefully.

2. Practice with Comparative Forms of Adverbs: Giving Advice

Write the following problem statements on word cards. Give the cards to students. Have each student read the problem to the class; then call on another student to give advice, using the appropriate comparative adverb.

Example:

    (problem):   Joe never says *Thank you* or *You're welcome.*
    (advice):   "He should try to speak more politely."

Problems:

1. Bill's friends don't want to play cards with him because he sometimes plays dishonestly.
2. My grandmother drives very carelessly.
3. Mary likes Sam. She wants to go out on a date with him, but her parents think he dresses sloppily.
4. Ted arrives late at the office every day. His boss always gets mad at him.
5. When Jim talks, everybody gets an earache.
6. Ronald types very fast, but he makes a lot of mistakes.
7. Janet is a good student, but sometimes she speaks impolitely.
8. When Karen washes the dishes, she always breaks something.
9. Larry is shy. He speaks so softly that his friends can't hear him.
10. Gertrude is lazy. She's afraid her boss might fire her.
11. Jane wants to get a new job, but she works very slowly.
12. Roger likes to play his radio very loud, but when he plays his radio loud, his brothers and sister can't do their homework.

READING: *Trying Harder*

FOCUS

> • Adverbs
> • Comparatives of adverbs

NEW VOCABULARY

awkward	furthermore
director	in general
do well	

PREVIEWING THE STORY (optional)

Have students talk about the story title and/or illustrations. Introduce new vocabulary.

READING THE STORY

1. Have students read silently, or follow along silently as the story is read aloud by you, by one or more students, or on the tape.
2. Ask students if they have any questions; check understanding of vocabulary.
3. Check students' comprehension, using some or all of the following questions:

    a. What does Michael's boss think about his work?
    b According to Michael's boss, how does he type?
    c. What should he do?
    d. How does he file?
    e. What should he do?
    f. How does he speak on the telephone?
    g. What should he do?

    h. What does Stella's director think about her work?
    i. According to Stella's director, how does she speak?
    j. What should she do?
    k. How does she walk?
    l. What should she do?
    m. How does she dance?
    n. What should she do?

    o. What does Billy's teacher think about his behavior at school?
    p. According to Billy's teacher, when does he arrive at school?
    q. What should he do?
    r. How does he dress?
    s. What should he do?
    t. How does he speak?
    u. What should he do?

CHECK-UP

Q & A

1. Call on a pair of students to present the model.
2. Have students work in pairs to create new dialogs.
3. Call on pairs to present their new dialogs to the class.

Opposites

1. later
2. slower
3. impolitely
4. carelessly
5. neatly
6. loudly
7. gracefully

Text Page 69: *If*

FOCUS

> Introduction of *if-* clauses to express present real conditions:
> - Use of simple present tense in the *if-* clause
> - Use of *will* in the result clause

GETTING READY

Review *will* using the following conversational model:

> A. Will _____ be there soon?
> B. Yes. _____ be there in a few minutes.

Ask the following questions and have students respond chorally and individually, using the appropriate contraction with *will*.

Will the train be there soon? (Yes. It'll be there in a few minutes.)   Will Bob be there soon?
Will Mrs. Larson be there soon?   Will we be there soon?
Will Mary and Jane be there soon?   Will you be there soon?

INTRODUCING THE MODEL

1. Have students look at the model illustration.
2. Set the scene: "This husband and wife are going to have a baby soon. They might have a boy, or they might have a girl."
3. Present the model.
4. Full-Class Choral Repetition.
5. Ask students if they have any questions; check understanding of new vocabulary: *if*.
6. Group Choral Repetition.
7. Choral Conversation.
8. Call on one or two pairs of students to present the dialog.

    (For additional practice, do Choral Conversation in small groups or by rows.)

SIDE BY SIDE EXERCISES

Answer Key

> 1. A. How are you going to get to school tomorrow?
>   B. If it rains, I'll take the bus.
>   If it's sunny, I'll walk.

2. A. What's Bob going to do this Saturday afternoon?
   B. If the weather is good, he'll go to the beach.
      If the weather is bad, he'll go to the movies.

3. A. What's Carmen going to have for dinner tonight?
   B. If she's very hungry, she'll have a big dinner.
      If she isn't very hungry, she'll have a sandwich.

4. A. What's Fred going to do tomorrow?
   B. If he feels better, he'll go to work.
      If he doesn't feel better, he'll go to the doctor.

5. A. When are you going to go to sleep tonight?
   B. If I'm tired, I'll go to sleep early.
      If I'm not tired, I'll go to sleep late.

6. A. What are they going to wear tomorrow?
   B. If it's hot, they'll wear short pants (shorts).
      If it's cool, they'll wear long pants.

1. **Exercise 1:** Introduce the new expression *get to*. Call on two students to present the dialog. Then do Choral Repetition and Choral Conversation Practice.

2. **Exercise 2:** Same as above.

3. **Exercises 3–6:**

   > **New vocabulary:**   5. *go to sleep*   6. *short pants (shorts)*

   Either Full-Class Practice or Pair Practice.

HOW ABOUT YOU?

1. For homework, have students write answers to the questions.
2. Have students present their answers in the next class without referring to their written homework. Call on pairs of students to ask and answer.

WORKBOOK

Pages 77–79

Exercise Notes

Workbook p. 78: In Exercise J, students practice *if* and *will* by completing sentences with any vocabulary they wish. Have students compare their answers.

Workbook p. 79: In Exercises K and L, students practice the present real conditional (*if* _____ *will*).

EXPANSION ACTIVITY

Tell a Story: The Boss's Family Is Coming for Dinner

1. Set the scene:
   "Herbert's new boss and his family are coming to Herbert's house for dinner this Saturday. Herbert is

very worried because he doesn't know what to cook. He's going to try to speak to his boss soon to ask what kind of food his boss's family likes."

2. Continue telling the story as you write all of the word cues below on the board. For each cue say: "If they like _____ food, Herbert will cook _____." For example: "If they like Italian food, Herbert will cook spaghetti."

   Cues:

Italian spaghetti	**French** an omelette
Chinese chicken and rice	**American** hamburgers and french fries

3. Call on pairs of students to ask and answer questions about Herbert's plans. For example:

   A. What's Herbert going to do if they like Italian food?
   B. If they like Italian food, he'll cook spaghetti.

   A. What's Herbert going to do if they like Chinese food?
   B. If they like Chinese food, he'll cook chicken and rice.

4. Have students make suggestions for other possible menus and write them on the board. For example:

German potatoes	**Hungarian** stew

5. Have pairs of students role play Herbert talking with a friend. For example:

   A. Herbert, what are you going to do if your boss and his family like American food?
   B. If they like American food, I'll cook hamburgers and french fries.

Text Page 70: *If You Drive Too Fast, You Might Have an Accident*

FOCUS

> Practice using *if*-clauses with *might*

INTRODUCING THE MODEL

1. Have students look at the model illustration.
2. Set the scene: "A mother and son are talking in the car."
3. Present the model.
4. Full-Class Choral Repetition.
5. Ask students if they have any questions; check understanding of new vocabulary: *shouldn't, Oh?, accident, Hmm, You're probably right.*

   ### Language Note

   > *Too:* The adverb *too* is used to mean *excessively* and has a negative connotation: *If you drive too fast, you might have an accident.* Students sometimes confuse this word with *very*, which does not normally have this negative connotation.

6. Group Choral Repetition.
7. Choral Conversation.
8. Call on one or two pairs of students to present the dialog.

   (For additional practice, do Choral Conversation in small groups or by rows.)

SIDE BY SIDE EXERCISES

Examples

---

1. A. You know . . . you shouldn't work so slowly.
   B. Oh?
   A. Yes. If you work too slowly, you might lose your job.
   B. Hmm. You're probably right.

2. A. You know . . . you shouldn't sing so loud.
   B. Oh?
   A. Yes. If you sing too loud, you might get a sore throat.
   B. Hmm. You're probably right.

---

1. **Exercise 1:** Introduce the new expression *lose your job.* Call on two students to present the dialog. Then do Choral Repetition and Choral Conversation Practice.
2. **Exercise 2:** Same as above.
3. **Exercises 3–8:**

New vocabulary: 3. *worry, ulcer*   5. *mistakes*   7. *headphones, ear*   8. *scary, nightmare*

Either Full-Class Practice or Pair Practice.

4. **Exercise 9:**   Have students use the model as a guide to create their own conversations, using vocabulary of their choice. Encourage students to use dictionaries to find new words they want to use. This exercise can be done orally in class or for written homework. If you assign it for homework, you should do one example in class to make sure students understand what's expected. Have students present their conversations in class the next day.

WORKBOOK

Page 80

Exercise Note

Workbook p. 80:   Students practice *if* and *might* by completing sentences with any vocabulary they wish. Have students compare their answers.

EXPANSION ACTIVITY

Sentence Game: The Missing **If-***Clause*

Say each *might* clause below. Call on two or three students to create different possible *if*-clauses that could come before or after them. For example:

"If you work too slowly, you might lose your job."
"You might lose your job if you're late for work very often."

1. "You might lose your job."
2. "The teacher might get mad at you."
3. "You might get a sore throat."
4. "You might have nightmares."
5. "You might get a stomachache."
6. "You might break your leg."
7. "You might catch a cold."
8. "You might meet a new friend."
9. "You might have a wonderful time."
10. "You might get an earache."

Text Pages 71–72

READING: *Too Bad!*

FOCUS

If-clauses

NEW VOCABULARY

Arizona	far away	rent (n)
bank account	left	stay up
enough	lonely	Too bad!
evict	New Jersey	until
	oversleep	

PREVIEWING THE STORY (optional)

Have students talk about the story title and/or illustrations. Introduce new vocabulary.

READING THE STORY

1. Have students read silently, or follow along silently as the story is read aloud by you, by one or more students, or on the tape.
2. Ask students if they have any questions; check understanding of vocabulary.
3. Check students' comprehension, using some or all of the following questions:

   a. What does Ronald want to do?
   b. What will happen if he stays up late to watch a movie?
   c. What will happen if he doesn't get to bed until after midnight?
   d. What will happen if he's tired in the morning?
   e. What will happen if he oversleeps?
   f. What will happen if he's late for work?

   g. What does Barbara want to do?
   h. What will happen if she buys a new car?
   i. What will happen if she has to take a lot of money out of her bank account?
   j. What will happen if she doesn't have much left?
   k. What will happen if she doesn't have enough to pay the rent?

   l. What do Mr. and Mrs. Watson want to do?
   m. What will happen if they move to Arizona?
   n. What will happen if they're far away from their children and grandchildren in New Jersey?
   o. What will happen if they don't see them very often?

CHECK-UP

Choose

1.	a	4.	a
2.	b	5.	b
3.	b	6.	a

Listening

Have students complete the exercises as you play the tape or read the following:

Listen and choose the best answer to complete the sentences.

1. If Ronald stays up late tonight . . . (a)
2. If Barbara doesn't have enough money to pay the rent . . . (b)
3. If the Watsons move to Arizona . . . (b)
4. If I do my homework carelessly . . . (b)
5. If Johnny doesn't feel better tomorrow . . . (a)
6. If he doesn't translate accurately . . . (b)

IN YOUR OWN WORDS

1. Make sure students understand the instructions.
2. Have students do the activity as written homework, using a dictionary for any new words they wish to use.
3. Have students present and discuss what they have written, in pairs or as a class.

Text Page 73

ON YOUR OWN: *Superstitions*

FOCUS

> Review of *if* and *will*

ON YOUR OWN ACTIVITY

1. Introduce the three GOOD LUCK superstitions.*
   a. Go over the new vocabulary: *good luck, four-leaf clover, horseshoe.*
   b. Read from the book or play the tape one or more times.
   c. Ask students to tell about any other *good luck* superstitions they know.

2. Introduce the four BAD LUCK superstitions.
   a. Go over the new vocabulary: *bad luck, under, ladder, open.*
   b. Read from the book or play the tape one or more times.
   c. Ask students to tell you about any other *bad luck* superstitions they know.

3. Introduce the other superstitions.
   a. Go over the new vocabulary: *itch, ear, somebody, say good things, say bad things, knife, falls, fork, spoon, mirror, spill, throw, over, shoulder.*
   b. Read from the book or play the tape one or more times.
   c. Ask students to tell about any other superstitions they know.

WORKBOOK

Page 81

Exercise Note

Workbook p. 81: For additional oral practice with Exercise N, have students act out the conversations.

Check-Up Test: Pages 82–83

---

*In the United States, as in countries all over the world, *superstitions* are part of the folk culture passed on through word of mouth. Students usually enjoy discussing these colorful beliefs.

WORKBOOK ANSWER KEY AND LISTENING SCRIPTS

Page 72   A.   WHAT DO YOU THINK?

1. terribly	7. fast
2. gracefully	8. well
3. carelessly	9. beautiful
4. slowly	10. patient
5. accurately	11. good
6. sloppily	12. hard

Page 73   B.   ANSWER   CAREFUL (CAREFULLY)

1. terrible, sloppily
2. dishonestly
3. slow, well
4. graceful, beautifully
5. cheaply
6. terribly, good
7. badly, patiently
8. carefully, careless

Page 73   C.   LISTEN

Listen and put a circle around the correct answer.

1. He isn't a sloppy painter. He's very . . .
2. I can't read their homework because they write very . . .
3. David never makes mistakes. He's very . . .
4. At the concert last night Antonio played the piano . . .
5. I don't dance very well because I'm not . . .
6. She isn't a good tennis player. She plays tennis very . . .
7. Your homework is very interesting, but it's . . .
8. Mr. and Mrs. Smith always dress . . .
9. Leave the party early and drive home . . .
10. She's a good worker, but she's . . .
11. A. Mary skated carelessly yesterday.
    B. That's strange. She's usually . . .
12. Ted does his homework . . .

Answers

1. neat	7. sloppy
2. sloppily	8. elegantly
3. accurate	9. safely
4. beautifully	10. slow
5. graceful	11. careful
6. badly	12. easily

Page 75   E.   THE BOSS IS ANGRY

1. neater/more neatly
2. louder/more loudly
3. earlier
4. more carefully
5. slower/more slowly
6. later
7. more politely

Page 77   G.   WHAT'S THE WORD?

1. I move, I'll live
2. you call
3. we'll drive
4. it rains
5. I'll write
6. isn't
7. they're, won't go
8. he'll buy

Page 77   H.   IF

1. go, we'll
2. do, will be
3. is, will go
4. goes, he'll have
5. you'll be
6. they're
7. rains
8. eat, you'll
9. drink, I'll
10. have, we'll name

Page 78   I.   SCRAMBLED SENTENCES

1. If she misses the bus, she'll walk.
2. If he goes to the concert, he'll wear his suit.
3. If she isn't tired, she'll cook dinner.
4. If I'm not busy, I'll visit you.
5. If you don't finish school, you'll be sorry.
6. If he works hard, he'll get a good job.

Page 81 N. PLEASE DON'T!

1. I eat, I'll
   I get, I'll
2. they're, they'll
   they tell, he'll/she'll
3. he reads, he'll
   he's
   he doesn't, he'll
   he's, he'll

CHECK-UP TEST: *CHAPTERS 7–8*

Page 82 A.

1. gracefully
2. terribly
3. sloppily
4. hard

Page 82 B.

1. good
   badly
2. quickly
   accurate
3. beautifully
   neatly
4. safely
   careless

Page 82 C.

1. later
2. more politely
3. faster
4. louder

Page 82 D.

1. is
2. watch
   you'll
3. I'm
4. does
   will be

Page 82 E.

1. we go
   we'll buy
2. doesn't, she'll go
3. might get
4. feel
   might visit

Page 83 F.

Listen and fill in the correct places.

1. Mrs. Johnson was at the park on Park Street. She walked up Park Street to Third Avenue and turned right. She walked along Third Avenue to the building between the pet shop and the post office. Where did she go?

2. Arthur was at the TV station on River Street. He walked down River Street to Second Avenue and turned right. He walked along Second Avenue to the building across from the beauty parlor. Where did he go?

3. Mr. and Mrs. Schultz were at the supermarket on Second Avenue. They walked along Second Avenue to Park Street and turned left. They walked up Park Street to Third Avenue and turned right. They walked along Third Avenue to the building across from the motel. Where did they go?

4. Frieda was at the zoo on Third Avenue. She walked along Third Avenue to Park Street and turned right. She walked down Park Street to Second Avenue and turned left. She walked along Second Avenue to the building next to the beauty parlor. Where did she go?

5. Mr. and Mrs. Williams were at the hotel on Park Street. They walked up Park Street to Second Avenue and turned right. They walked along Second Avenue to River Street and turned left. They walked up River Street to the building next to the TV station, at the corner of River Street and Third Avenue. Where did they go?

Answers
1. motel
2. shoe store
3. shopping mall
4. cafeteria
5. hospital

TEACHER'S NOTES

GRAMMAR

Past Continuous Tense

What	was	I he she it	doing?
	were	we you they	

I He She It	was	eating.
We You They	were	

Reflexive Pronouns

I You He She It We You They	took a walk by	myself. yourself. himself. herself. itself. ourselves. yourselves. themselves.

While-Clauses

I lost my wallet **while I was jogging through the park**.
He cut himself **while he was shaving**.

FUNCTIONS

Asking for and Reporting Information

What were you doing *last night at 8:00*?
What was *Doris* doing *last night* when *the lights went out*?

I saw *you yesterday*.
   When?
At about *2:30*.

Yesterday at 2:30 I was *cooking dinner*.

Which *apartment* do you live in?
   Apartment 1.

Were you *home at the time of the robbery*?
   No, I wasn't.   I was *washing my clothes at the laundromat*.

What did *the burglars take*?
   They took some money.
How much?
   About *three hundred dollars*.

What did you do yesterday?
Who did you *go bowling* with?

I had a bad day today.
   Why?   What happened?

I *lost my wallet* while I was *jogging through the park*.

Sympathizing

I'm sorry to hear that.
That's too bad.
How awful!
That's terrible!
What a shame!
What a pity!

Initiating a Topic

You look upset.

Admitting an Error

I guess I made a mistake.

NEW VOCABULARY

about *2:30*
all over town
at all
attend
away
blackout
bleed
break into
burglar
burn (v)
college student
crash (into) (v)
drawer
drop (v)
elderly
faint
flat tire
fortunately
get on
get out of
gone
go out

have an accident
herself
himself
intersection
itself
jog
lady
lights
merry-go-round
myself
nose
Ohio
ourselves
out of town
package
police car
robbery
saw (see)
stop (v)
stop sign
superstitious

take
take care of
taxi
themselves
through
trip (v)
unfortunate
unlucky
wallet
which
while
yourself
yourselves

do yourself a favor
have no idea
How awful!
poke *himself* in the eye
That's terrible!
That's too bad.
What a pity!
What a shame!

Text Page 76: *The Blackout*

FOCUS

> Introduction of the past continuous tense

INTRODUCING THE MODEL

There are two model conversations. Introduce and practice each separately. For each model:

1. Have students look at the model illustration.
2. Introduce the new vocabulary: *blackout, lights went out, all over town.*
3. Set the scene: "Last night there was a blackout in Centerville. The lights went out all over town."
4. Present the model.
5. Full-Class Choral Repetition.

   ### Language Note

   > *Use of the Past Continuous Tense:* The past continuous tense is commonly used to show the duration of a past activity in contrast with a particular point in time. For example: *Doris was taking a bath when the lights went out.*

6. Ask students if they have any questions; check understanding of vocabulary.
7. Group Choral Repetition.
8. Choral Conversation.
9. Call on one or two pairs of students to present the dialog.

   (For additional practice, do Choral Conversation in small groups or by rows.)
10. Make sentences using the past continuous forms in the box at the top of the page. Have students repeat chorally and individually.

SIDE BY SIDE EXERCISES

Answer Key

1. A. What was Ted doing last night when the lights went out?
   B. He was shaving.
2. A. What was Irene doing last night when the lights went out?
   B. She was brushing her teeth.
3. A. What were Bob and Judy doing last night when the lights went out?
   B. They were having dinner.
4. A. What were you doing last night when the lights went out?
   B. I was feeding my cat.
5. A. What was Joe doing last night when the lights went out?
   B. He was cooking dinner.
6. A. What were your parents doing last night when the lights went out?
   B. They were watching TV.
7. A. What was your younger sister doing last night when the lights went out?
   B. She was studying English.

8. A. What was your father doing last night when the lights went out?
   B. He was cleaning the apartment.
9. A. What were Mr. and Mrs. Jones doing last night when the lights went out?
   B. They were washing their clothes at the laundromat.

1. **Exercise 1:** Call on two students to present the dialog. Then do Choral Repetition and Choral Conversation Practice.
2. **Exercise 2:** Same as above.
3. **Exercises 3–9:** Either Full-Class Practice or Pair Practice.
4. **What were you doing last night at 8:00?** Have students tell about themselves.

WORKBOOK

Pages 84–85 (Exercises A, B, C)

Exercise Note

Workbook p. 85: Students practice the past continuous tense.

EXPANSION ACTIVITIES

1. *Role Play with Visuals: What Were You Doing?*

   Have students create role plays based on the conversations on text page 76.
   a. For conversation cues, select visuals from *Side by Side* Picture Cards 18–41, 121–139, and 147–171, or make your own appropriate visuals; for example: *fix _____ car, do _____ exercises, clean _____ apartment, play cards.*
   b. Hold up a visual and call on two students to create a conversation. An example:

      (visual: *listen to the radio*)
      A. What were you doing last night when the lights went out?
      B. I was listening to the radio.

2. *Picture Story: A Blackout at the PRESTO Office*

   a. Put these story cues on the board:

Tom type a letter	Roger read the newspaper	Toshi talk on the telephone	Mrs. Blake eat in the cafeteria
Linda ride in the elevator	Miss Green translate letters	Frank fix his tie in the men's room	Barbara brush her hair in the ladies' room

b. Point to the cues as you begin the story, **A Blackout at the PRESTO Office**.

"Last week there was a blackout at the PRESTO Office in New York. Everybody was working late. They were tired, and they wanted to go home. When the lights went out, everybody was very upset."

c. Call on pairs of students to ask and answer about the people in the story. For example:

A. What was Tom doing when the lights went out?
B. He was typing a letter.

d. Have one or two pairs of students role play a conversation in which Student A pretends to be one of the people in the story and Student B is a newspaper reporter who is doing an interview about the blackout. Encourage students to be imaginative and add additional details to the story.

Text Page 77: *I Saw You Yesterday, but You Didn't See Me*

FOCUS

> Practice with the past continuous tense

INTRODUCING THE MODEL

1. Have students look at the model illustration.
2. Set the scene: "Two friends are talking."
3. Present the model.
4. Full-Class Choral Repetition.
5. Ask students if they have any questions; check understanding of new vocabulary: *saw (see), at about 2:30, get out of, taxi.*
6. Group Choral Repetition.
7. Choral Conversation.
8. Call on one or two pairs of students to present the dialog.

   (For additional practice, do Choral Conversation in small groups or by rows.)

SIDE BY SIDE EXERCISES

Examples

---

1. A. I saw you yesterday, but you didn't see me.
   B. Really? When?
   A. At about 2:30. You were walking into the post office.
   B. That wasn't me. Yesterday at 2:30 I was fixing my car.
   A. Hmm. I guess I made a mistake.

2. A. I saw you yesterday, but you didn't see me.
   B. Really? When?
   A. At about 2:30. You were walking out of the laundromat.
   B. That wasn't me. Yesterday at 2:30 I was cleaning my apartment.
   A. Hmm. I guess I made a mistake.

---

1. **Exercise 1:** Introduce the new expression *walking into*. Call on two students to present the dialog. Then do Choral Repetition and Choral Conversation Practice.
2. **Exercise 2:** Introduce the new expression *walking out of*. Same as above.
3. **Exercises 3–7:**

New vocabulary: 3. *get on*   4. *merry-go-round*   5. *jog, through*   7. *police car*

Either Full-Class Practice or Pair Practice.

4. **Exercise 8:** Have students use the model as a guide to create their own conversations, using vocabulary of their choice. Encourage students to use dictionaries to find new words they want to use. This exercise can be done orally in class or for written homework. If you assign it for homework, you should do one example in class to make sure students understand what's expected. Have students present their conversations in class the next day.

WORKBOOK

Pages 86–88 (Exercises D, E, F)

Exercise Note

Workbook p. 88: Students practice the past continuous tense.

EXPANSION ACTIVITY

Role Play with Visuals: A Bad Accident

Use *Side by Side* Picture Cards 9–17, 59–74, 204–220, your own visuals, or word cards as cues for locations in the community.

1. Set the scene: "There was a car accident in (your city) last Saturday. It happened at 3:30 in the afternoon. The streets were very busy. I was walking into the laundromat when the accident happened. There was a very loud noise. Did you hear it? What were you doing?"

2. Write on the board:

walk $\begin{cases} \text{into} \\ \text{out of} \end{cases}$

3. Point to different visuals as you ask students:

   "What were you doing when the accident happened?"

   Have students answer, using the past continuous tense and the location on the visual. For example:

   "At 3:30 I was walking into the post office."
   "I was walking out of the supermarket when the accident happened."

4. Hold up visuals and call on pairs of students to ask and answer.

Text Page 78

READING: *A Robbery*

FOCUS

> Past continuous tense

NEW VOCABULARY

attend	college student	lady
away	elderly	out of town
broke (break) into	gone	robbery
burglar	have no idea	unfortunate

PREVIEWING THE STORY (optional)

Have students talk about the story title and/or illustration. Introduce new vocabulary.

READING THE STORY

1. Have students read silently, or follow along silently as the story is read aloud by you, by one or more students, or on the tape.
2. Ask students if they have any questions; check understanding of vocabulary.
3. Check students' comprehension, using some or all of the following questions:

    a. Were the tenants home yesterday when burglars broke into the building?
    b. What was the man in Apartment 1 doing?
    c. What was the woman in Apartment 2 doing?
    d. What were the people in Apartment 3 doing?
    e. What was the man in Apartment 4 doing?
    f. What were the college students in Apartment 5 doing?
    g. What was the elderly lady in Apartment 6 doing?

CHECK-UP

Q & A

1. Call on a pair of students to present the model.
2. Have students work in pairs to create new dialogs. Students should use their imaginations to think of objects that were stolen from the different apartments.
3. Call on pairs to present their new dialogs to the class.

Text Page 79: *He Went to the Movies by Himself*

FOCUS

> Introduction of reflexive pronouns

INTRODUCING THE MODEL

1. Have students look at the model illustration.
2. Set the scene: "Two people are talking about John."
3. Present the model.
4. Full-Class Choral Repetition.
5. Ask students if they have any questions; check understanding of new vocabulary: *by himself.*

    ### Language Note

    Who did he go to the movies with? The pronoun *who* rather than *whom* is widely used in informal conversation. The pronoun *whom* as the object of a preposition is used in more formal speech.

6. Group Choral Repetition.
7. Choral Conversation.
8. Call on one or two pairs of students to present the dialog.

    (For additional practice, do Choral Conversation in small groups or by rows.)
9. Read the reflexive pronouns in the box at the top of the page. Have students repeat chorally and individually.

SIDE BY SIDE EXERCISES

Examples

> 1. A. What did Patty do yesterday?
>   B. She went to the beach.
>   A. Oh. Who did she go to the beach with?
>   B. Nobody. She went to the beach by herself.
> 2. A. What did Peter do yesterday?
>   B. He went to the ballgame.
>   A. Oh. Who did he go to the ballgame with?
>   B. Nobody. He went to the ballgame by himself.

1. **Exercise 1:** Call on two students to present the dialog. Then do Choral Repetition and Choral Conversation Practice.
2. **Exercise 2:** Same as above.
3. **Exercises 3–8:** Either Full-Class Practice or Pair Practice.

4. **Exercise 9:** Have students use the model as a guide to create their own conversations, using vocabulary of their choice. Encourage students to use dictionaries to find new words they want to use. This exercise can be done orally in class or for written homework. If you assign it for homework, you should do one example in class to make sure students understand what's expected. Have students present their conversations in class the next day.

WORKBOOK

Page 89 (Exercise G)

EXPANSION ACTIVITIES

1. *Practice with Reflexives*

   a. With books closed, have students repeat:

      "He went to the movies by himself."

   b. Next, signal substitution of *I, you, she, we, they,* and have students substitute the new pronouns and repeat the sentences chorally. For example:

      You: "I"
      Class: "I went to the movies by myself."

      You: "She"
      Class: "She went to the movies by herself."

2. *Practice with Visuals: I Did It by Myself*

   Use visuals as cues for activities such as *fix _____ sink, fix _____ car, fix _____ TV, do _____ homework, clean _____ apartment, wash _____ dishes.* You can use *Side by Side* Picture Cards, your own visuals, or word cards.

   a. Write this conversational model on the board:

      > A. Did anybody help you _____?
      > B. No. Nobody helped me. I _____ by myself.

   b. Introduce the model as you point to a visual; have students repeat chorally and individually. For example:

      A. Did anybody help you fix the sink?
      B. No. Nobody helped me. I fixed it by myself.

   c. Hold up visuals and call on pairs of students to create conversations based on the model.

   d. Practice other pronouns by holding up a visual and asking the question, using people's names. Have students answer chorally or individually. For example:

      A. Did anybody help Mrs. Jones fix her car?
      B. No. Nobody helped her. She fixed it by herself.

Text Pages 80–81: *I Had a Bad Day Today*

FOCUS

- Introduction of *while*-clauses with the past continuous tense
- Practice with reflexive pronouns

INTRODUCING THE MODEL

There are two model conversations. Introduce and practice each separately. For each model:

1. Have students look at the model illustration.
2. Set the scene:

    1st model: "A man is talking with a friend about what happened this morning."
    2nd model: "Two people are talking about why Harry is upset."

3. Present the model.
4. Full-Class Choral Repetition.
5. Ask students if they have any questions; check understanding of new vocabulary:

    1st model: *lost (lose), wallet, while*
    2nd model: *That's too bad!*

Language Note

While-clauses: *While* is commonly used to introduce a clause in the past continuous tense. Although *when* can be substituted in its place, *while* emphasizes the duration of an activity.

6. Group Choral Repetition.
7. Choral Conversation
8. Call on one or two pairs of students to present the dialog.
9. Introduce the new expressions *How awful! That's terrible! What a shame! What a pity!* Have pairs of students practice the models again, using the new expressions.

   (For additional practice, do Choral Conversation in small groups or by rows.)

SIDE BY SIDE EXERCISES

Examples

---

1. A. You look upset.
   B. I had a bad day today.
   A. Why? What happened?
   B. I burned myself while I was cooking dinner.
   A. I'm sorry to hear that.*

2. A. Sheila looks upset.
   B. She had a bad day today.
   A. Why? What happened?
   B. She dropped her packages while she was walking out of the supermarket.
   A. I'm sorry to hear that.*

*Or: How awful!/That's terrible!/What a shame!/What a pity!

---

1. **Exercise 1:** Introduce the new expression *burn myself.* Call on two students to present the dialog. Then do Choral Repetition and Choral Conversation Practice.

2. **Exercise 2:** Introduce the new words *drop, package.* Same as above.

3. **Exercises 3–12:**

> **New vocabulary:** 3. *hurt himself* 4. *flat tire, over, bridge* 5. *faint*
> 6. *gray hairs* 7. *have an accident* 10. *trip (v), fell (fall)*

Language Note

Although *hair* is usually considered a non-count noun, in Exercise 6 it is used as a count noun since it refers to individual strands of hair that can be counted.

Either Full-Class Practice or Pair Practice.

HOW ABOUT YOU?

Have students do the activity in pairs or as a class.

WORKBOOK

Pages 89–92 (Exercises H, I, J, K)

Exercise Notes

Workbook p. 91: Students practice reflexive pronouns.

Workbook p. 92: Students practice pronouncing the sounds [i] as in l*ea*ve and [ɪ] as in l*i*ve. Note that the sentences on the left give practice with the [i] sound, and those on the right give practice with [ɪ]. For additional practice, have students ask and answer questions about the pictures.

EXPANSION ACTIVITIES

1. Picture-Story: The Larsons' Terrible Vacation

   a. Put these cues on the board:

Mr. Larson
(swim)
cut himself
on a broken bottle

Mrs. Larson
(ride)/boat
got seasick

Elizabeth
(play) football/beach
lost her glasses

Arthur
(jog)/beach
fell and hurt himself

Bobby
(sleep)/beach
got a sunburn

the dog
(swim)
a fish bit him

b. Point to the cues as you tell the story of **The Larsons' Terrible Vacation**.

> "Last year the Larsons had a terrible vacation in Hawaii.
>   Something bad happened to everybody."

1. While Mr. Larson was swimming, he cut himself on a broken bottle.
2. While Mrs. Larson was riding in a boat, she got very seasick.
3. While Elizabeth was playing football on the beach, she lost her glasses.
4. While Arthur was jogging on the beach, he fell and hurt himself.
5. While Bobby was sleeping on the beach, he got a terrible sunburn.
6. While their dog Rover was swimming, a fish bit him.

c. Ask students questions about the story. For example:

> A. Where did the Larsons go for their vacation?
> B. They went to Hawaii.
>
> A. What happened to Mr. Larson?
> B. He cut himself on a broken bottle while he was swimming.
>
> A. How did Bobby get a sunburn?
> B. He got a sunburn while he was sleeping on the beach.

d. Call on pairs of students to create conversations about the story.

e. Have a few students role play characters in the story and tell what happened. Encourage students to expand the story, using any vocabulary they wish. For example:

> (Mrs. Larson:) "While I was riding in a boat, I got very seasick. Then I fainted!"

2. *Personal Activities*

a. Write on the board:

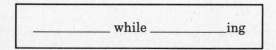

b. Tell the class something factual about yourself, using the structures on the board. For example:

> "I listened to the radio while I was driving to school today."
> "I read the newspaper while I was eating dinner last night."

c. Have students tell things about themselves, using the past continuous tense and *while*.

3. *Interview Game*

The activity above may also be done as an *interview game*.

a. Have students write on a piece of paper something true about themselves, using the past continuous tense and *while*. For example:

> "I studied English while I was eating breakfast today."
> "I ate candy while I was watching TV last night."

b. Collect the pieces of paper and copy all the sentences on the board or on a handout for students.

c. Have students *interview* others in the class to find out *who did what*. For example:

> Student A: Did you study English while you were eating breakfast today?
> Student B: No, I didn't.

d. The first student to identify everybody is the winner of the game.

READING: *Friday the 13th*

FOCUS

- Reflexive pronouns
- Past continuous tense
- *While*-clauses

NEW VOCABULARY

do yourself a favor	superstitious
poke himself in the eye	unlucky

PREVIEWING THE STORY (optional)

Have students talk about the story title and/or illustrations. Introduce new vocabulary.

READING THE STORY

1. Have students read silently, or follow along silently as the story is read aloud by you, by one or more students, or on the tape.
2. Ask students if they have any questions; check understanding of vocabulary.

   Culture Note

   In the United States, if the thirteenth day of the month falls on a Friday, it is considered an unlucky day.

3. Check students' comprehension, using some or all of the following questions:
   a. What day was yesterday?
   b. What do many people believe?
   c. What happened to the writer of the story yesterday?
   d. What happened to his wife?
   e. What happened to his son?
   f. What happened to his daughter?
   g. What happened to both his children?
   h. What happened to his entire family?
   i. According to the writer, what should you do the next time it's Friday the 13th?

CHECK-UP

Q & A

1. Call on a pair of students to present the model.

2. Have students work in pairs to create new dialogs.

3. Call on pairs to present their new dialogs to the class.

HOW ABOUT YOU?

Have students answer the questions in pairs or as a class.

What's the Word?

1.	a
2.	c
3.	b
4.	b
5.	c
6.	c

Listening

Have students complete the exercises as you play the tape or read the following:

Listen to the conversations. What happened to these people? Listen and choose the best answer.

1. A. How did you do that?
   B. I did it while I was shaving. (a)

2. A. When did it happen?
   B. While I was getting off a bus. (a)

3. A. What were they doing?
   B. They were playing outside. (b)

4. A. Why do you think it happened?
   B. It was a very hot day. (b)

5. A. The park isn't as safe as it used to be.
   B. I agree. (a)

READING: *An Accident*

FOCUS

- Past continuous tense
- *While*-clauses

NEW VOCABULARY

at all	fortunately	saw (see)
bleed	intersection	stop
crash (into)	nose	stop sign

PREVIEWING THE STORY (optional)

Have students talk about the story and/or illustrations. Introduce new vocabulary.

READING THE STORY

1. Have students read silently, or follow along silently as the story is read aloud by you, by one or more students, or on the tape.
2. Ask students if they have any questions; check understanding of vocabulary.
3. Check students' comprehension, using some or all of the following questions:

   a. What did the writer see this morning?
   b. Where was the writer standing?
   c. How was the woman driving?
   d. What kind of car was she driving?
   e. What was the man driving?
   f. How was the man driving?

   g. How did the accident happen?
   h. Was the woman seriously hurt?
   i. Was the man seriously hurt? What was he doing?
   j. When did the writer leave?

CHECK-UP

True, False, or Maybe?

1. True
2. False
3. Maybe
4. False
5. Maybe
6. True
7. Maybe

HOW ABOUT YOU?

Have students answer the questions, in pairs or as a class.

Page 84 A. BAD WEATHER

1. She was washing her car.
2. He was planting flowers.
3. We were playing baseball.
4. He was waiting for the bus.
5. They were having a picnic.
6. She was riding her bicycle.
7. They were taking a walk.
8. He was swimming.

Page 86 C. WHAT WERE THEY DOING?

1. were waiting
2. was washing
3. were playing
4. was taking
5. were leaving
6. was looking for
7. were making
8. was talking

Page 86 D. WHAT'S THE WORD?

1. into
2. out of
3. off
4. into
5. on
6. along
7. out of

Page 87 E. TOO EARLY

1. She was cleaning the living room.
2. She was washing clothes.
3. He was shaving.
4. They were doing their homework.
5. She was baking a cake.
6. He was taking a shower.

Page 89 G. NOBODY WANTS TO

1. myself
2. herself
3. ourselves
4. yourself
5. themselves
6. himself
7. yourselves

Page 89 H. WHAT'S THE WORD?

1. on
2. over
3. on
4. to
5. in
6. at
   in
7. under
8. by

Page 90 I. WHAT HAPPENED?

1. she was skating
2. I was walking
3. she was riding
4. he was shaving
5. they were dancing
6. cut, I was shaving
7. burned
   they were baking
8. had
   he was sleeping

Page 92 K. LOUD AND CLEAR

1. Rita, eat
   three pieces
   pizza
2. This dinner
   delicious
   didn't finish it
3. police, thief
   stealing
   Green Street
4. Ginger is
   office with
   children
   Smith, busy
5. Rio
   leave between
   three fifteen
6. sister, is
   live in
   building
   big city

GRAMMAR

Could

Could	I he she it we you they	lift the suitcase?

Yes,	I he she it we you they	could.

No,	I he she it we you they	couldn't.

Be Able to

Was	I he she it	able to go swimming?
Were	we you they	

No,	I he she it	wasn't	able to.
	we you they	weren't	

Have Got to

I've We've You've They've He's She's It's	got to work.

I'll He'll She'll It'll We'll You'll They'll	be able to help you.

I He She It We You They	won't be able to help you.

Too + Adjective

He was too short. She was too busy.

FUNCTIONS

Inquiring about Ability

Could you *finish your homework last night*?
Were you able to *do the grammar exercises*?

Expressing Ability

I'm sure I'll be able to *move by myself*.

Expressing Inability

No, I couldn't.
No, I wasn't able to.

I couldn't do it.

He won't be able to *get to the airport on time*.
She can't *get into her apartment*.
He won't be able to *find a job*.
He couldn't *dance in the school play*.

Expressing Regret

I'm afraid *I won't be able to help you move
tomorrow*.

Expressing Certainty

I'm sure *I'll be able to move by myself*.

Describing

I was too *short/sick/young/. . . .*

Inquiring about Satisfaction

Did you enjoy yourself *at the tennis match*?

Expressing Obligation

I had to *fix a flat tire*.

I've got to *take my son to the doctor*.

Describing Feelings-Emotions

George is upset/frustrated/disappointed.

NEW VOCABULARY

a while
able to
assistant
ballet
classmate
clumsy
could
couldn't
dance (n)
dark
full moon
got to
grammar

key
lesson
lift
moon
ocean
operation
pipe
policeman
promise (v)
repair truck
school play
side

someone
spicy
symphony
team
tennis match
theater
vet
weak
windy

Don't worry about it!
for quite a while

Text Page 86: *They Couldn't*

FOCUS

- Introduction of *could* and *couldn't*
- *Too* + adjective

GETTING READY

Introduce *could* and *couldn't*.

1. Write on the board:

> Jimmy
>
> 2 years old—walk
> 5 years old—write his name
> 7 years old—read
> 8 years old—ride a bicycle

2. Say "When Jimmy was two years old, he could walk." Then have students repeat chorally.
3. Ask and have students answer:

   "What could Jimmy do when he was two years old?/when he was five years old?/when he was seven years old?/when he was eight years old?"

4. Ask Yes/No questions about Jimmy and have students answer "Yes, he could" or "No, he couldn't." For example:

   "Could Jimmy walk when he was two years old?"   ("Yes, he could.")
   "Could Jimmy ride a bicycle when he was two years old?"   ("No, he couldn't.")

INTRODUCING THE MODEL

1. Have students look at the model illustration.
2. Set the scene: "Two people are talking about Peter."
3. Present the model.
4. Full-Class Choral Repetition.
5. Ask students if they have any questions; check understanding of new vocabulary: *team.*
6. Group Choral Repetition.
7. Choral Conversation.
8. Call on one or two pairs of students to present the dialog.

   (For additional practice, do Choral Conversation in small groups or by rows.)

SIDE BY SIDE EXERCISES

Examples

> 1. A. Could Henry go to work yesterday?
>   B. No, he couldn't. He was too sick.
>
> 2. A. Could Rita go out with her boyfriend last weekend?
>   B. No, she couldn't. She was too busy.

1. **Exercise 1:** Call on two students to present the dialog. Then do Choral Repetition and Choral Conversation Practice.
2. **Exercise 2:** Same as above.
3. **Exercises 3–8:**

> **New vocabulary:** 6. *operation, weak* 7. *policeman*

Either Full-Class Practice or Pair Practice.

WORKBOOK

Pages 93–94

Exercise Note

Workbook p. 94: Students practice *couldn't* and *too* + adjective.

EXPANSION ACTIVITIES

1. Practice Could: *Harvey the Genius*

a. Bring a magazine picture of a man to class or draw a face on the board. Point to the man and say, "This is Harvey. Harvey is (45) years old and he works in a bank. What's so special about Harvey? When he was a little boy, people thought he was a genius."

b. Write these models for questions on the board:

> When could Harvey _____?
> What could Harvey do when he was _____?

c. Call on pairs of students to create conversations about Harvey, using any vocabulary they wish. Encourage students to exaggerate and be playful in describing the abilities of *Harvey the Genius*. For example:

> A. When could Harvey read?
> B. He could read when he was one year old.
>
> A. What could Harvey do when he was three years old?
> B. He could play the guitar.

2. Personal Data

a. Write the following on the board:

> (When you were young . . .)
>
> ride a bicycle
> stay up late
> swim
> speak English
> drive
> _____

b. Ask students to think about the time when they were very young. Ask questions using the verbs on the board. For example:

> Teacher: Could you ride a bicycle when you were young?

Have students answer truthfully, using either affirmative or negative answers.

> Student: Yes, I could. (or) No, I couldn't.

c. Have students ask others in the class, using the verbs on the board or any others they wish.

Continue with more _recent_ questions.

d. Write on the board:

> (last . . .)
>
> finish your homework
> watch a late movie on TV
> vote
> walk to school
> _____

e. Ask questions using the verbs on the board, and have students answer truthfully. Encourage students to give reasons for their answers. For example:

> Teacher: Could you finish your homework last night?
> Student: No, I couldn't. It was too difficult.

> Teacher: Could you come to the school dance last weekend?
> Student: No, I couldn't. I had too much homework to do.

f. Have students ask others in the class the questions, using the verbs on the board or any others they wish.

Text Page 87: *They Weren't Able to*

FOCUS

> Introduction of $\left\{\begin{array}{l}\textit{was/were}\\ \textit{wasn't/weren't}\end{array}\right\}$ *able to*

GETTING READY

Introduce the forms of *was able to.*

1. Have students practice Exercise 8 on text page 86 again.

2. Change *could* to *was able to* and have students repeat:

   A. Was Stuart able to eat at his wedding?
   B. No, he wasn't able to. He was too nervous.

3. Do the same for Exercise 3 on text page 86. Have students practice the exercise; then change *could* to *were able to* and have students repeat:

   A. Were Mr. and Mrs. Jones able to finish their dinner?
   B. No, they weren't able to. They were too full.

4. Practice all the forms of *was able to.* Have students repeat:

I was able to.	I wasn't able to.
He was able to.	He wasn't able to.
She was able to.	She wasn't able to.
We were able to.	We weren't able to.
You were able to.	You weren't able to.
They were able to.	They weren't able to.

INTRODUCING THE MODEL

1. Have students look at the model illustration.
2. Set the scene: "Jimmy's grandmother arrived by plane this morning. Jimmy met her at the airport."
3. Present the model.
4. Full-Class Choral Repetition.
5. Ask students if they have any questions; check understanding of new vocabulary: *lift.*
6. Group Choral Repetition.
7. Choral Conversation.
8. Call on one or two pairs of students to present the dialog.
   (For additional practice, do Choral Conversation in small groups or by rows.)

SIDE BY SIDE EXERCISES

Examples

> 1. A. Was Louise able to paint her house yesterday afternoon?
>   B. No, she wasn't able to. It was too windy.
>
> 2. A. Was Carl able to sit down on the bus this morning?
>   B. No, he wasn't able to. It was too crowded.

1. **Exercise 1:** Introduce the new word *windy*. Call on two students to present the dialog. Then do Choral Repetition and Choral Conversation Practice.

2. **Exercise 2:** Introduce the new expression *sit down*. Same as above.

3. **Exercises 3–8:**

> **New vocabulary:** 3. *ocean* 4. *spicy* 5. *dark* 6. *grammar exercises*
> 7. *full moon* 8. *dance* (n)

Either Full-Class Practice or Pair Practice.

WORKBOOK

Page 95

Exercise Note

Workbook p. 95: Students use any vocabulary they wish to complete these sentences. Have students compare their answers.

EXPANSION ACTIVITIES

1. *SIDE BY SIDE Again*

   Do Side by Side Exercises 1–8 on Student Text page 87 again, using *able to* in place of *could*.

2. *Practice* **Too + Adjective:** *Finish the Sentence.*

   a. Write the sentence fragments below on word cards.

   b. Have a student read the sentence fragment on each card; then call on several students to finish the sentence, using expressions with *too*.

   1. They weren't able to find their friends at the movie theater because _____.
   2. Joe couldn't eat his dinner last night because _____.
   3. Hilda wasn't able to lift her suitcase because _____.
   4. Roger and Dan couldn't do their homework last night because _____.
   5. Mrs. Wong couldn't finish her meatball sandwich yesterday because _____.
   6. Mario wasn't able to play soccer yesterday because _____.
   7. Bill couldn't sing in the concert last night because _____.
   8. Peggy couldn't wear her sister's dress to the job interview because _____.
   9. Jane and Ginger weren't able to go skiing yesterday because _____.

3. *Larry's Terrible Night Out*

a. Write the following on the board:

go to his favorite restaurant	(busy)
order his favorite dish	(expensive)
sit near the window	(crowded)
drink the coffee	(cold)
get a taxi home	(late)
find his house key	(dark)
go to sleep	(upset)

b. Set the scene: "Larry went to a restaurant last weekend because it was his birthday. But he didn't have a very good evening. First, he wasn't able to go to his favorite restaurant because it was too busy."

c. Have students use the cues on the board to tell more about what Larry wasn't able to do and why.

d. You can also have students ask each other questions about Larry. For example:

    A. Was Larry able to go to his favorite restaurant?
    B. No, he wasn't.
    A. Why not?
    B. Because it was too busy.

e. Have someone pretend to be Larry and have other students ask him questions. For example:

    A. Were you able to drink the coffee?
    B. No, I wasn't.
    A. Why not?
    B. Because it was too cold.

Text Page 88: *She Had to Study for an Examination*

FOCUS

> - Review of *wasn't/weren't able to* and *couldn't*
> - Introduction of *had to*
> - Review of reflexive pronouns

GETTING READY

Review reflexive pronouns, using the new expression *enjoy ____-self/selves.*

1. Say "Mary had a party last weekend, and everybody had a wonderful time. I really enjoyed myself."
2. Ask "Did David have a good time?" Then have students repeat:

    "Yes, he enjoyed himself."
3. Ask the questions below and have students respond according to the pattern:

    "Yes, ____ enjoyed ____self/selves."
    a. Did Sally have a good time?
    b. Did Bob have a good time?
    c. Did Mr. and Mrs. Jones have a good time?
    d. Did we have a good time?
4. Then ask individual students: "Did you have a good time at Mary's party?"

INTRODUCING THE MODEL

1. Have students look at the model illustration.
2. Set the scene: "Two people are talking about what Barbara did last night."
3. Present the model using *wasn't able to*. Then present the model using *couldn't*.
4. Full-Class Choral Repetition.
5. Ask students if they have any questions; check understanding of new vocabulary: *enjoy herself, study for an examination.*
6. Group Choral Repetition.
7. Choral Conversation.
8. Call on one pair of students to present the dialog using *wasn't able to*. Then have another pair present the dialog using *couldn't*.

    (For additional practice, do Choral Conversation in small groups or by rows.)

SIDE BY SIDE EXERCISES

Examples

> Students may use either *wasn't able to* or *couldn't* in the dialogs.
>
> 1. A. Did Ronald enjoy himself at the baseball game yesterday?

B. Unfortunately, he $\left\{ \begin{array}{l} \text{wasn't able to} \\ \text{couldn't} \end{array} \right\}$ go to the baseball game yesterday. He had to go to the dentist.

2. A. Did you enjoy yourself at the tennis match last week?
   B. Unfortunately, I $\left\{ \begin{array}{l} \text{wasn't able to} \\ \text{couldn't} \end{array} \right\}$ go to the tennis match last week. I had to visit my boss in the hospital.

1. **Exercise 1:** Call on two students to present the dialog. Then do Choral Repetition and Choral Conversation Practice.

2. **Exercise 2:** Introduce the new expression *tennis match*. Same as above.

3. **Exercises 3–8:**

New vocabulary:	3. *symphony*	4. *theater*	6. *classmate*

   Language Note

   Exercise 4: In this exercise, the word *theater* refers to the place where plays are presented on a stage.

   Either Full-Class Practice or Pair Practice.

4. **Exercise 9:** Have students use the model as a guide to create their own conversations, using vocabulary of their choice. Encourage students to use dictionaries to find new words they want to use. This exercise can be done orally in class or for written homework. If you assign it for homework, you should do one example in class to make sure students understand what's expected. Have students present their conversations in class the next day.

WORKBOOK

Pages 96–97 (Exercises D, E)

Exercise Note

Workbook p. 97: In Exercise E, students complete the sentences with any vocabulary they wish. Have students compare their answers.

EXPANSION ACTIVITIES

1. *Review of* **Had to:** *The Secretary*

   a. Write this schedule on the board:

9:00–10:00	make coffee/type letters
10:00–11:00	answer the telephone/make appointments
11:00–12:00	go to the post office/mail some packages
(Lunch)	
1:00–2:30	translate a few letters
2:30–3:30	go shopping/buy paper and pens for the office
3:30–5:00	meet some visitors at the airport/recommend hotels and restaurants

b. Introduce the new word *secretary*. Use *Side by Side* Picture Card 112 or your own visual. Practice the story with both *he* and *she* by introducing the secretary first as a man; then repeat the exercise using a woman's name.

c. Set the scene: "(*Bob Smith/Lois Schultz*) is a secretary for a big company in Washington, D.C. (He/she) has to work very hard. Here's what (he/she) had to do last Friday."

d. Point to the cues on the board as you begin the story:

"From 9 o'clock to 10 o'clock, (he/she) had to make coffee and type letters."

e. Call on students to tell each additional part of the story as you point to the cues.

f. Practice questions; call on a few pairs of students to create conversations. For example:

> A. What did Bob have to do from 9 o'clock to 10 o'clock?
> B. He had to make coffee and type letters.

g. Call on a few individuals to role play the secretary. Have other students ask questions about last Friday.

h. Optional homework activity: Have students choose a different profession and write a list of things someone in that profession had to do on a typical day last week.

2. *Review of Past Ability: A Telephone Apology*

a. Write this conversational framework on the board:

> A. Hi, _____. This is _____.
> B. Hi, _____.
> A. I'm really sorry I $\begin{Bmatrix} \text{couldn't} \\ \text{wasn't able to} \end{Bmatrix}$ go to the _____ with you last _____.
> B. Don't worry about it! The _____ was terrible and I didn't enjoy myself at all.
> A. Oh really? Then I'm glad I couldn't go!

b. Have pairs of students role play this conversation, using the following cues. Either write them on the board or say them.

concert/music   night club/music
theater/play   lecture/professor
restaurant/food   symphony/music
beach/weather   zoo/weather

Example:

> A. Hi, Susan. This is Richard.
> B. Hi, Richard.
> A. I'm really sorry I couldn't go to the concert with you last Saturday.
> B. Don't worry about it! The music was terrible and I didn't enjoy myself at all.
> A. Oh really? Then I'm glad I couldn't go!

Text Page 89

READING: *Mrs. Murphy's Students Couldn't Do Their Homework*

FOCUS

Could

NEW VOCABULARY

lesson
promise (v)

PREVIEWING THE STORY (optional)

Have students talk about the story title and/or illustration. Introduce new vocabulary.

READING THE STORY

1. Have students read silently, or follow along silently as the story is read aloud by you, by one or more students, or on the tape.
2. Ask students if they have any questions; check understanding of vocabulary.
3. Check students' comprehension, using some or all of the following questions:

   a. Why didn't Mrs. Murphy know what to do with her students today?
   b. Why couldn't Bob do his homework?
   c. Why couldn't Sally do her homework?
   d. Why couldn't John do his homework?
   e. Why couldn't Donna do her homework?
   f. Why couldn't all the other students do their homework?
   g. What do the students promise Mrs. Murphy?

CHECK-UP

Q & A

1. Call on a pair of students to present the model.
2. Have students work in pairs to create new dialogs.
3. Call on pairs to present their new dialogs to the class.

Listening

Have students complete the exercise as you play the tape or read the following:

Listen and choose the best answer.

1. I couldn't sit down. (a)
2. We couldn't see the sun. (b)
3. Did she enjoy her hamburger? (b)
4. He wasn't able to lift it. (a)
5. Why weren't the plumbers able to fix it? (a)

Choose

1. d
2. a
3. d
4. a
5. b

Text Pages 90–91: *I'm Afraid I Won't Be Able to Help You*

FOCUS

- Introduction of *will/won't be able to*
- Introduction of *have got to*

GETTING READY

1. Introduce *have got to,* using the box at the top of the page.

   a. Write on the board:

      > have to = have got to

   b. Have students listen and repeat:

"I've got to work."	"He's got to work."
"We've got to work."	"She's got to work."
"You've got to work."	"It's got to work."
"They've got to work."	

2. Introduce *will/won't be able to.*

   a. Say "I can't go shopping today, but I'll be able to go shopping tomorrow." Then, read the sentence fragments below and have students finish them, using *will be able to.*

      1. He can't study today, _____.
      2. She can't come to class today, _____.
      3. We can't work late today, _____.
      4. They can't go swimming today, _____.
      5. I can't call him today, _____.
      6. You can't visit her today, _____.

   b. Say "I can go jogging today, but I won't be able to go jogging tomorrow." Then do the same as above, using *won't be able to.*

      1. He can help you today, _____.
      2. She can visit them today, _____.
      3. We can go shopping today, _____.
      4. They can work today, _____.
      5. I can come to class early today, _____.
      6. You can go today, _____.

INTRODUCING THE MODEL

1. Have students look at the model illustration.
2. Set the scene: "Two friends are talking. One of them has some bad news."
3. Present the model.
4. Full-Class Choral Repetition.
5. Ask students if they have any questions; check understanding of new vocabulary: *Don't worry about it!*

Language Note

Have to/have got to:
   a. Both of these expressions are used to express obligation: *I have to work, I've got to work.*
   b. Tell your students they will sometimes hear *got to* pronounced *gotta* in informal speech.
   c. *Have got to* is not normally used in negative sentences.

6. Group Choral Repetition.
7. Choral Conversation.
8. Call on one or two pairs of students to present the dialog.

(For additional practice, do Choral Conversation in small groups or by rows.)

SIDE BY SIDE EXERCISES

Examples

---

1. A. I'm afraid I won't be able to help you clean your garage tomorrow.
   B. You won't? Why not?
   A. I've got to go to the office.
   B. Don't worry about it! I'm sure I'll be able to clean my garage by myself.

2. A. I'm afraid I won't be able to help you paint your living room tomorrow.
   B. You won't? Why not?
   A. I've got to fly to Chicago.
   B. Don't worry about it! I'm sure I'll be able to paint my living room by myself.

---

1. **Exercise 1:** Call on two students to present the dialog. Then do Choral Repetition and Choral Conversation Practice.
2. **Exercise 2:** Introduce the new word *fly.* Same as above.
3. **Exercises 3–9:**

New vocabulary: 6. *Christmas dinner*   7. *ballet*   9. *vet (veterinarian)*

Culture Note

Christmas dinner, buy presents (Exercise 6):   These expressions refer to the special meal and gift-giving that characterize the celebration of the Christmas holiday.

Language Note

Vet (Exercise 9):   This word is the common abbreviation of *veterinarian.*

Either Full-Class Practice or Pair Practice.

4. **Exercise 10:** Have students use the model as a guide to create their own conversations, using vocabulary of their choice. Encourage students to use dictionaries to find new words they want to use. This exercise can be done orally in class or for written homework. If you assign it for homework, you should do one example in class to make sure students understand what's expected. Have students present their conversations in class the next day.

WORKBOOK

Pages 97–99 (Exercises F, G, H)

Exercise Note

Workbook p. 98: For additional practice with Exercise G, have students suggest other activities that Carmen *will* and *won't be able to* do this month. Students can also role play Carmen (*I'm upset because I won't be able to go jogging every morning,* etc.).

EXPANSION ACTIVITIES

1. **Practice** Have Got to: *What Have They Got to Do?*

   a. Write this conversational model on the board:

   > A. _____ want(s) to be the best _____ in _____.
   > B. Then _____ got to practice.
   > A. You're right. _____ got to _____ every day.

   b. Put the cues below on word cards. Give the word cards to pairs of students and have them create conversations based on the model. (Note: 13 is *open-ended;* students can use any vocabulary they wish.)

   Cues:

   1. Helen/piano player/_____/play the piano
   2. George/typist/_____/type
   3. my sisters/actresses/_____/act
   4. Paul/baseball player/_____/play baseball
   5. Mrs. Lopez/English teacher/_____/speak English
   6. Carl/violinist/_____/play the violin
   7. Susan/plumber/_____/fix sinks
   8. Tom/mechanic/_____/fix cars
   9. Jack and Jane/singers/_____ sing
   10. I/dancer/_____/dance
   11. our English teacher/swimmer/_____/swim
   12. Frank/chef/_____/cook
   13. _____/_____/_____/_____

   Examples:

   A. Helen wants to be the best piano player in (England).
   B. Then she's got to practice.
   A. You're right. She's got to play the piano every day.

   A. I want to be the best dancer in (our school).
   B. Then you've got to practice.
   A. You're right. I've got to dance every day.

2. **Practice** Will/Won't Be Able to: *Maybe . . . Maybe Not*

   a. Write this conversational model on the board:

   > A. Do you think _____ will be able to _____ soon?
   > B. { I don't know. / I'm really not sure. } Maybe _____ will, and
   >   maybe _____ won't. We'll just have to wait and see.

b. Call on pairs of students. For each pair, say one of the cues below and have students use the cue to create a conversation based on the model.

Cues:

1. Roger/get a new job
2. Doris/find an apartment
3. Mr. and Mrs. Wilson/move to Paris
4. you/go to the beach this weekend
5. we/speak English well
6. Cynthia and Charlie/get married
7. Hilda/visit her cousins in Mexico
8. you/buy a color TV
9. I/take a vacation
10. the Johnsons/paint their living room
11. Jeff/go skiing

Example:

A. Do you think Roger will be able to get a new job soon?
B. I don't know. (OR: I'm really not sure.) Maybe he will, and maybe he won't. We'll just have to wait and see.

c. Call on a few pairs of students to create conversations based on the model, using any vocabulary they wish.

3. Role Play: *I Won't Be Able to Help You*

a. Divide the class into pairs.

b. Give the cue cards below to the pairs and have them create role plays based on the situations.

1.

Your friend is here to see you. You're excited because he or she is going to help you carry your new refrigerator into the house. You've got to do it this morning because you're having a party tonight and you have to buy food and put it in the refrigerator.

You're really sorry. You can't help your friend today. Your back hurts and you've got to go to the doctor.

2.

Your friend is here to see you. You're pleased because he or she is going to help you fix your car. You have to fix it today because tomorrow you've got to go to your cousin's wedding.

You're very sorry. You can't help your friend. You weren't able to finish your homework last night, and you have to do it today. Tell your friend you can help tomorrow.

Text Page 92

READING: *The Bathroom Pipe Is Broken*
The Television Is Broken

FOCUS

> Be able to

NEW VOCABULARY

Story 1	Story 2
broke (break)	repair truck
for quite a while	side
pipe	

PREVIEWING THE STORIES (optional)

Have students talk about the story titles and/or illustrations. Introduce new vocabulary.

READING THE STORIES

1. Have students read silently, or follow along silently as the stories are read aloud by you, by one or more students, or on the tape.
2. Ask students if they have any questions; check understanding of vocabulary.

CHECK-UP

Answer These Questions

1. No, she couldn't. She was sick.
2. No, she can't. She's too busy.
3. No, she won't be able to. Tomorrow is Sunday.
4. No, he couldn't. He was fixing televisions on the other side of town.
5. No, he can't. His repair truck is broken.
6. No, he won't be able to. He'll be out of town.

Choose

1.	a	5.	b
2.	b	6.	a
3.	b	7.	b
4.	b		

Text Page 93

ON YOUR OWN: *Frustrated, Disappointed, and Upset*

FOCUS

> Review of expressions of ability:
>
> - Present ability   *can/can't*
> - Past ability   *could/couldn't*
>   *was/wasn't able to*
> - Future ability   *will/won't be able to*

ON YOUR OWN ACTIVITY

For each situation:

1. Have students follow along in the text as you read or play the tape one or more times.
2. Ask students if they have any questions; check understanding of new vocabulary.

> **New vocabulary:**   2. *key*   5. *school play, clumsy*

Culture Note

School play (Exercise 6): In many schools in the United States, students participate in theatrical productions as an extracurricular activity.

3. Ask questions about each situation. For example:

> 1. Is George happy?
>   Why is George upset?
>   Where does George want to go?
>   Will he be able to get to the airport on time?
>
> 2. What's the matter with Rita?
>   Can she get into her apartment?
>   Why not?
>
> 3. Who is Mrs. Brown?
>   What's the matter with Mrs. Brown?
>   Is Mrs. Brown's English class happy?
>   Why are they upset?
>
> 4. How does Sidney feel?
>   What did Sidney want to do?
>   Was he able to find a job in New York?
>   What did he have to do?
>
> 5. Could Ted dance in the school play last year?
>   Was he disappointed?
>   What did his teacher say?
>   Do you think his teacher was too honest?

4. For homework, have students write about situations in their own lives. In the next class, have students talk about their situations, and encourage the other students to ask questions.

WORKBOOK

Pages 99–100 (Exercises I, J, K)

Exercise Note

Workbook p. 100:   Students practice *able to* and *had to*.

Check-Up Test: Pages 101–102

WORKBOOK ANSWER KEY AND LISTENING SCRIPTS

Page 93 A. WHAT'S THE WORD?

1. couldn't
   can
2. Could
   could
3. couldn't
4. can
5. couldn't
6. could
7. can
   can't
8. Could
   couldn't
9. couldn't
   could
10. can
11. couldn't
12. could
13. can't

Page 94 C. YOU DECIDE: *Why Weren't They Able to?*

1. wasn't able to, . . .
2. weren't able to, . . .
3. wasn't able to, . . .
4. weren't able to, . . .
5. wasn't able to, . . .
6. wasn't able to, . . .
7. weren't able to, . . .
8. wasn't able to, . . .
9. weren't able to, . . .
10. weren't able to, . . .
11. wasn't able to, . . .

Page 96 D. WHEN THEY WERE YOUNG

1. couldn't/wasn't able to
   had to
2. couldn't/wasn't able to
   had to
3. couldn't/weren't able to
4. had to
5. could/were able to
   couldn't/wasn't able to, had to
6. couldn't/wasn't able to
7. could/were able to
   could/were able to
   had to
8. couldn't/wasn't able to
   had to

Page 97 E. YOU DECIDE: *Why Didn't They Enjoy Themselves?*

1. myself, . . .
2. themselves, . . .
3. herself, . . .
4. himself, . . .
5. myself, . . .
6. ourselves, . . .

Page 97 F. THEY'LL BE ABLE TO

1. couldn't, she'll be able to
2. couldn't, we'll be able to
3. couldn't, I'll be able to
4. couldn't, they'll be able to
5. couldn't, he'll be able to

Page 98 G. CARMEN

1. She won't be able to go jogging every morning.
2. She won't be able to ride her bicycle to school every day.
3. She won't be able to play soccer on the school team.
4. She won't be able to swim every afternoon.
5. She won't be able to do exercises every morning.

6. She'll be able to play the guitar.
7. She'll be able to write her own songs.
8. She'll be able to bake delicious cakes and pies.
9. She'll be able to make her own clothes.

Page 99 H. I'M SORRY

1. won't be able to
   We've got to
2. won't be able to
   She's got to
3. won't be able to
   They've got to
4. won't be able to
   he's got to
5. won't be able to
   We've got to

Listen to each story twice and then answer the questions you hear.

MR. AND MRS. SMITH'S VACATION

Mr. and Mrs. Smith aren't enjoying their vacation at the beach. They couldn't go swimming all week because the ocean was too cold. According to tomorrow's weather forecast, it's going to be hot and sunny. But Mr. and Mrs. Smith won't be able to go swimming tomorrow because they've got to leave early in the morning.

1. Mr. and Mrs. Smith couldn't go swimming on their vacation because . . .
2. The weather tomorrow is probably going to be . . .
3. Mr. and Mrs. Smith won't be able to go swimming tomorrow because . . .

HELEN'S ENGLISH EXAMINATION

Helen wasn't able to study for her English examination last night because she couldn't find her glasses. When she got to school this morning, she looked in her briefcase and her glasses were there. Unfortunately it was too late. Helen didn't have any time to study in the morning, and she made a lot of mistakes on the examination. Poor Helen is very embarrassed.

4. Helen couldn't study for her examination because she lost her . . .
5. When did she find her glasses?
6. Helen is very embarrassed because . . .

Answers
1. c   2. a   3. b
4. c   5. a   6. c

CHECK-UP TEST: *CHAPTERS 9–10*

Page 101   A.

1. were painting
2. was driving
3. were studying
4. was skating
5. was riding
6. were walking
7. was making

Page 101   B.

1. ourselves
2. himself
3. yourselves
4. themselves
5. herself
6. yourself

Page 101   C.

1. into
2. off
3. out of
4. into
5. out of
6. couldn't
7. couldn't
8. couldn't, had to

Page 102   D.

1. wasn't
2. were
3. weren't
4. I'll be
5. won't be
   I've
6. you've
7. won't be
   She's

Page 102   E.

Listen to the story twice and then answer the questions you hear.

POOR BILL!

Poor Bill! He was driving over the State Street Bridge a few minutes ago when he got a flat tire. He tried to fix it by himself, but he couldn't, and he had to call a mechanic. Now he's really frustrated because he doesn't think he'll get to the airport on time.

1. Bill is . . .
2. While he was driving he . . .
3. He called . . .
4. He's probably going to be . . .
5. He might miss his . . .

Answers
1. b   4. b
2. c   5. a
3. c

GRAMMAR

Must

I He She It We You They	must work.

I He She It We You They	mustn't eat ice cream.

Count/Non-Count Nouns

Non-Count

He must eat	more less	bread. fish. meat.

Count

He must eat	more fewer	cookies. potatoes. eggs.

FUNCTIONS

Asking for Advice

Should I *stop eating rich desserts*?

What should I do?

Offering Advice

You should *go to my doctor*.

Inquiring about Obligation

Do you have to *stop eating ice cream*?

Expressing Obligation

You must *go on a diet*.
You must *stop eating rich desserts*.

I mustn't *eat as much ice cream as I did before*.

Asking for and Reporting Information

The doctor told *him he's a little too heavy*.

What did *the doctor* say?

Expressing Worry

I'm really worried about *your heart*.

Expressing Want-Desire

I want to *get a medical checkup*.

Greeting People

Hello, *Roger*.

NEW VOCABULARY

annual
awful
back
beef stew
blood
blood pressure
blood test
bloody nose
blueprints
brick
build
cardiogram
cement
checkup
chest
chest X-ray
come in
complete (adj)
construction
cookbook
diet
dog biscuit
draw blood
electrical wiring
exactly
examination room
examine

fall down
fatty
fewer
finger
fruit
grapefruit
hearing (n)
heart
height
hiccups
hospital gown
ice
ingredients
instructions
last (v)
lead (v)
lean (adj)
less
lose weight
lungs
margarine
materials
measure
medical checkup
move away
must
mustn't

nurse
overweight
own (adj)
physical examination
potato chips
pulse
require
rich
rub
scale
serious
shake *your* hand
snack foods
stethoscope
supposed to
take off
water
weight
wiring (n)
wood
worried
X-ray
yearly

as a matter of fact
take life a little easier

Text Pages 96–97: *Diets*

FOCUS

- Introduction of *must*
- Introduction of $\begin{cases} less \text{ with non-count nouns} \\ fewer \text{ with count nouns} \end{cases}$

GETTING READY

1. Introduce *must.*

   a. Write on the board:

      must = $\begin{cases} \text{have to} \\ \text{have got to} \end{cases}$

   b. Give a few examples of strong obligations or rules from your students' experience. For example:

      "The school says we must study hard, we must do our homework, and we must not be late for class."

      "The President says if there is a war, we must fight for our country."

2. Introduce *less, fewer.*

   a. Write on the board:

      less

      Say: "Yesterday Tom drank too much coffee and he felt terrible. Today he's going to drink *less coffee.*"

      "Last week Judy bought too much milk. She didn't need all of it. This week she's going to buy *less milk.*"

   b. Write on the board:

      fewer

      Say: "In 1987 Susan had 4 accidents while she was driving. In 1988 she had *fewer* accidents–she had only 2!"

      "Last night Antonio made vegetable stew, but he put in too many onions. Next week he's going to put in *fewer onions.*"

INTRODUCING THE MODEL

1. Have students look at the illustration for Exercise 1.
2. Set the scene: "Somebody is talking about Henry."
3. Present the model.
4. Ask students if they have any questions; check understanding of new vocabulary: *yearly checkup, diet, potato chips, snack foods, fish, vegetables, fruit.*

5. Talk about Henry's diet. Write the diet on the board.

    a. Point to *bread* and say: "He must eat less bread." Have students repeat chorally.

    b. Point to *cookies* and say: "He must eat fewer cookies." Have students repeat chorally.

    c. Point to each of the other foods in the left column and have students respond chorally and individually:

$$\text{"He must eat} \left\{ \begin{array}{l} \text{less} \\ \text{fewer} \end{array} \right\} \underline{\hspace{2cm}} \text{."}$$

    d. Point to each of the foods in the right column and have students respond chorally and individually:

        "He must eat more _____."

Culture Note

    Diet, go on a diet: This lesson reflects the desire of many people in the United States to reduce their weight.

EXERCISES

Answer Key

---

2. (−) She must eat less fatty meat, fewer potatoes, less rice, and fewer rich desserts.
   (+) Also, she must eat more lean meat, more grapefruit, and more green vegetables.

3. (−) He must eat less butter, fewer eggs, less cheese, and less ice cream.
   (+) Also, he must eat more margarine, he must drink more skim milk, and he must eat more yogurt.

4. (−) He must eat less fatty meat and fewer dog biscuits.
   (+) Also, he must eat more lean meat, and he must drink more water.

Exercises 2–4:

For each exercise:

1. Have students look at the illustration in the book.
2. Read the introduction.
3. Ask students if they have any questions; introduce new vocabulary.

New vocabulary: 2. *annual, fatty meat, rich, lean meat, grapefruit*
   3. *worried, heart, margarine* 4. *dog biscuit, water*

Language Note

    Rich desserts: When referring to desserts, the adjective *rich* usually means that the dessert is made with a lot of butter or cream.

4. Call on individual students to tell about each food item. For example:

    fatty meat: "She must eat less fatty meat."

(For additional practice, do Choral Repetition.)

5. After telling about each individual food, call on one or two students to tell the whole diet.

Exercise 5: Read the introduction. Ask students if they have any questions; check understanding of new vocabulary: *physical examination, overweight.* Call on individual students to tell about their *diets.*

WORKBOOK

Pages 103–105

Exercise Note

Workbook p. 104: Students practice count/non-count nouns with *fewer* and *less.*

EXPANSION ACTIVITIES

1. ***Food Confessions***
   a. Set the scene: "I always eat too many cookies. My doctor says I must eat fewer cookies and more fruit."
   b. Write on the board:

   > I always (eat/drink) too (much/many) _____.
   > My doctor says I must (eat/drink) (less/fewer) _____ and more _____.

   c. Give each student a word card with two food cues, such as those below. Have each student make a *food confession,* using the model on the board.

   Cues:

ice cream/apples	candy/cheese	butter/margarine
rice/vegetables	potato chips/grapefruit	salt/pepper
potatoes/carrots	rich desserts/fruit	chocolate cake/oranges
beer/milk	wine/tea	french fries/green vegetables
coffee/water	fatty meat/fish	

   Call on students to make *food confessions,* using any vocabulary they wish.

2. ***Rules and Regulations***
   a. Write the following on the board:

   > pay taxes
   > get a passport to travel overseas
   > _____

   b. Talk about government rules and regulations with your students. Model: "What are some things you must do? You must pay taxes. You must get a passport to travel overseas."
   c. Write on the board and tell your students:

   > you must = a person must

   d. Call on students to tell you other rules and regulations, using *you must.*

Text Page 98

READING: *Carol's Apple Cake*
          Paul's Beef Stew

FOCUS

> Fewer/less

NEW VOCABULARY

Story 1	Story 2
cookbook	awful
enough	beef stew
ingredients	
instructions	
require	
supposed to	

PREVIEWING THE STORIES (optional)

Have students talk about the story titles and/or illustrations. Introduce new vocabulary.

READING THE STORIES

1. Have students read silently, or follow along silently as the stories are read aloud by you, by one or more students, or on the tape.
2. Ask students if they have any questions; check understanding of vocabulary.
3. Check students' comprehension, using some or all of the following questions:

Story 1
a. What did Carol bake yesterday?
b. Why couldn't she follow all the instructions in her cookbook?
c. What did she use?
d. What was the result?

Story 2
a. What did Paul cook yesterday?
b. Why couldn't he follow all the instructions in his cookbook?
c. What did he use?
d. What was the result?

CHECK-UP

What's the Word?

1. less	4. fewer
2. fewer	5. less
3. less	6. fewer

Listening

Have students complete the exercises as you play the tape or read the following:

Listen and choose the best words to complete the sentences.

1. This tastes terrible. I used too much . . . (b)
2. You know . . . the next time you bake this, you should try to use fewer . . . (a)
3. You're a little too heavy. You must eat less . . . (b)
4. This pie is delicious! I can't believe it has so many . . . (a)
5. This tastes better than it did the last time I made it. I think it's because I used fewer . . . (a)
6. Remember, we couldn't finish everything the last time we ate here. This time let's order less . . . (b)

Text Page 99: *I Must Lose Some Weight*

FOCUS

> Introduction of *mustn't*

INTRODUCING THE MODEL

1. Have students look at the model illustration.
2. Set the scene: "A wife and husband are talking."
3. Present Exercise 1 as a model. Read or play the tape one or more times:

> A. I had my yearly checkup today.
> B. What did the doctor say?
> A. He told me I'm a little too heavy and I must lose some weight.
> B. Do you have to stop eating ice cream?
> A. No, but I mustn't eat as much ice cream as I did before.

4. Full-Class Choral Repetition.
5. Ask students if they have any questions; check understanding of new vocabulary: *told (tell), lose weight, stop eating, as much/many _____ as.*

   ### Language Note

   Mustn't/don't have to: Although *must* and *have to* are very similar in meaning, the negative forms of these verbs have very different meanings.
   a. *Mustn't* = a strong obligation or necessity *not* to do something. For example, *You mustn't go there* implies *Do NOT go there.*
   b. *Don't have to* = no obligation or necessity to do something. For example, *You don't have to go there* implies *It's not necessary to go there.*

6. Group Choral Repetition.
7. Choral Conversation.
8. Call on one or two pairs of students to present the dialog.

   (For additional practice, do Choral Conversation in small groups or by rows.)

SIDE BY SIDE EXERCISES

Examples

> 2. A. I had my yearly checkup today.
> B. What did the doctor say?
> A. He (she) told me I'm a little too heavy and I must lose some weight.
> B. Do you have to stop eating cookies?
> A. No, but I mustn't eat as many cookies as I did before.

3. A. I had my yearly checkup today.
   B. What did the doctor say?
   A. He (she) told me I'm a little too heavy and I must lose some weight.
   B. Do you have to stop eating butter?
   A. No, but I mustn't eat as much butter as I did before.

1. **Exercise 2:** Call on two students to present the dialog. Then do Choral Repetition and Choral Conversation Practice.

2. **Exercise 3:** Same as above.

3. **Exercises 4–8:**

   Either Full-Class Practice or Pair Practice.

4. **Exercise 9:** Have students use the model as a guide to create their own conversations, using vocabulary of their choice. Encourage students to use dictionaries to find new words they want to use. This exercise can be done orally in class or for written homework. If you assign it for homework, you should do one example in class to make sure students understand what's expected. Have students present their conversations in class the next day.

WORKBOOK

Pages 106–107

Exercise Notes

Workbook p. 106:   In Exercise D, students must decide which words are most appropriate based on the fact that Miss Primm's school is very strict and the Flower School is not.

Workbook p. 107:   In Exercises E and F, students complete the sentences using any vocabulary they wish. Have students compare their answers.

EXPANSION ACTIVITIES

1. *Rules of the School*

   a. Have students make up a set of rules for an imaginary school. (Have students give the school a name.) Write the rules on the board as students say them. For example:

      "The students mustn't talk during class."
      "The students mustn't eat during class."

   b. Write on the board:

      A. Can the students at _____ _____?
      B. { Yes, they can.
         { No! They mustn't _____.

   c. Call on pairs of students to create conversations about the school. For example:

      A. Can the students at _____ eat during class?
      B. Yes, they can. They can eat whenever they want.

      A. Can the students at _____ have long hair?
      B. No! They mustn't have long hair. They must have short hair.

2. *More Rules and Regulations*

a. Write on the board:

> You mustn't _____.

b. Tell students you're going to talk about more rules and regulations . . . about things people MUSTN'T do. Give a few examples, such as:

> "You mustn't smoke on the bus."
> "You mustn't drive over the speed limit."
> "You mustn't talk in the library."

c. Call on students to tell other rules and regulations they know, using *You mustn't*.

Text Pages 100–101: *The Checkup*
Your Checkup

FOCUS

- Steps in a complete physical checkup
- Review of the future and past tenses

INTRODUCING THE MODEL

Introduce the Telephone Conversation

1. Have students look at the model illustration of the two people talking on the telephone.
2. Set the scene: "Two friends are talking on the telephone."
3. Present the model.
4. Full-Class Choral Repetition.
5. Ask students if they have any questions; check understanding of new vocabulary: *medical checkup, move away, complete.*
6. Group Choral Repetition.
7. Choral Conversation.
8. Call on one or two pairs of students to present the dialog.

    (For additional practice, do Choral Conversation in small groups or by rows.)

Introduce the Checkup Steps 1–10

1. Have students look at the illustration.
2. Set the scene before presenting Step 1: "Roger is telling his friend what will happen if he goes to Dr. Anderson's office for a checkup."
3. Have students listen as you read or play the tape for each step one or more times.
4. Have students repeat each step chorally.
5. For each step, ask students if they have any questions; check understanding of new vocabulary:

New vocabulary: 1. *nurse, lead, examination room*
  2. *scale, measure, height, weight*
  3. *take off, hospital gown*   4. *come in, shake your hand*
  5. *examine*   6. *stethoscope*   7. *pulse*   8. *blood pressure*
  9. *blood, blood test*   10. *chest X-ray, cardiogram*

Culture Note

> *Cardiogram* (Step 10): This refers to a procedure used to detect and diagnose heart problems. It is sometimes referred to as an "E.K.G."

6. Call on a few students to present each step in the checkup.

7. Review the steps, using these key words on the board:

---

1. nurse/lead/examination room
2. stand/scale/so/measure/height/weight
3. leave/take off/put on
4. Dr. A _____/come in/shake/say
5. examine/eyes/ears/nose/throat

6. listen/heart/stethoscope
7. take/pulse
8. then/take/blood pressure
9. after/draw blood/blood test
10. take/chest X-ray/do/cardiogram

---

a. With students' books closed, point to each step and have them listen and repeat chorally as you read 1–10 again.

b. Next, have students retell the steps. Point and call on individual students.

c. Review the checkup by asking questions. For example:

> "Where will Dr. Anderson examine you?"
> "What do you have to wear during the examination?"
> "What will the doctor say when he sees you?"
> "Why do you have to stand on the scale?"
> "How will the doctor listen to your heart?"
> "Will he take your blood pressure?"
> "Will he take your pulse?"

YOUR CHECKUP (text page 101)

1. Introduce these irregular past tense forms:

---

lead–led
take–took
come–came
shake–shook
say–said
stand–stood

Write the words on the board; then have students repeat them after you.

2. Students pretend they had a checkup yesterday and tell what happened.

a. Have students look at the illustrations.

b. Call on individual students to present each checkup step.

c. Do Choral Repetition.

d. Call on one or two students to tell about the whole checkup—steps 1–10.

WORKBOOK

Page 108

EXPANSION ACTIVITY

Telephone Role Play: Calling Dr. Lee's Office for an Appointment

1. Write the following conversational model on the board or on a large poster:

A. Dr. Lee's office. May I help you?
B. Yes. I'd like to make an appointment for a checkup with Dr. Lee.
A. Will this be your first visit to Dr. Lee?
B. Yes, it will. A friend recommended him to me.
A. What is your name?
B. _____ _____.
A. Okay. (Mr./Miss/Mrs./Ms.) _____.
    Would you be able to come to the office on _____ at _____?
B. On _____ at _____? Yes. That will be fine.
A. What is your telephone number, please?
B. _____.
A. Thank you very much (Mr./Miss/Mrs./Ms.) _____.
    We'll see you on _____ at _____.
B. Thank you. Good-bye.
A. Good-bye.

---

2. Present the dialog with one of your students, using any date, time, and telephone number you wish.
3. Ask students if they have any questions; check understanding of *I'd like to = I want to.*
4. Divide the class into pairs and have students practice both part A and part B.
5. Call on a few pairs to present their dialogs to the class. For added realism, have students hold telephone receivers as they present their dialogs.

Text Page 102: *Really, Doctor?*

FOCUS

> Contrast between *should* and *must*

INTRODUCING THE MODEL

1. Have students look at the model illustration.
2. Set the scene: "Mr. Jones is in the doctor's office. He had a checkup a few minutes ago, and now the doctor is talking to him."
3. Present the model.
4. Full-Class Choral Repetition.
5. Ask students if they have any questions; check understanding of new vocabulary: *stop, serious.*
6. Group Choral Repetition.
7. Choral Conversation.
8. Call on one or two pairs of students to present the dialog.

   (For additional practice, do Choral Conversation in small groups or by rows.)

SIDE BY SIDE EXERCISES

Examples

1. A. I'm really worried about your lungs.
   B. Really, Doctor? Should I stop smoking?
   A. (Mr./Miss/Mrs./Ms.) _____. You MUST stop smoking! If you don't, you're going to have serious problems with your lungs some day.

2. A. I'm really worried about your back.
   B. Really, Doctor? Should I start doing exercises?
   A. (Mr./Miss/Mrs./Ms.) _____. You MUST start doing exercises! If you don't, you're going to have serious problems with your back some day.

1. **Exercise 1:** Introduce the new word *lungs*. Call on two students to present the dialog. Then do Choral Repetition and Choral Conversation Practice.
2. **Exercise 2:** Introduce the new words *back, start doing*. Same as above.
3. **Exercises 3–5:**

   > **New vocabulary:** 3. *feet*   4. *take life a little easier*   5. *hearing* (n)

   Either Full-Class Practice or Pair Practice.
4. **Exercise 6:** Have students use the model as a guide to create their own conversations, using vocabulary of their choice. Encourage students to be *playful* as well as realistic. Possible cues include:

blood pressure	teeth	weight
stop eating so much salt	stop eating so much candy	go on a diet

eyes   back
stop reading by candlelight   stop lifting heavy things

This exercise can be done orally in class or for written homework. If you assign it for homework, you should do one example in class to make sure students understand what's expected. Have students present their conversations in class the next day.

WORKBOOK

Pages 109–110

Exercise Notes

Workbook p. 109:   For additional oral practice with Exercise I, have students ask and answer questions about the pictures.

Workbook p. 110:   In Exercise J, students practice *must*. In Exercise K, they practice *must* and the past tense.

EXPANSION ACTIVITIES

1. *Students Talk about Themselves: You Can Do It*

   a. Write on the board:

   A. I know I should _____, but I can't.
   B. I don't believe that. If you REALLY want to _____, you CAN!
       As my _____ always says, you should stop TALKING about it and DO it!

   ---

   b. Call on pairs of students to create conversations about themselves.

   Examples:

   A. I know I should go on a diet, but I can't.
   B. I don't believe that! If you REALLY want to go on a diet, you CAN!
       As my Uncle Albert always says, you should stop TALKING about it and DO it!

   A. I know I should study harder, but I can't.
   B. I don't believe that. If you REALLY want to study harder, you CAN!
       As my grandmother always says, you should stop TALKING about it and DO it!

2. *Practice Must: What Do They Tell Everybody?*

   Have students listen as you read the first situation below. Then read each of the others and call on a student to complete the answer according to the model.

   1. Mary stopped smoking because she had problems with her lungs. Now she tells everyone:
      "You MUST stop smoking! If you don't stop smoking, you'll have problems with your lungs!"

   2. George stopped eating rich foods because he had problems with his heart. Now he tells everyone:
      "_____!"

   3. Ellen stopped eating candy because she had problems with her teeth. Now she tells everyone:
      "_____!"

   4. Peter stopped eating salt because he had problems with his blood pressure. Now he tells everyone: "_____!"

5. Helen stopped jogging because she had problems with her feet. Now she tells everyone:
   "_____!"

6. Jack started doing exercises because he had problems with his back. Now he tells everyone:
   "_____!"

7. Jane started swimming because she had problems with her weight. Now she tells everyone:
   "_____!"

ON YOUR OWN: *Home Remedies*

FOCUS

Students give advice about home remedies for common ailments and emergencies

ON YOUR OWN ACTIVITY

1. Have students look at the illustrations at the top of the page.
2. Set the scene: "What do you do when you burn your finger?"
3. Have students listen as you read the three remedies.
4. Model each line and have students repeat chorally.
5. Ask students if they have any questions; check understanding of new vocabulary: *finger, rub, ice.*
6. Introduce Exercise 1 in class. Role play the person in the book and have a few students give you advice. For example:

> You: "I have a cold. What should I do?"
> Students: "You should go home and go to sleep."
> "You should wear a heavy sweater."
> "You should drink a lot of tea."

7. For homework, have students write home remedies for Exercises 1–5. Encourage students to tell what you *shouldn't* do, as well as what you *should* do. Have students use dictionaries to find new words they want to use.
8. In the next class, call on students to present their remedies without referring to their written homework. Encourage students to agree or disagree and tell why.

WORKBOOK ANSWER KEY AND LISTENING SCRIPTS

**Page 103 A. GEORGE IS WORRIED
ABOUT HIS HEALTH**

1.	fewer	12.	less
2.	less	13.	fewer
3.	fewer	14.	less
4.	more	15.	more
5.	more	16.	more
6.	less	17.	fewer
7.	fewer	18.	less
8.	less	19.	less
9.	more	20.	more
10.	more	21.	more
11.	more		

Page 105 C. THEY CAN'T WORK HERE

1. must type accurately and speak Spanish
2. must work quickly and dress neatly
3. must speak English and have a car
4. must be patient and kind
5. must act, sing, and dance very well

**Page 106 D. TWO VERY DIFFERENT
SCHOOLS**

1.	must	9.	must
2.	must	10.	mustn't
3.	don't have to	11.	must
4.	must	12.	mustn't
5.	must	13.	must
6.	mustn't	14.	don't have to
7.	must	15.	must
8.	don't have to	16.	don't have to

Page 108 G. THE CHECKUP

1. examination room
2. clothes, hospital gown
3. scale, measure, weight
4. pulse
5. heart
6. blood, blood test
7. chest
8. pressure
9. examination

**Page 108 H. SCRAMBLED MEDICAL
WORDS**

1. cardiogram
2. stethoscope
3. chest
4. pulse
5. pressure
6. examine

Page 69 I. LOUD AND CLEAR

1. hire Helen
   her

2. hungry, Who
   hamburger
   whole

3. Harry hurt
   head, hockey

4. Hilda, her
   husband, healthy

5. Henry hopes
   his homework
   half

6. Hello, happy
   here, Honolulu
   Hawaii

GRAMMAR

Future Continuous Tense

(I will)	I'll	
(He will)	He'll	
(She will)	She'll	
(It will)	It'll	be working.
(We will)	We'll	
(You will)	You'll	
(They will)	They'll	

Time Expressions

I'll be staying	for	a few months.
		a few more hours.
		a few more minutes.
	until	Friday.
		10 o'clock.
		I finish this.

We'll be arriving	at 7 A.M.
	in a few days.

FUNCTIONS

Asking for and Reporting Information

Will you *be home this evening*?
 Yes, I will. I'll be *reading*.

I won't *be home this evening*.

How long will *your Aunt Gertrude be staying with us*?
How much longer will *you be working on my car*?
How late will *your husband be working tonight*?
Where will *you be getting off*?
When will *we be arriving in Paris*?
How far will *we be driving today*?
How soon will *Santa Claus be coming*?

Inquiring about Intention

How long will you *be staying with us*?

Expressing Intention

I won't *come over at five*.

Inquiring about Ability

When can you *come over*?

Expressing Ability

I can *come over at* _____ *o'clock*.

Offering a Suggestion

How about _____ *o'clock*?

Asking for Permission

Can I *come over and visit this evening*?

Inquiring about Agreement

Is that okay?
Will that be okay?

Expressing Agreement

Fine.
That'll be fine.

Greeting People

Hi, *Gloria*. This is *Arthur*.

Hi, *Uncle Frank*! How are you?
 Fine!

Leave Taking

Good-bye.
I'll see you then.
See you at *five*.

Offering to Help

I'll be glad to help.

Expressing Want-Desire

I want to *return the tennis racket I borrowed from you*.

Indicating Understanding

I see.

Initiating a Topic

By the way, . . .

NEW VOCABULARY

actually
adult
age
borrow
career
chapter
coffee pot
come over
cot
couch
Detroit
dictionary
disturb
get older
Good-bye.
Grandma
Grandpa

guest room
hammer
have children
holiday weekend
how far
how late
how long
how much longer
how soon
knit
middle-aged
plenty (of)
reach
relative
retire
senior citizen
several

sometime
stay
Thanksgiving
videotape
work on
young adult

by the way
from top to bottom
"Happy Thanksgiving!"
how quickly time flies
I see.
I'll see you then.
Is that okay?
See you at *five*.
take it easy
That's great!

LANGUAGE NOTE

Use of the Future Continuous Tense

This verb tense is commonly used to:

1. emphasize the ongoing nature or duration of an activity in the future:

   Will you be home today at about five o'clock?
   Yes, I will. I'll be cooking dinner.
   They'll be staying in San Francisco until Friday.

2. express a polite tone in talking about future events:

   Where will you be getting off (the bus)?
   I'll be getting off at the last stop.

   When will we be arriving in London?
   We'll be arriving in London at 7 A.M..

Text Page 106: *Will They Be Home This Evening?*

FOCUS

> Introduction of the future continuous tense

INTRODUCING THE MODEL

1. Have students look at the model illustration.
2. Set the scene: "Two people are talking about this evening."
3. Present the model.
4. Full-Class Choral Repetition.
5. Ask students if they have any questions.
6. Group Choral Repetition.
7. Choral Conversation.
8. Call on one or two pairs of students to present the dialog.

   (For additional practice, do Choral Conversation in small groups or by rows.)
9. Use the words in the box at the top of the page to form sentences with the future continuous tense. Have students repeat chorally. For example:

   "I'll be working."
   "He'll be working."

SIDE BY SIDE EXERCISES

Answer Key

1. A. Will Sharon be home this evening?
   B. Yes, she will. She'll be watching TV.
2. A. Will Steven be home this evening?
   B. Yes, he will. He'll be studying English.
3. A. Will Mr. and Mrs. Williams be home this evening?
   B. Yes, they will. They'll be cleaning their apartment/cleaning their house.
4. A. Will Bob be home this evening?
   B. Yes, he will. He'll be fixing his sink.
5. A. Will you be home this evening?
   B. Yes, we will. We'll be playing cards.
6. A. Will Kathy be home this evening?
   B. Yes, she will. She'll be practicing/playing the piano.
7. A. Will Jack be home this evening?
   B. Yes, he will. He'll be listening to records.
8. A. Will you be home this evening?
   B. Yes, I will. I'll be cooking.
9. A. Will Mrs. McDonald be home this evening?
   B. Yes, she will. She'll be doing her exercises.

10. A. Will you and your brother be home this evening?
    B. Yes, we will. We'll be playing chess.
11. A. Will Dave be home this evening?
    B. Yes, he will. He'll be doing his laundry/washing his clothes.

1. **Exercise 1:** Call on two students to present the dialog. Then do Choral Repetition and Choral Conversation Practice.

2. **Exercise 2:** Same as above.

3. **Exercises 3–11:** Either Full-Class Practice or Pair Practice.

4. **Exercise 12:** Have students use the model as a guide to create their own conversations, using vocabulary of their choice. Encourage students to use dictionaries to find new words they want to use. This exercise can be done orally in class or for written homework. If you assign it for homework, you should do one example in class to make sure students understand what's expected. Have students present their conversations in class the next day.

WORKBOOK

Page 111

EXPANSION ACTIVITIES

1. *Practice with Visuals*

   Use *Side by Side* Picture Cards, your own visuals, or word cards to review the future continuous tense. Suggested visuals are:

fix _____ car	listen to the radio
fix _____ sink	paint
clean _____ apartment	plant flowers
clean _____ yard	play cards
wash _____ car	read
wash _____ clothes	study
do _____ exercises	watch TV
cook	write letters

   a. Write on the board:

   > A. Will _____ be home tomorrow morning?
   > B. I think so. _____ probably be _____ all morning.

   b. Give visuals to pairs of students and have them create conversations about themselves, using the visuals as cues. For example:

   > A. Will you be home tomorow morning?
   > B. I think so. I'll probably be washing my clothes all morning.

   c. Have pairs of students create conversations about other students who are holding visuals. For example:

   > A. Will Yoko be home tomorrow morning?
   > B. I think so. She'll probably be writing letters all morning.

   > A. Will Bill and Richard be home tomorrow morning?
   > B. I think so. They'll probably be studying all morning.

2. Next Year

a. Write the following cues on the board and tell this story:

Maria Lopez

This year . . .	Next year . . .
live in Mexico City	live in London
speak Spanish	speak English
eat Mexican food	eat English food/drink tea
study in high school	study at the university

"Maria Lopez is from Mexico City. Next year she's going to go to school in London. A lot of things are going to change in Maria's life. This year she lives in Mexico City. Next year she'll be living in London."

b. Call on students to continue the story about Maria Lopez, using the cues on the board.

c. Have students think of other things Maria Lopez will be doing in London next year.

Text Pages 107–108: *Hi, Gloria. This Is Arthur.*
When Can You Come Over?

FOCUS

Review of the future continuous tense

INTRODUCING THE MODEL (text page 107)

1. Have students look at the illustration.
2. Set the scene: "Arthur wants to go out on a date with Gloria, but Gloria doesn't want to go out with him."
3. Present the model.
4. Full-Class Choral Repetition.
5. Ask students if they have any questions; check understanding of new vocabulary: *come over, Good-bye, I see.*
6. Call on different pairs of students to present portions of the dialog.
7. Call on one or two pairs of students to present the entire dialog.

SIDE BY SIDE EXERCISE (text page 108)

In this exercise, students complete the conversation, using any vocabulary they wish.

1. Role play the conversation with one of your better students.
2. Ask students if they have any questions; check understanding of new vocabulary: *Is that okay? I'll see you then.*
3. Divide the class into pairs and have students role play the conversation.
4. Call on one or two pairs to present their role plays to the class.

WORKBOOK

Pages 112–113

Exercise Notes

Workbook p. 112:   In this exercise, students fill in their choice of verbs in the future continuous tense. For additional oral practice, have students act out the conversation between Arthur and Louise.

Workbook p. 113:   Students practice the future continuous tense.

EXPANSION ACTIVITIES

1. Role Play: Invitations

a. Write on the board:

> A. I'm _____ing Saturday $\begin{Bmatrix} \text{morning} \\ \text{afternoon} \end{Bmatrix}$. Would you like to come?
>
> B. I'd really like to, but I can't. I'll be _____ing all day.
>
> A. That's too bad. Maybe we can _____ together some time soon.

b. Call on pairs of students to role play invitations, using the conversational model on the board and any vocabulary they wish.

Examples:

A. I'm going to the movies Saturday afternoon. Would you like to come?
B. I'd really like to, but I can't. I'll be painting my apartment all day.
A. That's too bad. Maybe we can go to the movies together some time soon.

A. I'm going jogging Saturday morning. Would you like to come?
B. I'd really like to, but I can't. I'll be taking care of my younger sister all day.
A. That's too bad. Maybe we can go jogging together some time soon.

2. Trying to Make an Appointment

a. Write the following on the board:

> | | |
> |-------|------------------|
> | 9:00 | read his mail |
> | 10:00 | talk to a client |
> | 11:00 | dictate letters |
> | 12:00 | have lunch |
> | 1:00 | have lunch |
> | 2:00 | go to a meeting |
> | 3:00 | see a client |
> | 4:00 | play golf |
> | 5:00 | _____ |

b. Set the scene: "You're trying to find a time to meet with your lawyer to talk about something important. But your lawyer is VERY busy."

c. Model the following:

A. Can I see you at 9 o'clock tomorrow?
B. I'm sorry. I'll be reading my mail at 9 o'clock.
A. Hmm. How about 10 o'clock?
B. I'm sorry. I'll be talking to a client at 10 o'clock.

d. Have pairs of students continue the conversation, using the cues on the board and any others they wish, until they have *finally* arranged a time to meet.

Text Page 109: *How Long Will Your Aunt Gertrude Be Staying with Us?*

FOCUS

- Review of the future continuous tense
- Introduction of time expressions with *for* and *until*:

  for a few more months/a few more hours/a few more minutes
  until Friday/10 o'clock/I finish this

INTRODUCING THE MODEL

1. Have students look at the illustration.
2. Set the scene: "A husband and wife are talking. The husband is upset because his wife's Aunt Gertrude just arrived for a visit."
3. Present the model.
4. Full-Class Choral Repetition.
5. Ask students if they have any questions; check understanding of new vocabulary: *how long, staying, for a few months.*
6. Group Choral Repetition.
7. Choral Conversation.
8. Call on one or two pairs of students to present the dialog.

   (For additional practice, do Choral Conversation in small groups or by rows.)

SIDE BY SIDE EXERCISES

Examples

1. A. How long will they be staying in San Francisco?
   B. They'll be staying in San Francisco until Friday.

2. A. How much longer will you be working on my car?
   B. I'll be working on your car for a few more hours.

1. **Exercise 1:** Introduce the new words *stay, until.* Call on two students to present the dialog. Then do Choral Repetition and Choral Conversation Practice.
2. **Exercise 2:** Introduce the new expression *how much longer.* Same as above.
3. **Exercises 3–10:**

   New vocabulary: 4. *last, stop* (n) 6. *how late* 8. *how much longer, chapter*
   9. *how far, reach, Detroit* 10. *how soon*

   Either Full-Class Practice or Pair Practice.

Pages 114–116

Exercise Note

Workbook p. 116: Students practice the future continuous tense and time expressions with *for*.

EXPANSION ACTIVITY

Role Play: At the Airport

Have students use the model below and cues on the board to role play conversations at the airport.

1. Write on the board:

> A.   Are you taking a trip?
> B.   Yes. I'll be leaving for _____ in a few minutes.
> A.   How long _____ staying?
> B.   _____ $\begin{Bmatrix} \text{for} \\ \text{until} \end{Bmatrix}$ _____.
> A.   That's great! What _____ doing while you're there?
> B.   _____.
> A.   Well, I hope you have a wonderful time!

2. Set the scene: "You're at the airport and you're going on a trip. You see a friend and begin talking."

3. Call on pairs of students to role play, using the cues on the board. Students can use any vocabulary of their choice to tell about what they'll be doing in these places.

Cues:

1. Tokyo 7 days _____	5. Washington, D.C. 5 days _____	9. Caracas Sunday night _____
2. Mexico City Saturday _____	6. Stockholm Sunday _____	10. Cairo 12 days _____
3. Honolulu 2 weeks _____	7. Geneva 3 weeks _____	11. Moscow Friday _____
4. Rio de Janeiro Wednesday _____	8. Athens a month _____	12. Beijing a week _____

Examples:

> A.   Are you taking a trip?
> B.   Yes. I'll be leaving for Paris in a few minutes.
> A.   How long will you be staying?
> B.   I'll be staying for 3 months.
> A.   That's great! What will you be doing while you're there?
> B.   I'll be studying French.
> A.   Well, I hope you have a wonderful time!

A. Are you taking a trip?
B. Yes. I'll be leaving for London in a few minutes.
A. How long will you be staying?
B. I'll be staying until Sunday.
A. That's great! What will you be doing while you're there?
B. I'll be visiting my cousins and going to museums.
A. Well, I hope you have a wonderful time!

Text Page 110

READING: *Happy Thanksgiving!*

FOCUS

Future continuous tense

NEW VOCABULARY

actually	Grandma	relative
cot	Grandpa	several
couch	guest room	Thanksgiving
from top to bottom	holiday weekend	"Happy Thanksgiving"

PREVIEWING THE STORY (optional)

Have students talk about the story title and/or illustrations. Introduce new vocabulary.

READING THE STORY

1. Have students read silently, or follow along silently as the story is read aloud by you, by one or more students, or on the tape.
2. Ask students if they have any questions; check understanding of vocabulary.

   ### Culture Note

   Thanksgiving is a holiday that is celebrated in the United States on the third Thursday in November. This holiday dates back to the seventeenth century, when the Pilgrim settlers in the original colonies that became the United States celebrated the harvest season. Thanksgiving is a time when families traditionally gather to share a festive holiday meal.

3. Check students' comprehension, using some or all of the following questions:

   a. What holiday is this week?
   b. Who will be staying with them during the long holiday weekend?
   c. How long will Uncle Frank be staying?
   d. Where will he be sleeping?
   e. How long will his wife's parents be staying?
   f. Where will they be sleeping?
   g. How long will cousin Bertha be staying?
   h. Where will she be sleeping?
   i. What will his wife be doing for the next few days?
   j. What will he be doing for the next few days?

CHECK-UP

Q & A

1. Call on a pair of students to present the model.
2. Have students work in pairs to create new dialogs.
3. Call on pairs to present their new dialogs to the class.

HOW ABOUT YOU?

Have students answer the questions, in pairs or as a class.

FOCUS

> Review of the future continuous tense

INTRODUCING THE MODEL

1. Have students look at the illustration.
2. Set the scene: "Julie is calling Richard on the telephone. She has Richard's tennis racket, and she wants to give it back to him."
3. Present the model.
4. Full-Class Choral Repetition.
5. Ask students if they have any questions; check understanding of new vocabulary: *return, borrow, disturb.*

   Language Note

   At five: This is a shorter way of saying *at five o'clock.*

6. Group Choral Repetition.
7. Choral Conversation.
8. Call on one or two pairs of students to present the dialog.

SIDE BY SIDE EXERCISES

In these exercises students can use their own names and any times they wish.

Examples

> 1. A. Hello (Mary). This is (Sally). I want to return the dictionary I borrowed from you last week. Will you be home today at about (two) o'clock?
>   B. Yes, I will. I'll be doing the laundry.
>   A. Oh. Then I won't come over at (two).
>   B. Why not?
>   A. I don't want to disturb you. You'll be doing the laundry!
>   B. Don't worry. You won't disturb me.
>   A. Okay. See you at (two).
>
> 2. A. Hello (David). This is (Michael). I want to return the videotape I borrowed from you last week. Will you be home today at about (one) o'clock?
>   B. Yes, I will. I'll be watching my favorite TV program.
>   A. Oh. Then I won't come over at (one).
>   B. Why not?
>   A. I don't want to disturb you. You'll be watching your favorite TV program!
>   B. Don't worry. You won't disturb me.
>   A. Okay. See you at (one).

1. **Exercise 1:** Introduce the new word *dictionary.* Call on two students to present the dialog. Then do Choral Repetition and Choral Conversation Practice.

2. **Exercise 2:** Introduce the new word *videotape.* Same as above.

3. **Exercises 3–5:**

   > **New vocabulary:**   3. *hammer*   4. *coffee pot, knit*

   Either Full-Class Practice or Pair Practice.

4. **Exercise 6:** Have students use the model as a guide to create their own conversations, using vocabulary of their choice. Encourage students to use dictionaries to find new words they want to use. This exercise can be done orally in class or for written homework. If you assign it for homework, you should do one example in class to make sure students understand what's expected. Have students present their conversations in class the next day.

WORKBOOK

Pages 117–119

Exercise Note

Workbook p. 117:   For additional oral practice with Exercise G, have students act out the conversations.

EXPANSION ACTIVITY

Telephone Role Play: They Can't Come to the Phone

1. Write this conversational model on the board:

   > A. Hello. Can I speak to _____, please?
   > B. I'm sorry. _____ is _____ right now, and (he/she) can't come to the phone.
   > A. How much longer will (he/she) be _____?
   > B. (He'll/She'll) probably be _____ $\begin{Bmatrix} \text{for} \\ \text{until} \end{Bmatrix}$ _____.
   > A. I'll call back later. Thank you very much.

2. Have pairs of students role play the telephone conversation. You can give students cues such as those below on word cards or let students use any vocabulary they wish. For added realism, bring telephones to class. Use Full-Class Practice or Pair Practice.

   Cues:

   > Dave/eat dinner

   > Bill/practice the violin

   > Sharon/work in the garden

   > Mr. Smith/take a shower

Kathy/wash the floor	Joe/bake bread
Charlie/wash his hair	Stanley/paint the living room
Sally/fix the car	Margaret/sleep

Example:

- A. Hello. Can I speak to Dave, please?
- B. I'm sorry. Dave is eating dinner right now, and he can't come to the phone.
- A. How much longer will he be eating dinner?
- B. He'll probably be eating dinner (for thirty minutes/until 8 o'clock).
- A. I'll call back later. Thank you very much.

Text Page 113

READING: *Growing Up*

FOCUS

> Future continuous tense

NEW VOCABULARY

adult	have children	retire
age	how quickly time flies	senior citizen
career	middle-aged	take it easy
get older		young adult

PREVIEWING THE STORY (optional)

Have students talk about the story title and/or illustrations. Introduce new vocabulary.

READING THE STORY

1. Have students read silently or follow along silently as the story is read aloud by you, by one or more students, or on the tape.
2. Ask students if they have any questions; check understanding of vocabulary.
3. Check students' comprehension, using some or all of the following questions:

   a. What will Jessica be doing soon?
   b. Will she be a baby very much longer?
   c. What will Tommy be doing soon?
   d. Will he be a little boy very much longer?
   e. What will Kathy be doing soon?
   f. Will she be a teenager very much longer?
   g. What will Peter and Sally be doing soon?
   h. Will they be young adults very much longer?
   i. What will Walter be doing soon?
   j. Will he be middle-aged very much longer?

Listening

Have students complete the exercises as you play the tape or read the following:

> Listen and choose the best answer.
>
> 1. When will we be arriving in Tokyo? (b)
> 2. When will they be getting married? (a)
> 3. How late did you work last night? (a)
> 4. How much longer will the pies be baking? (b)
> 5. Will they be leaving soon? (a)
> 6. When will the boss be retiring? (b)

HOW ABOUT YOU?

Have students answer the question, in pairs or as a class.

WORKBOOK ANSWER KEY AND LISTENING SCRIPTS

Page 111   A.   THEY'LL ALL BE BUSY

1. Yes, they will. They'll be painting their kitchen.
2. Yes, she will. She'll be fixing her car.
3. Yes, we will. We'll be washing our windows.
4. Yes, they will. They'll be shopping at the supermarket.
5. Yes, I will. I'll be planting flowers.
6. Yes, they will. They'll be practicing the violin.
7. Yes, she will. She'll be teaching.
8. Yes, she will. She'll be taking care of her little brother.

Page 114   D.   UNTIL WHEN?

1. I'll be working, until
2. He'll be reading, until
3. She'll be practicing, for
4. They'll be getting, at
5. He'll be playing, until
6. I'll be getting off, at
7. We'll be waiting for, for
8. She'll be arriving, in

Page 115   E.   WHAT'S THE QUESTION?

1. will you be taking a bath
2. will you be arriving in Paris
3. will they be shopping in the city
4. will she be studying
5. will he be skiing in Europe
6. will you be visiting your family
7. will they be working on her car
8. will he be coming to visit them
9. will we be sailing

Page 117   G.   WHY DON'T YOU . . . ?

1. he'll be practicing the piano
   practices the piano
2. he'll be baking cookies
   bakes cookies
3. she'll be studying English
   studies English

4. he'll be doing his exercises
   does his exercises
5. they'll be washing their clothes
   wash their clothes
6. she'll be cleaning the house
   cleans the house
7. she'll be washing her car
   washes her car

Page 118   H.   LISTEN

Listen and fill in the blanks with the words you hear.

ON THE AIRPLANE

Good afternoon. This is Captain Harris speaking. Our plane will be leaving in just a few minutes. Soon we'll be flying over New York City, and you'll be able to see the baseball stadium on your right and Central Park on your left. We'll be flying over the Atlantic Ocean for three and a half hours. In a little while, you'll be having dinner, and after dinner you'll be seeing a movie. We'll be arriving in San Juan at 8:35. The weather in San Juan this evening is 70°F./21° C. and cloudy. It'll probably be raining when we get there.

IN THE HOSPITAL

Now Mr. Jones, after your operation, you'll probably be feeling weak for a few days. But don't worry! We'll be taking good care of you. Tomorrow you'll be staying in bed and resting comfortably all day. The nurses will be taking your pulse and blood pressure, and we'll be giving you a lot of soup and juice. The day after tomorrow you'll be walking and you'll be able to eat ice cream and yogurt. If everything is okay you'll be leaving the hospital on Saturday. Do you have any questions?

YOU'LL FIND ME

When you come into the restaurant, you'll know who I am. I'll be wearing dark glasses and a raincoat. I'll be sitting by myself at a table in the corner, and I'll be drinking a glass of water and reading a newspaper. And I'll be looking for you. You'll find me. Don't worry!

Answers

On the Airplane

1. will be
2. we'll be
3. you'll be able
4. right
5. left
6. over
7. for
8. In a little while
9. having
10. you'll be seeing
11. We'll be arriving
12. It'll
13. be raining

In the Hospital

1. you'll
2. be feeling
3. for a few days
4. We'll be taking
5. you'll be staying
6. comfortably
7. will be taking
8. blood
9. we'll be giving
10. a lot of
11. you'll be walking
12. you'll be able to
13. is
14. you'll be leaving
15. any

You'll Find Me

1. into
2. you'll know
3. I'll be wearing
4. I'll be sitting
5. in the corner
6. I'll be drinking
7. reading
8. I'll be looking
9. You'll find

GRAMMAR

Pronoun Review

Subject Pronouns	Object Pronouns	Possessive Adjectives	Possessive Pronouns	Reflexive Pronouns
I	me	my	mine	myself
you	you	your	yours	yourself
he	him	his	his	himself
she	her	her	hers	herself
it	it	its	its	itself
we	us	our	ours	ourselves
you	you	your	yours	yourselves
they	them	their	theirs	themselves

Some/Any

There's **something** wrong with my washing machine.
I'm sure you'll find **somebody/someone** who can fix it.

I don't know **anything** about washing machines.
Do you know **anybody/anyone** who can help me?

FUNCTIONS

Asking for and Reporting Information

There's something wrong with *my washing machine.*

Do you know *anybody who can help me?*

I won't *be home tomorrow morning.*
I'll be *taking my son to the dentist.*

Where do you live?
156 Grove Street in Centerville.

What's the name?
Helen Bradley.
And what's the address again?
156 Grove Street in Centerville.
And the phone number?
237–9180.

Offering to Help

Do you need any help?
Can I help you?
I'll be glad to help you.

Expressing Ability

I can *do my homework* by myself.

Expressing Inability

I can't *help you.*
I couldn't *fall asleep last night.*

Inquiring about Agreement

Is that okay?

Expressing Agreement

That's fine.

Expressing Disagreement

Not really.

Initiating a Topic

You look tired today.

Expressing Hope

I hope *you sleep better tonight.*

Expressing Regret

I'm afraid *I won't be home tomorrow morning.*

Offering Advice

You should *look in the phone book.*

Identifying

Armstrong Plumbing Company.

NEW VOCABULARY

address book
anybody
anyone
argue
brakes (n)
camera
canary
cassette player
charge (v)
dishwasher
electrician
everything
faucet

flood (v)
garbage
grateful
hall
lift weights
moving company
next door neighbor
notebook
phone book
repair person
ring (n)
since
sneakers

somebody
steering wheel
take out
turn (v)
weights
yellow pages

as soon as possible
for example
No, that's okay.
Not really.
That's fine.
there's something wrong with

LANGUAGE NOTE

Some—/Any— Words: Something, Somebody, Someone, Anything, Anybody, Anyone

In this chapter, the usage of these words can be summarized as follows:

1. The *some*–words are used in affirmative statements:

    There's something wrong with my washing machine.

2. The *any*–words are used in questions and negative statements:

    Do you know anybody who can help me?
    I don't know anything about stoves.

In addition to the usage presented in this chapter, the *some*– words are also commonly used in questions when the speaker expects a positive answer.

    Are you looking for someone?
    Is there something I can do for you?

Text Page 116: *I'll Be Glad to Help*

FOCUS

> Review of subject, object, and reflexive pronouns

INTRODUCING THE MODEL

1. Have students look at the illustration.
2. Set the scene: "Johnny's grandmother and mother are talking about him."
3. Present the model.
4. Full-Class Choral Repetition.
5. Ask students if they have any questions; check understanding of new vocabulary: *No, that's okay.*
6. Group Choral Repetition.
7. Choral Conversation.
8. Call on one or two pairs of students to present the dialog.

   (For additional practice, do Choral Conversation in small groups or by rows.)

SIDE BY SIDE EXERCISES

Examples

> 1. A. What's your husband doing?
>   B. He's fixing the TV.
>   A. Does he need any help?
>   I'll be glad to help him.
>   B. No, that's okay. He can fix the TV by himself.
>
> 2. A. What's your daughter doing?
>   B. She's feeding the canary.
>   A. Does she need any help?
>   I'll be glad to help her.
>   B. No, that's okay. She can feed the canary by herself.

1. **Exercise 1:** Call on two students to present the dialog. Then do Choral Repetition and Choral Conversation Practice.
2. **Exercise 2:** Introduce the new word *canary*. Same as above.
3. **Exercises 3–8:**

   > **New vocabulary:**   6. *take out the garbage*

   Either Full-Class Practice or Pair Practice.

4. **Exercise 9:** Have students use the model as a guide to create their own conversations, using vocabulary of their choice. Encourage students to use dictionaries to find new words they want to use. This exercise can be done orally in class or for written homework. If you assign it for homework, you should do one example in class to make sure students understand what's expected. Have students present their conversations in class the next day.

WORKBOOK

Pages 120–121 (Exercise A)

EXPANSION ACTIVITY

Role Play: What Happened?

Use this role play exercise to provide additional review of pronouns.

1. Write on the board:

> A. Where's _____?
> _____ (isn't/aren't) in school/at work today.
> B. Oh. Didn't you hear what happened to _____?
> A. No! What happened?
> B. _____.
> A. Are you sure?
> B. Yes, I am. (His/Her/Their) _____ told me.
> A. That's too bad! I hope _____ (get/gets) back to school/work soon.

2. Call on pairs of students to create conversations about fictitious people. You may have students use any names and information they wish, or you can give them the cues below. Have students expand the details of what happened. You can either say the cues or write them on the board before calling on students.

> 1. George
>   broke his leg
>
> 2. Betsy
>   tripped and fell
>
> 3. Mary
>   cut herself
>
> 4. Jack and his brother
>   got seasick
>
> 5. Jim and David
>   had a serious accident
>
> 6. Mr. Romero
>   a dog bit him
>
> 7. Bill
>   got sick
>
> 8. Mrs. Schultz
>   had an operation

Example:

> A. Where's George? He isn't in school today.
> B. Oh. Didn't you hear what happened to him?
> A. No! What happened?
> B. He broke his leg while he was skating in the park yesterday.
> A. Are you sure?
> B. Yes, I am. His brother told me.
> A. That's too bad! I hope he gets back to school soon.

Text Page 117: *I Just Found This Watch*

FOCUS

Review of possessive nouns and possessive pronouns

INTRODUCING THE MODEL

1. Have students look at the illustration.
2. Set the scene: "Two friends are talking. One of the them just found a watch."
3. Present the model.
4. Full-Class Choral Repetition.
5. Ask students if they have any questions.
6. Group Choral Repetition.
7. Choral Conversation.
8. Call on one or two pairs of students to present the dialog.

   (For additional practice, do Choral Conversation in small groups or by rows.)

SIDE BY SIDE EXERCISES

Examples

1. A. I just found this umbrella. Is it yours?
   B. No, it isn't mine. But it might be Susan's. She lost hers a few days ago.
   A. Really? I'll call her right away.
   B. When you talk to her, tell her I said "Hello."

2. A. I just found this briefcase. Is it yours?
   B. No, it isn't mine. But it might be John's. He lost his a few days ago.
   A. Really? I'll call him right away.
   B. When you talk to him, tell him I said "Hello."

1. **Exercise 1:** Call on two students to present the dialog. Then do Choral Repetition and Choral Conversation Practice.
2. **Exercise 2:** Same as above
3. **Exercises 3–11:**

   New vocabulary: 5. *camera* 6. *notebook* 7. *ring* 8. *cassette player* 9. *address book* 10. *sneakers*

Either Full-Class Practice or Pair Practice.

4. **Exercise 12:** Have students use the model as a guide to create their own conversations, using vocabulary of their choice. Encourage students to use dictionaries to find new words they want to use. This exercise can be done orally in class or for written homework. If you assign it for homework, you should do one example in class to make sure students understand what's expected. Have students present their conversations in class the next day.

WORKBOOK

Pages 121–122 (Exercises B, C)

Exercise Note

Workbook p. 121:   For additional practice with Exercise B, have students act out the conversation.

EXPANSION ACTIVITIES

1. **Role Play: Help**

   Use this role play to provide additional review of possessive pronouns.

   a. Write on the board:

   A. I have a problem. I need a _____, but _____.
   (I can't find mine/mine is broken/somebody took mine and didn't return it . . .)
   B. Would you like to borrow mine?
   A. That's very nice of you, but I'm sure you'll need yours.
   _____ has one. I'll ask _____ if I can borrow _____.

   ---

   b. Call on pairs of students to role play the conversation, using any vocabulary they wish. Encourage students to use names of real people. For example:

   A. I have a problem. I need a typewriter, but mine is broken.
   B. Would you like to borrow mine?
   A. That's very nice of you, but I'm sure you'll need yours.
   David has one. I'll ask him if I can borrow his.

2. **Conversation Chain: Is This Yours?**

   a. Collect a personal item from every student in the class. For example: a notebook, a pen, a glove, a watch.

   b. Starting with the first student, hold the item and model the following:

   Teacher: Is this yours?
   Student A: No. It isn't mine. But it might be (his/hers).
   Teacher: Ask (him/her).

   (Student A takes the item from the teacher and shows it to Student B.)

   Student A: Is this yours?
   Student B: No. It isn't mine. But it might be (his/hers).
   Student A: Ask (him/her).

   c. Continue the *chain* until a student actually *does* get his or her own item. Have that student respond: "Yes. It's mine. Thank you."

   d. Continue the practice with other items.

Text Pages 118–119: *I Couldn't Fall Asleep Last Night*

FOCUS

```
Review of verb tenses
```

INTRODUCING THE MODEL

1. Have students look at the model illustration.
2. Set the scene: "Two friends are talking. One of them is very upset about what happened last night."
3. Present the model.
4. Full-Class Choral Repetition.
5. Ask students if they have any questions; check understanding of new vocabulary: *argue, complain.*
6. Group Choral Repetition.
7. Choral Conversation. Call on one or two pairs of students to present the dialog.

    (For additional practice, do Choral Conversation in small groups or by rows.)

SIDE BY SIDE EXERCISES

Examples

---

1. A. You look tired today.
    B. Yes, I know. I couldn't fall asleep last night.
    A. Why not?
    B. My neighbor's son was practicing the violin.
    A. How late did he practice the violin?
    B. Believe it or not, he practiced the violin until 2 A.M.!
    A. That's terrible! Did you call and complain?
    B. No, I didn't. I don't like to complain.
    A. Well, I hope you sleep better tonight.
    B. I'm sure I will. My neighbor's son doesn't practice the violin very often.

2. A. You look tired today.
    B. Yes, I know. I couldn't fall asleep last night.
    A. Why not?
    B. My neighbor's dog was barking.
    A. How late did it bark?
    B. Believe it or not, it barked until 4:30 A.M.!
    A. That's terrible! Did you call and complain?
    B. No, I didn't. I don't like to complain.
    A. Well, I hope you sleep better tonight.
    B. I'm sure I will. My neighbor's dog doesn't bark very often.

---

1. **Exercise 1:** Call on two students to present the dialog. Then do Choral Repetition and Choral Conversation Practice.
2. **Exercise 2:** Same as above.
3. **Exercises 3–9:**

New vocabulary:	6. *hall*	7. *next door neighbor*	9. *weights*

Either Full-Class Practice or Pair Practice.

4. **Exercise 10:** Have students use the model as a guide to create their own conversations, using vocabulary of their choice. Encourage students to use dictionaries to find new words they want to use. This exercise can be done orally in class or for written homework. If you assign it for homework, you should do one example in class to make sure students understand what's expected. Have students present their conversations in class the next day.

WORKBOOK

Pages 122–124 (Exercise D)

EXPANSION ACTIVITY

Tell a Story: The Worst Day

1. Write on the board:

"Yesterday was one of the worst days _____ can remember!"

2. Divide the class into small groups of 3–5 students. Have each group create a story of at least ten sentences about a character who had a very bad yesterday. Encourage students to use any vocabulary they wish and draw from their own experiences in describing the unlucky events.
3. Have one person from each group present the story to the class.
4. Have the class decide which character had *the worst day*.

FOCUS

Introduction of *something* *anything* $\left\{\begin{matrix} somebody \\ someone \end{matrix}\right\}$ $\left\{\begin{matrix} anybody \\ anyone \end{matrix}\right\}$

GETTING READY

Introduce words with *some–* and *any–*.

1. Write on the board:

2. Form sentences with all the pronouns in each group. Have students repeat the sentences chorally.
   For example:

   "Do you see anything?"
   "Do you see anybody?"
   "Do you see anyone?"

3. Call on pairs of students to practice the sentences conversationally.

   A. Do you see anything?
   B. No. I don't see anything.
   A. I'm sure you'll see something soon.

   A. Do you see anybody?
   B. No. I don't see anybody.
   A. I'm sure you'll see somebody soon.

   A. Do you see anyone?
   B. No. I don't see anyone.
   A. I'm sure you'll see someone soon.

4. Create other conversations with your students, using similar patterns. For example:

> "Do you hear anything/anybody/anyone?"
> "Did you find anything/anybody/anyone?"

INTRODUCING THE MODEL

1. Have students look at the model illustration.
2. Set the scene: "Two friends are talking. One of them is having a problem with his washing machine."
3. Present the model.
4. Full-Class Choral Repetition.
5. Ask students if they have any questions; check understanding of new vocabulary: *there's something wrong with, phone book.*
6. Group Choral Repetition.
7. Choral Conversation.
8. Call on one or two pairs of students to present the dialog.
9. Introduce the new expression *in the Yellow Pages.* Have one or two pairs of students practice the model using this expression in place of *in the phone book.*
10. Substitute *anyone* and *someone* in place of *anybody* and *somebody.* Call on one or two pairs of students to present the dialog, using these words.

   (For additional practice, do Choral Conversation in small groups or by rows.)

SIDE BY SIDE EXERCISES

In these exercises, students can use *somebody/someone* and *anybody/anyone* interchangeably.

Examples

---

1. A. There's something wrong with my stove.
   B. I'm sorry. I can't help you. I don't know ANYTHING about stoves.
   A. Do you know anybody/anyone who can help me?
   B. Not really. You should look in the phone book/yellow pages.
      I'm sure you'll find somebody/someone who can fix it.

2. A. There's something wrong with my TV.
   B. I'm sorry. I can't help you. I don't know ANYTHING about TVs.
   A. Do you know anybody/anyone who can help me?
   B. Not really. You should look in the phone book/yellow pages.
      I'm sure you'll find somebody/someone who can fix it.

---

1. **Exercise 1:** Call on two students to present the dialog. Then do Choral Repetition and Choral Conversation Practice.
2. **Exercise 2:** Same as above.
3. **Exercises 3–8:**

   New vocabulary: 6. *dishwasher*

Either Full-Class Practice or Pair Practice.

4. **Exercise 9:** Have students use the model as a guide to create their own conversations, using vocabulary of their choice. Encourage students to use dictionaies to find new words they want to use. This exercise can be done orally in class or for written homework. If you assign it for homework, you should do one example in class to make sure students understand what's expected. Have students present their conversations in class the next day.

WORKBOOK

Pages 124–126 (Exercises E, F)

EXPANSION ACTIVITY

Role Play: *Help! Somebody Stole My* _____!

1. Write on the board:

A. (Mr./Mrs./Miss/Ms.) _____. What happened last night?
B. Somebody/Someone stole my _____.

A. Did you $\begin{Bmatrix} \text{see} \\ \text{hear} \end{Bmatrix}$ $\begin{Bmatrix} \text{anything strange} \\ \text{anybody} \\ \text{anyone} \end{Bmatrix}$ at your house last night?

B. Yes. I think I $\begin{Bmatrix} \text{saw} \\ \text{heard} \end{Bmatrix}$ $\begin{Bmatrix} \text{something} \\ \text{somebody} \\ \text{someone} \end{Bmatrix}$ in the _____ at about _____ o'clock.

A. Is that all you can tell us?

B. $\begin{Bmatrix} \text{Yes, that's all.} \\ \text{There's one more thing.} \underline{\hspace{6cm}} \end{Bmatrix}$

A. Okay. Thank you, (Mr./Mrs./Miss/Ms.) _____. Someone from the station will call you if we find your _____.

2. Set the scene: "Somebody stole something from your house last night. You called the police, and they told you to come to the police station. You're at the police station now, and someone is asking you questions about last night."

3. Call on pairs of students to role play the dialog, using any vocabulary they wish. An example:

A. Mr. Rodriguez. What happened last night?
B. Somebody stole my car.
A. Did you hear anything strange at your house last night?
B. Yes. I think I heard someone in the garage at about 12 o'clock.
A. Is that all you can tell us?
B. There's one more thing. I found this black glove.
A. Okay. Thank you, Mr. Rodriguez. Someone from the station will call you if we find your car.

Text Pages 121–122: *Can You Send a Plumber?*

FOCUS

Review of verb tenses

INTRODUCING THE MODEL

1. Have students look at the illustration.
2. Set the scene: "Someone is calling the plumber."
3. Present the model.
4. Full-Class Choral Repetition.
5. Ask students if they have any questions; check understanding of new vocabulary: *as soon as possible, Not really, that's fine.*
6. Group Choral Repetition.
7. Choral Conversation.
8. Call on one or two pairs of students to present the dialog.

   (For additional practice, do Choral Conversation in small groups or by rows.)

SIDE BY SIDE EXERCISES

In these exercises, students use their own names and addresses; also students should make up times and excuses.

1. **Exercise 1:** Introduce the new expression *repair person*. Call on two students to present the dialog. Then do Choral Repetition and Choral Conversation Practice.
2. **Exercise 2:** Introduce the new word *electrician*. Same as above.
3. **Exercise 3:** Same as above.

   Either Full-Class Practice or Pair Practice.

   Culture Note

   Repair person (Exercise 3) is a term used instead of *repairman* to refer to both males and females. Other similar non-sexist terms such as this have come into the language in recent years, reflecting the fact that many women have entered what were traditionally male professions. Some examples are fire fighter (instead of fireman), mail carrier (instead of mailman), and weather forecaster (instead of weatherman).

Example

1. A. General Radio and TV. Can I help you? B. Yes. There's something wrong with my TV. Can you send a repair person to fix it as soon as possible? A. Where do you live? B. (209 Main Street) in (Littleton). A. I can send a repair person tomorrow morning. Is that okay? B. Not really. I'm afraid I won't be home tomorrow morning. I'll be (working).

A. How about tomorrow afternoon?
B. Tomorrow afternoon? What time?
A. Between (two) and (five).
B. That's fine. Somebody will be here then.
A. What's the name?
B. (Roger Watson).
A. And what's the address again?
B. (209 Main Street) in (Littleton).
A. And the phone number?
B. (398–7630).
A. Okay. We'll have somebody there tomorow afternoon.
B. Thank you.

WORKBOOK

Pages 126–130 (Exercises G, H, I, J, K)

Exercise Notes

Workbook pp. 126–128: In Exercises G and I, students are given one side of a conversation and must fill in appropriate responses. In order to figure out what Speaker B might be saying, students will have to look ahead to Speaker *A's* next line, and then go back to see what would make sense. There are several possible responses for each line. Call on different students to present their ideas.

Workbook p. 127: Students review subject pronouns, object pronouns, reflexive pronouns, and possessive adjectives.

Workbook p. 130: Students practice *anybody/anyone* with questions and negatives and *somebody/someone* with positive statements.

EXPANSION ACTIVITIES

1. **Role Play: Wrong Number**

    a. Write on the board:

    A. Hello.
    B. Hello. May I please speak to _____?
    A. I think you have the wrong number. There's nobody named _____ here.
    B. Oh. I'm sorry.

    b. Call on pairs of students to role play, using any names they wish.

2. **Role Play: It's Broken Again**

    a. Write on the board:

    A. I can't believe it. Our _____ is broken again
    B. Are you SURE?! The _____ just fixed it last week.
    A. I guess (he/she) isn't a very good _____. Maybe we should call sombody/someone else next time.

b. Have pairs of students role play the conversation. Begin by giving each pair one of the cues below, either on the board or on a word card. Then have one or two pairs do the role play, using any vocabulary they wish.

Cues:

1.	sink plumber	5.	stove electrician
2.	car mechanic	6.	washing machine repair person
3.	TV repair person	7.	piano piano tuner
4.	shower plumber	8.	light electrician

Text Pages 123–124

READING: *Trouble With Cars*

FOCUS

Pronoun review

NEW VOCABULARY

brakes
charge
since
steering wheel
turn (v)

PREVIEWING THE STORY (optional)

Have students talk about the story title and/or illustrations. Introduce new vocabulary.

READING THE STORY

1. Have students read silently, or follow along silently as the story is read aloud by you, by one or more students, or on the tape.
2. Ask students if they have any questions; check understanding of vocabulary.
3. Check students' comprehension, using some or all of the following questions:

    a. What's wrong with Charlie's car?
    b. What did he try to do?
    c. Was he able to?
    d. Why not?
    e. What did he finally do?
    f. What did the mechanic do?
    g. Why is Charlie annoyed?

    h. What's wrong with Betty's car?
    i. What did she try to do?
    j. Was she able to?
    k. Why not?
    l. What did she finally do?
    m. What did the mechanic do?
    n. Why is Betty annoyed?

    o. What's wrong with Mark and Nancy's car?
    p. What did they try to do?
    q. Were they able to?
    r. Why not?
    s. What did they finally do?
    t. What did the mechanic do?
    u. Why are Mark and Nancy annoyed?

v. What's wrong with my car?
w. What did I try to do?
x. Was I able to?
y. Why not?
z. What did I finally do?
aa. What did the mechanic do?
bb. Why am I annoyed?

CHECK-UP

What's the Word?

1. his/himself
2. them/their
3. her/her
4. my/mine (It)
5. them/myself
6. our/ourselves/our

Listening

Have students complete the exercises as you play the tape or read the following:

I. Listen and choose and word you hear.

1. Do you know him well? (a)
2. Did you see them today? (b)
3. Yours will be ready at five o'clock. (a)
4. Careful! You might hurt yourselves! (b)
5. I'll be glad to help him. (b)
6. We're having trouble with her car. (b)

II. Listen and choose what the people are talking about.

1. I'm going to have to call the plumber. (b)
2. It's broken. It won't get cold. (a)
3. She plays very well. (b)
4. Careful! It's raining. Don't let it get wet! (a)
5. He parked in the yard all night. (b)

HOW ABOUT YOU?

Have students answer the questions, in pairs or as a class.

IN YOUR OWN WORDS: *That's What Friends Are For*

FOCUS

- Tense review
- Review of pronouns
---

1. Have students read silently, or follow along silently as the situations are read aloud by you or by one or more students.
2. Ask students if they have any questions; check understanding of new vocabulary: *everything, faucet, flood (v), for example, grateful, moving company.*
3. Make sure students understand the instructions.
4. Have students do the activity as written homework, using a dictionary for any new words they wish to use.
5. Have students present and discuss what they have written, in pairs or as a class.

WORKBOOK

Check-Up Test: Pages 131–132

WORKBOOK ANSWER KEY AND LISTENING SCRIPTS

Page 120 A. HELP

1. His
   him
   himself
2. Their
   them
   themselves
3. Her
   her
   herself
4. Our
   us
   ourselves
5. him, his
   himself
6. myself
   my
   me
7. yourself
   you
8. you
   your
   yourselves

Page 121 B. THE LOST UMBRELLA

1. yours
2. mine
3. hers
4. his
5. theirs
6. ours

Page 121 C. SCRAMBLED SENTENCES

1. When is their sister going to visit her?
2. Are these brown gloves yours?
3. He wants to give her his book.
4. We didn't send him her address.
5. We enjoyed ourselves because our friends were with us.
6. He cooks dinner by himself because his children don't help him.
7. They're writing with their father's pen because they lost theirs.

Page 122 D. NOISY NEIGHBORS

1. neighbor's
2. is playing
3. played
4. for
5. wasn't
6. fall
7. hard
8. at
9. upstairs
10. weights
11. quieter
12. to complain
13. lifts
14. to
15. her
16. are dancing
17. danced
18. until
19. might
20. loud
21. noisy
22. to be tired
23. I'm practicing
24. during
25. until
26. I eat
27. a few
28. tells
29. have to
30. for
31. don't
32. won't be
33. well
34. quietly

Page 124 E. WHAT'S THE WORD?

1. anything
   anybody
   Nobody
2. something
   anything
   nobody
3. Somebody
   Nobody
4. nobody
   Everyone
5. somebody
   any
6. anything
   anything
7. Somebody
   nobody
   anybody
   Everybody

Page 125 F. LISTEN: *The School Picnic*

Listen and put a circle around the correct answer.

1. Did you have a good time at the school picnic last Saturday?
2. Was there anything good to eat?
3. How late did you stay?
4. Why did you leave so early?
5. Do you think next year's picnic will be better?

Answers
1. b.   2. c   3. b

Page 128   J.   WHAT'S THE  WORD?

1. week, weak
2. They're, their
3. ate, eight
4. right, write
5. hear, here
6. Where, wear
7. You're, Your
8. read, red
9. flower, flour
10. Our, hour
11. pear, pair
12. know, No
13. buy, by
14. four, for
15. Two, too
16. hole, whole

CHECK-UP TEST: *CHAPTERS 12–13*

Page 131   A.

1. They'll be painting
2. She'll be studying
3. He'll be practicing
4. We'll be taking care of
5. I'll be working

Page 131   B.

1. will she be working
2. will you be reading
3. will he be coming
4. will they be driving
5. will you be staying in New York

Page 131   C.

1. less
   fewer, less
2. don't have to

3. mustn't, much
4. don't have to
5. until
6. for
7. at
8. in
9. anything
10. somebody
11. Someone
12. mine
13. their
    hers
14. her

Page 132   D.

Listen and fill in the missing words.

ON THE BUS

Good morning. This is your bus driver, Jim Smith, speaking. I'm glad you'll be riding with us on this special weekend visit to New York City. We'll be leaving in just a few minutes and we'll be arriving in New York City at noon, in time for a delicious lunch at the Park Avenue Cafe. After lunch we'll be visiting the United Nations, and in the evening we'll be having dinner at one of New York's finest restaurants. Don't forget! You'll be staying at the Fifth Avenue Hotel across the street from the beautiful Museum of Modern Art. I'm sure you're all going to enjoy yourselves very much. If I can do anything to help you, please ask.

Answers
1. you'll be riding
2. We'll be leaving
3. we'll be arriving
4. we'll be visiting
5. we'll be having
6. you'll be staying
7. yourselves
8. anything
9. please ask

TEACHER'S NOTES

BOOK 2 FINAL TEST

A. Put a circle around the correct answer.

1. $\boxed{\begin{array}{c}\text{This}\\\text{These}\end{array}}$ cookies $\boxed{\begin{array}{c}\text{is}\\\text{are}\end{array}}$ delicious. I'm going to have a $\boxed{\begin{array}{c}\text{little}\\\text{few}\end{array}}$ more.

2. How many $\boxed{\begin{array}{c}\text{loaf}\\\text{loaves}\end{array}}$ of bread do we need?

3. I don't think I'll go skiing this weekend. I'm afraid I $\boxed{\begin{array}{c}\text{might}\\\text{should}\\\text{must}\end{array}}$ hurt myself.

4. Betty isn't as $\boxed{\begin{array}{c}\text{old}\\\text{older}\end{array}}$ as her sister, but she's much $\boxed{\begin{array}{c}\text{tall}\\\text{taller}\end{array}}$.

5. Louise $\boxed{\begin{array}{c}\text{couldn't}\\\text{can't}\\\text{won't be able to}\end{array}}$ go out on a date last year because she was too $\boxed{\begin{array}{c}\text{young}\\\text{younger}\\\text{youngest}\end{array}}$.

6. You aren't $\boxed{\begin{array}{c}\text{accurate}\\\text{accurately}\end{array}}$ because you work too $\boxed{\begin{array}{c}\text{quick}\\\text{quickly}\end{array}}$.

7. If our friends $\boxed{\begin{array}{c}\text{visit}\\\text{will visit}\end{array}}$ us tomorrow, $\boxed{\begin{array}{c}\text{we}\\\text{we'll}\end{array}}$ have a picnic.

8. I usually get $\boxed{\begin{array}{c}\text{at}\\\text{up}\\\text{on}\end{array}}$ the bus at First Avenue.

9. David has a stomachache because he ate too $\boxed{\begin{array}{c}\text{much}\\\text{many}\end{array}}$ bread and too $\boxed{\begin{array}{c}\text{much}\\\text{many}\end{array}}$ potatoes.

10. There's $\boxed{\begin{array}{c}\text{anything}\\\text{something}\end{array}}$ wrong with my cassette player, and I don't know $\boxed{\begin{array}{c}\text{anything}\\\text{something}\end{array}}$ about cassette players.

11. We $\boxed{\begin{array}{c}\text{painted}\\\text{were painting}\end{array}}$ the house when it started to rain.

12. They'll be staying at the Park Hotel [in / for / until] next Sunday.

13. My dentist says I [mustn't / don't have to] eat too much candy because I have problems with my teeth.

14. [I gave / I give / I'll give] you flowers a year ago.

15. Will George be home tonight? Yes, he will. He'll [bake / be baking]

16. I [might / should / shouldn't] name my son John, or I [might / should / shouldn't] name him Jack. I really can't decide.

17. If it [won't / doesn't] rain tomorrow, she'll go sailing.

18. Will you be getting [up / off / out of] the train [at / in / until] the next stop?

19. My doctor thinks I should drink [less / fewer] coffee.

20. We've got to study [for / until] a few more hours.

21. My brother plays the violin very [bad / badly], but he thinks he plays [well / good]

22. Would you care for [a few / a little] more rice? Yes, please. [It's / They're] delicious.

23. The PRESTO Company makes the [quiet / quieter / quietest] fans in the world.

24. My house is across the street. I'll get [off / from / out of] the car now.

25. I'm sorry you [can't / couldn't / won't be able to] go swimming with us last Thursday.

26. I worked [for / until] 10 o'clock last night.

252

27. | Somebody / Anybody | stole my favorite pen.

28. You don't have to dress | beautiful / beautifully |, but you've got to dress more | neat / neater / neatly |.

29. I need your advice. | Might / Should / Will | I go out with Steve or Fred?

30. How | much / many | does a | bunch / head | of carrots cost?

31. I couldn't lift the suitcase because it was too | weak / heavy |.

32. I | mustn't / don't have to | stop eating snack foods, but I really think I should.

33. There | isn't / aren't | any crackers because you ate | it / them | all.

34. You should try to drive more | safe / safer / safely |.

35. The plane will be arriving | at / in / until | 4:00.

36. If I work too | hard / hardly | tonight, I | get / might get | a headache.

37. I'm terribly sorry. My husband and I | couldn't / weren't able to / won't be able to | go to the theater with you next Sunday.

38. We'll get married | in / until | a few days.

39. You | mustn't / don't have to | work overtime. You should do it only if you want to.

40. My brother | got / was getting | a flat tire while he was driving to work.

41. She walked | of / off / out of | the room when we started to play cards.

253

B. Complete the sentences.

Ex. Madrid is ____*warmer than*____ Stockholm.
                  warm

1. Carl is _____ Roger.
              friendly

2. Michael is _____ Mark.
              intelligent

3. Eleanor is _____ Frieda.
              energetic

4. My neighborhood is _____ yours.
              safe

5. Patty's recipe for apple pie is _____ mine.
              good

C. Complete the sentences.

Ex. This chair is ____*the most comfortable*____ one in our house.
              comfortable

1. Herbert is _____ violinist in Centerville.
              talented

2. Ginger is _____ person in our class.
              funny

3. My mother is _____ person in our family.
              generous

4. This wine is _____ wine you can buy.
              cheap

5. This stereo is _____ one in the store.
              good

D. Fill in the blanks.

Ex. She's a careless skier. She skis very ____*carelessly*____ .

1. She's a slow typist. She types very _____ .

2. He's a terrible skater. He skates _____ .

3. They're careful workers. They work very _____ .

4. They're fast swimmers. They swim very _____ .

5. I'm a good tennis player. I play tennis very _____ .

E. Fill in the blanks with a pronoun.

Ex. I always do my homework, but my brother never does ____*his*____ .

1. Jane's birthday is tomorrow. She hopes her husband will send _____ flowers.

2. Is this Mr. and Mrs. Smith's umbrella? No. I'm sure it isn't _____ .

3. Please don't help us. We want to clean the yard by _____ .

4. Peter is sick, but he'll feel better if I give _____ some hot tea.

5. I always forget my wallet, but my friend Mary never forgets _____ .

6. Martha couldn't go to work today because she hurt _____ yesterday evening.

7. Mr. and Mrs. Green enjoyed _____ on _____ vacation.

8. Nobody helped Albert fix his TV. He fixed it by _____ .

9. Did you call your grandparents? No. I'll call _____ right away.

F. Answer the questions.

Ex. What was Edward doing when the lights went out?

(study) _____ *He was studying* _____

1. What did you do last night?

(go to a party) _____

2. What was Mary doing when you arrived?

(dance) _____

3. What were you doing when I called?

(cook dinner) _____

4. What does Tom do every morning?

(brush his teeth) _____

5. What were your children doing when you got up?

(get dressed) _____

6. What will you and your wife be doing this afternoon?

(fix our car) _____

7. What will your son be doing after school?

(practice the piano) _____

8. What does your daughter usually do after school?

(practice the violin) _____

9. How did you get to work today?

(take the bus) _____

1. a. He stays home.
   b. He went bowling.
   c. He'll watch TV.

2. a. What a shame!
   b. That's wonderful!
   c. I feel terrible.

3. a. For a few minutes.
   b. In a little while.
   c. Until tomorrow.

4. a. I'll be visiting my cousin.
   b. I'm studying.
   c. I was listening to records.

5. a. I'll have a piece of pie.
   b. The celery is out of this world.
   c. The strawberries are excellent.

6. a. I got a new shirt.
   b. I'm really sorry.
   c. I'm glad to hear that.

7. a. I can't.
   b. I mustn't.
   c. I've got to.

8. a. Yes, please. I need a loaf of bread and some milk.
   b. Yes, please. But not too many.
   c. Yes, please. Just a few.

9. a. I know. He always says "Thank you."
   b. I know. He never says "Thank you."
   c. I know. He should try to speak louder.

10. a. I know. She left on Friday.
    b. I know. She's got to leave tomorrow.
    c. I know. She's going to stay until next summer.

BOOK 2 ALTERNATIVE FINAL TEST

Fill in the missing words.

Sally gets up early _____ morning. She _____ a shower, she _____ her
1   2   3

exercises, she _____ the newspaper, and then she eats _____ .
4   5

But not today! _____ morning Sally _____ up late. She couldn't fall
6   7

_____ last night _____ her neighbor _____ _____ the piano very
8   9   10   11

loudly. He doesn't usually _____ the piano at night, but last night he _____ the
12   13

piano until 4 a.m. Unfortunately, Sally is going to _____ very busy today, and she
14

_____ be able to rest until this evening.
15

_____ 10 o'clock she has _____ appointment with _____ daughter's
16   17   18

teacher at school. At noon she has to go home to wait _____ the _____ because her
19   20

kitchen sink _____ broken. At 1:30 she has to go to the _____ office for her yearly
21   22

physical examination, and at 3 o'clock she has to take her children to _____ violin lessons.
23

Before she goes home, she's got _____ go _____ the supermarket. She needs two
24   25

_____ of soup, a _____ eggs, and a _____ _____ wine.
          26   27   28   29

Sally is upset because she won't _____ able to buy anything for her husband's birthday.
                                      30

She didn't forget about _____ birthday, but she's _____ busy that she doesn't have
                              31   32

time to buy _____ a present.
                 33

ANSWER KEY AND LISTENING SCRIPTS

Book 2 Final Test Answer Key

A.
1. These, are, few
2. loaves
3. might
4. old, taller
5. couldn't, young
6. accurate, quickly
7. visit, we'll
8. on
9. much, many
10. something, anything
11. were painting
12. until
13. mustn't
14. I gave
15. be baking
16. might, might
17. doesn't
18. off, at
19. less
20. for
21. badly, well
22. a little, It's
23. quietest
24. out of
25. couldn't
26. until
27. Somebody

28. beautifully, neatly
29. Should
30. much, bunch
31. heavy
32. don't have to
33. aren't, them
34. safely
35. at
36. hard, might get
37. won't be able to
38. in
39. don't have to
40. got
41. out of

B.
1. friendlier than
2. more intelligent than
3. more energetic than
4. safer than
5. better than

C.
1. the most talented
2. the funniest
3. the most generous
4. the cheapest
5. the best

D.
1. slowly
2. terribly
3. carefully
4. fast
5. well

E.
1. her
2. theirs
3. ourselves
4. him
5. hers
6. herself
7. themselves, their
8. himself
9. them

F.
1. I went to a party.
2. She was dancing.
3. I was cooking dinner.
4. He brushes his teeth.
5. They were getting dressed.
6. We'll be fixing our car.
7. He'll be practicing the pian
8. She (usually) practices the
9. I took the bus.

Teacher Key to Listening Comprehension Exercise G.
Read or play the tape. Have students put a circle around the letter of the correct answer.

1. What's Mario going to do if the weather's bad?
2. My uncle got out of the hospital a few days ago.
3. When are you going to finish your book?
4. What were you doing at about 5:00 today?
5. What do you recommend for dessert?
6. You forgot my birthday.
7. I really should stop eating rich desserts, but...
8. I'm going shopping. Can I get anything for you?
9. Charlie really speaks impolitely.
10. Aunt Jane isn't going to be staying for a long time.

G.
1. c
2. b
3. b
4. c
5. c
6. b
7. a
8. a
9. b
10. b

Book 2 Alternative Final Test

1. every
2. takes
3. does
4. reads
5. breakfast
6. This
7. got
8. asleep
9. because
10. was
11. playing

12. play
13. played
14. be
15. won't
16. At
17. an
18. her
19. for
20. plumber
21. is
22. doctor's

23. their
24. to
25. to
26. cans
27. dozen
28. bottle
29. of
30. be
31. his
32. so
33. him

SIDE BY SIDE PICTURE CARDS

Numerical List

1. bedroom	56. warm	112. secretary	166. plant flowers
2. bathroom	57. cool	113. factory worker	167. rest
3. living room	58. cold	114. businessman	168. eat
4. dining room	59. school	115. businesswoman	169. sing
5. kitchen	60. church	116. salesman	170. drink
6. basement	61. police station	117. saleswoman	171. sit
7. yard	62. fire station	118. computer programmer	172. tomatoes
8. garage	63. train station	119. mailman	173. eggs
9. restaurant	64. bus station	120. painter	174. bananas
10. bank	65. laundromat	121. go to a movie	175. apples
11. supermarket	66. gas station	122. go to a baseball game	176. cheese
12. library	67. drug store	123. have lunch/dinner	177. milk
13. park	68. cafeteria	124. go swimming/swim	178. ice cream
14. movie theater	69. bakery	125. go dancing/dance	179. bread
15. post office	70. barber shop	126. go skating/skate	180. crackers
16. zoo	71. beauty parlor	127. go skiing/ski	181. beans
17. hospital	72. clinic	128. go shopping/shop	182. garlic
18. read	73. department store	129. go bowling/bowl	183. rice
19. cook	74. doctor's office	130. go sailing/sail	184. flour
20. study	75. nervous	131. go jogging/jog	185. cookies
21. eat	76. sad	132. go to the doctor	186. yogurt
22. watch TV	77. happy	133. go to the bank	187. soda
23. sleep	78. tired	134. visit a friend in the	188. orange juice
24. play the piano	79. sick	hospital	189. jam and jelly
25. play cards	80. cold	135. get up	190. beer
26. play baseball	81. hot	136. take a bath	191. mayonnaise
27. drink	82. hungry	137. take a shower	192. butter
28. dance	83. thirsty	138. put on clothes	193. wine
29. sing	84. angry	139. write	194. melon
30. listen to the radio	85. embarrassed	140. headache	195. lettuce
31. fix _____ car	86. cry	141. stomachache	196. pears
32. fix _____ sink	87. smile	142. toothache	197. celery
33. fix _____ TV	88. shout	143. backache	198. sugar
34. feed _____ dog	89. smoke	144. earache	199. coffee
35. clean _____ yard	90. shiver	145. sore throat	200. salt and pepper
36. clean _____ apartment	91. perspire	146. cold	201. tea
37. paint	92. yawn	147. work	202. onions
38. do _____ exercises	93. blush	148. cook	203. butcher shop
39. wash _____ car	94. mechanic	149. talk on the telephone	204. shoe store
40. wash _____ clothes	95. violinist	150. fix _____ car	205. high school
41. brush _____ teeth	96. singer	151. brush _____ teeth	206. university
42. tall–short	97. dancer	152. dance	207. museum
43. young–old	98. chef	153. smoke	208. hotel
44. heavy–thin	99. baker	154. watch TV	209. playground
45. new–old	100. actor	155. play cards	210. parking lot
46. pretty–ugly	101. actress	156. study	211. airport
47. handsome–ugly	102. teacher	157. shave	212. candy store
48. rich–poor	103. truck driver	158. smile	213. newsstand
49. large/big–small/little	104. bus driver	159. clean	214. hardware store
50. expensive–cheap	105. doctor	160. cry	215. pet shop
51. sunny	106. nurse	161. listen to the radio	216. motel
52. cloudy	107. dentist	162. yawn	217. shopping mall
53. raining	108. carpenter	163. shout	218. TV station
54. snowing	109. plumber	164. paint	219. courthouse
55. hot	110. scientist	165. wait for the bus	220. concert hall
	111. policeman		

Alphabetical List

actor (100)
actress (101)
airport (211)
angry (84)
apples (175)

backache (143)
baker (99)
bakery (69)
bananas (174)
bank (10)
barber shop (70)
basement (6)
bathroom (2)
beans (181)
beauty parlor (71)
bedroom (1)
beer (190)
big (49)
blush (93)
bowl (129)
bread (179)
brush _____ teeth (41, 151)
bus driver (104)
businesswoman (115)
businessman (114)
bus station (64)
butcher shop (203)
butter (192)

cafeteria (68)
candy store (212)
carpenter (108)
celery (197)
cheap (50)
cheese (176)
chef (98)
church (60)
clean (159)
clean _____ apartment (36)
clean _____ yard (35)
clinic (72)
cloudy (52)
coffee (199)
cold [adjective] (80)
cold [ailment] (146)
cold [weather] (58)
computer programmer (118)
concert hall (220)
cook (19, 148)
cookies (185)
cool (57)
courthouse (219)
crackers (180)
cry (86, 160)

dance (28, 125, 152)
dancer (97)
dentist (107)
department store (73)
dining room (4)

doctor (105)
doctor's office (74)
do _____ exercises (38)
drink (27, 170)
drug store (67)

earache (144)
eat (21, 168)
eggs (173)
embarrassed (85)
expensive (50)

factory worker (113)
feed _____ dog (34)
fire station (62)
fix _____ car (31, 150)
fix _____ sink (32)
fix _____ TV (33)
flour (184)

garage (8)
garlic (182)
gas station (66)
get up (135)
go bowling (129)
go dancing (125)
go jogging (131)
go sailing (130)
go shopping (128)
go skating (126)
go skiing (127)
go swimming (124)
go to a baseball game (122)
go to a movie (121)
go to the bank (133)
go to the doctor (132)

handsome (47)
happy (77)
hardware store (214)
have lunch/dinner (123)
headache (140)
heavy (44)
high school (205)
hospital (17)
hot [adjective] (81)
hot [weather] (55)
hotel (208)
hungry (82)

ice cream (178)

jam and jelly (189)
jog (131)

kitchen (5)

large (49)
laundromat (65)
lettuce (195)
library (12)

listen to the radio (30, 161)
little (49)
living room (3)

mailman (119)
mayonnaise (191)
mechanic (94)
melon (194)
milk (177)
motel (216)
movie theater (14)
museum (207)

nervous (75)
new (45)
newsstand (213)
nurse (106)

old (43, 45)
onions (202)
orange juice (188)

paint (37, 164)
painter (120)
park (13)
parking lot (210)
pears (196)
pepper (200)
perspire (91)
pet shop (215)
plant flowers (166)
play baseball (26)
play cards (25, 155)
playground (209)
play the piano (24)
plumber (109)
policeman (111)
police station (61)
poor (48)
post office (15)
pretty (46)
put on clothes (138)

raining (53)
read (18)
rest (167)
restaurant (9)
rice (183)
rich (48)

sad (76)
sail (130)
salesman (116)
saleswoman (117)
salt (200)
school (59)
scientist (110)
secretary (112)
shave (157)
shiver (90)
shoe store (204)

shop (128)
shopping mall (217)
short (42)
shout (88, 163)
sick (79)
sing (29, 169)
singer (96)
sit (171)
skate (126)
ski (127)
sleep (23)
small (49)
smile (87, 158)
smoke (89, 153)
snowing (54)
soda (187)
sore throat (145)
stomachache (141)
study (20, 156)
sugar (198)
sunny (51)
supermarket (11)
swim (124)

take a bath (136)
take a shower (137)
talk on the telephone (149)
tall (42)
tea (201)
teacher (102)
thin (44)
thirsty (83)
tired (78)
tomatoes (172)
toothache (142)
train station (63)
truck driver (103)
TV station (218)

ugly (46, 47)
university (206)

violinist (95)
visit a friend in the
   hospital (134)

wait for the bus (165)
warm (56)
wash _____ car (39)
wash _____ clothes (40)
watch TV (22, 154)
wine (193)
work (147)
write (139)

yard (7)
yawn (92, 162)
yogurt (186)
young (43)

zoo (16)

Categories

Adjectives

angry (84)
big (49)
cheap (50)
cold (80)
embarrassed (85)
expensive (50)
handsome (47)
happy (77)
heavy (44)
hot (81)
hungry (82)
large (49)
little (49)
nervous (75)
new (45)
old (43, 45)
poor (48)
pretty (46)
sad (76)
short (42)
sick (79)
small (49)
tall (42)
thin (44)
thirsty (83)
tired (78)
rich (48)
ugly (46, 47)
young (43)

Ailments

backache (143)
cold (146)
earache (144)
headache (140)
sore throat (145)
stomachache (141)
toothache (142)

Foods

apples (175)
bananas (174)
beans (181)
beer (190)
bread (179)
butter (192)
celery (197)
cheese (176)
coffee (199)
cookies (185)
crackers (180)
eggs (173)
flour (184)
garlic (182)
ice cream (178)
jam and jelly (189)
lettuce (195)
mayonnaise (191)

melon (194)
milk (177)
onions (202)
orange juice (188)
pears (196)
pepper (200)
rice (183)
soda (187)
sugar (198)
tea (201)
tomatoes (172)
wine (193)
yogurt (180)

Community

airport (211)
bakery (69)
bank (10)
barber shop (70)
beauty parlor (71)
bus station (64)
butcher shop (203)
cafeteria (68)
candy store (212)
church (60)
clinic (72)
concert hall (220)
courthouse (219)
department store (73)
doctor's office (74)
drug store (67)
fire station (62)
gas station (66)
hardware store (214)
high school (205)
hospital (17)
hotel (208)
laundromat (65)
library (12)
motel (216)
movie theater (14)
museum (207)
newsstand (213)
park (13)
parking lot (210)
pet shop (215)
playground (209)
police station (61)
post office (15)
restaurant (9)
school (59)
shopping mall (217)
supermarket (11)
train station (63)
TV station (218)
university (206)
zoo (16)

Home

basement (6)
bathroom (2)
bedroom (1)
dining room (4)
garage (8)
kitchen (5)
living room (3)
yard (7)

Professions

actor (100)
actress (101)
baker (99)
bus driver (104)
businessman (114)
businesswoman (115)
carpenter (108)
chef (98)
computer programmer (118)
dancer (97)
dentist (107)
doctor (105)
factory worker (113)
mailman (119)
mechanic (94)
nurse (106)
painter (120)
plumber (109)
policeman (111)
salesman (116)
saleswoman (117)
scientist (110)
secretary (112)
singer (96)
teacher (102)
truck driver (103)
violinist (95)

Verbs

blush (93)
bowl (129)
brush _____ teeth (41, 151)
clean (159)
clean _____ apartment (36)
clean _____ yard (35)
cook (19, 148)
cry (86, 160)
dance (28, 125, 152)
do _____ exercises (38)
drink (27, 170)
eat (21, 168)
feed _____ dog (34)
fix _____ car (31, 150)
fix _____ sink (32)
fix _____ TV (33)
get up (135)
go bowling (129)
go dancing (125)

go jogging (131)
go sailing (130)
go shopping (128)
go skating (126)
go skiing (127)
go swimming (124)
go to a baseball game (122)
go to a movie (121)
go to the bank (133)
go to the doctor (132)
have lunch/dinner (123)
jog (131)
listen to the radio (30, 161)
paint (37, 164)
perspire (91)
plant flowers (166)
play baseball (26)
play cards (25, 155)
play the piano (24)
put on clothes (138)
read (18)
rest (167)
sail (130)
shave (157)
shiver (90)
shop (128)
shout (88, 163)
sing (29, 169)
sit (171)
skate (126)
ski (127)
sleep (23)
smile (87, 158)
smoke (89, 153)
study (20, 156)
swim (124)
take a bath (136)
take a shower (137)
talk on the telephone (149)
visit a friend in the
  hospital (134)
wait for the bus (165)
wash _____ car (39)
wash _____ clothes (40)
watch TV (22, 154)
work (147)
write (139)
yawn (92, 162)

Weather

cloudy (52)
cold (58)
cool (57)
hot (55)
raining (53)
snowing (54)
sunny (51)
warm (56)